The Great British
Torso Mystery

To Foxy Lady,
faithful and well-beloved companion of my later days.

© Richard Whittington-Egan 2002

Published by The Bluecoat Press, Liverpool
Book design by March Design, Liverpool
Printed by MFP, Manchester

ISBN 1872568 912

The Great British Torso Mystery is Richard Whittington-Egan's latest re-examination of a famous murder case and is an addition to an already impressive collection of titles, including: *The Ordeal of Philip Yale Drew, The Riddle of Bridehurst Rise, The Identity of Jack the Ripper, William Roughead's Chronicles of Murder* and *The Oscar Slater Murder Story: New Light on a Classic Mystery* .

Acknowledgments

First and foremost, my greatest debt of gratitude must go to Mr Keith Smart and Mr Andrew Parry, both experts on the case, and both of whom not only generously shared their knowledge with me, but also did sterling research on the book's behalf.

To my old friend, Mr Jonathan Goodman, I am grateful for his having introduced me to the indispensable Keith Smart. Another old friend who was of considerable help in many directions is Mr James Morton. Mrs Betty Wilson has been an unfailing support in my endeavours. Mr Tom Kelly, late librarian of the *Daily Mail* Reference Library, was, like his predecessor, Mr Stanley Prior, ever ready with much-needed assistance. The late Nick Barrett, of Corse Court, Gloucestershire, very kindly shared with me his reminiscences of Brian Sullivan's early days with him in the motor-car business in London. Mr Philip Correll, and his brother, Mr John Correll, who retailed to me their boyhood memories of Brian Sullivan, whom they knew as Byron Smith. Mrs Ann Stephens, although young at the time of his disappearance, was able to recount some interesting details concerning her great-uncle, the late Captain William Butt. Mrs Elizabeth Marsh proved most valuable in the carrying out of researches into the latter years of the late Mrs Edith Butt. Mr Douglas Symes of the Dowty Cine Society is sincerely thanked for all his actions of cooperation. The late Bernard O'Donnell and the late Glyn Hardwicke, both friends of mine, and Mr Robin Brooks, all of whom have written either short references to, or articles about, the mysterious affair at Tower Lodge, must be accorded my warmest thanks.

I am particularly, and indeed very heavily, indebted to a number of those who were actually involved in the Haw Bridge Case, who agreed to my interviewing them at length, spoke freely, and put their memories and private papers at my disposal, but requested anonymity. I must acknowledge, too, my debt to the long-ago legions of hard-working journalists who originally covered the story as it broke, and, all unknowingly, distinguished themselves as the unsung chroniclers of history. One such historian whom I would wish to single out, is the late Ronald Camp, formerly of the *News Chronicle*. He was one of the reporters on the ground at the time, and it was he who first brought the mystery to my attention. To David and Morwenna Byram-Wigfield I am also grateful for many helpful acts.

Throughout the fret and fume of composition, there has always been available, just along the corridor in her study, a font of consultative stimulation and redemptive pacification, my guardian *ad litem*, fellow-author, and wife, Molly Whittington-Egan.

Finally, and sadly, I find myself unable to thank Her Majesty's current coroner for the Cheltenham Division of Gloucestershire, a Cheltenham solicitor, named A Lester Maddrell.

As there has been no previous book on this intriguing case, my sources must, therefore, be defined as those indicated above.

Richard Whittington-Egan

The Great British
Torso Mystery

Richard Whittington-Egan

The Bluecoat Press

Contents

List of Pictures

Prologue

Blood Over The Bridge

The overnight rain had finally died away and the Monday morning had broken fine and frosty. The fields and hedgerows of rural Gloucestershire were a'crackle with the sharp needles of mini-icicles. Far below the towering arc of Haw Bridge, the River Severn was running fast and high. It flowed and frothed, still menacingly dark, against the background of a rapidly lightening sky.

Silhouetted upon the bridge's arched back were two lone-looking figures. They walked slowly. One of them was pushing a bicycle.

The time was 6.55am.

The man with the bike was Hubert Jack Dudfield, salmon fisherman, who lived at a house named 'Fairfield' in the East Gloucestershire village of Tirley, on the west bank of the Severn, hard by Haw Bridge. With him was Henry Ball. It was he who spotted the shoe and the glove – lying close together on the tarmac footway beside the road, five yards from the first pillar of the Gloucester end of the bridge.

The shoe was of discoloured white canvas. It was the left foot shoe of a pair of what used to be called Oxford shoes. Its lace was unfastened. The glove – a left-hand-one – was of chamois-leather. Both articles were rain-soaked. Ball picked them up. Looked cursorily. Clearly they were of no value. He threw them back on the footway.

Dudfield and Ball continued on their way, heading in the direction of the Cheltenham end of the bridge. They had by-passed their chance of discoverers' fame.

Minute by minute the light from the East increased, picking out the verdant detail of hill, field, and boscage – woods, copses, isolate trees. Blobs in the dissolving morning dusk resolved themselves into clear-cut, woolly sheep. The blurred outlines of cattle and horses came into sharper focus and identified themselves.

7.30am, Monday 10 January 1938. Full day's light suffused the landscape. Along came another passer-by, Hubert Charles Price, a roadman in the employ of Gloucestershire County Council, trudging, upstream side, towards Cheltenham. He crossed Haw Bridge, the solitary route over the surging Severn between Tewkesbury in the north and Gloucester to the south, *en route* to his day's work.

He was about 40 yards from the Gloucester side of the bridge, when second his early morning eye beheld the shoe and the glove. He picked both off the ground, just as Ernest Clayton, of 'Steps', in Tirley, rode up on his pedal cycle.

"Half a minute, here's something here I want you to look at," Hubert greeted him.

Haw Bridge, where the first clues to the murder were discovered.

And while Ernest was examining the items, something more sinister caught Hubert's eye. On the vertical iron railings of the bridge, at the precise spot beside the north-side kerb of the narrow footway where the shoe and glove had lain ... bloodstains. On the horizontal rail running along the top of the iron uprights; on the uprights themselves, jutting out beyond it; on the tarmac below it, were more bloodstains. The deep red streaks were unmistakable. There also appeared to be some fragments of flesh, minute but equally unmistakable, on the path. That these small clues to misadventure were still there was pure chance. Only a slightly more savage, more prolonged downpour, and they could have been washed clean away.

"I'm damned!" said Price. "Look at this blood on the rails. There has been foul play here. Somebody has been flung over into the water."

"It looks funny," Clayton agreed, but he was in a hurry, and rode off to Gloucester.

Price, who lived at Hazel Cottage, Haw Bridge, gathered up the shoe and glove and took them to the Pike House at the end of the bridge. He placed them on a heap of granite chippings there, and locked them in the old turnpike house. He, too, then went along to work.

But, as the morning wore on and he pondered his unusual discovery in retrospect, he became progressively more uneasy, more discomfortably convinced that he ought to tell the police about the blood spots on the bridge.

Accordingly, when at half-past twelve he went home to dinner, taking the shoe and glove with him, he sat down and wrote a note to PC Frederick Thomas Knight, who was in charge of the small police station at Corse, on the Worcestershire border, six miles north-west of Gloucester.

He had intended to get the letter delivered by the driver of the local bus. However, after a little more mulling, he decided that it would be better to telephone through to Constable Knight. He got a friend, Oliver Gaskins, to whom on his way home to dinner he had shown the shoe and glove at the public-house by the bridge, to do it for him.

Knight, who received the call at about one o'clock, promptly contacted Gloucester Police Headquarters, and, while PC Price waited on Haw Bridge to meet with Knight and point out the bloodstains to him, another friend of his, Joe Ball, went back to Price's house and fetched the shoe and the glove. Both were, in due course, handed over to Knight.

That afternoon, Chief Superintendent Albert James Wayman and Detective Inspector David Millar Wagstaff, of the Gloucester Police, motored up to Haw in a fast police car, arriving there at about half-past two. They were met by Inspector Charles F Large, of Tewkesbury, and PC Knight.

Wayman took possession of the shoe – a man's, size seven, and containing a metatarsal arch support sock – and the glove, also a man's, size eight. Upon scrutiny, the glove was found to present a potential clue. Inside it, in indelible black marking-ink was written 'CLR 614', which, he conjectured, was likely to be a cleaner's or a laundry mark.

He also carried out a close examination of the bloodied area. He found that three of the railings bore smears of blood, at points varying between two feet and two feet nine inches from the ground level. There were more traces of blood on the parapet immediately above the railings, and also on the water-facing side of the stone ledge at the base of the railings. On the footway, close to the railings, Wayman turned up a tiny triangular piece of flesh, without skin or hair, adhering to a splinter of bone. There was also a second sliver of clean bone, a fragment of bloodstained cloth, apparently torn from a garment, and a few strands of some sort of fibre.

While a police party, which included Inspector Large, PC Moyte, and the surprisingly aptly – positively Shakespeareanly – named PC Midwinter, waited on the bridge in the bone shaving wind and gathering darkness, careful scrapings of the bloodstained paint of the rail and railings, and of blood from the footway, were taken by the light of an electric torch. And these, together with the shoe, glove, and flesh and bone minutiae, painstakingly wrapped in a sheet of newspaper, and the cloth and fibre placed in a matchbox, were borne off by Wagstaff to Gloucester Royal Infirmary, where they were handed over to Mr Gale, assistant to Dr Davey, the pathologist.

On the Tuesday afternoon, 11 January, Chief Superintendent Wayman returned to Haw Bridge, accompanied this time by Detective Sergeant Philip Benjamin Grocey Franklin. Monday's overnight rain had washed away most of the blood marks. Only a few traces remained visible on the top rail and on the parapet. The Superintendent received a two-and-a-half-foot length of red braid with a loop in the centre. Mr Price had picked it up about 30 yards from the place where the

Hubert Charles Price, who made the grim discovery, pointing out the bloodstains on the bridge.

bloodstains had been found, stuffed it in his pocket, and forgotten all about it. He was handed also a brown button, about half an inch in diameter, which had been discovered on the Tirley side bank of the bridge. Attached to it were some strands of purplish fabric.

Investigating the land at the respective ends of Haw Bridge, the police officers came up with another potential clue. On the grass verge of the left-hand-side of the road going towards Apperley, at a distance of some 400 yards from the bridge, they found a woman's tweed belt. It was of a similar purplish fabric to that attached to the brown button.

Later that Tuesday night, Superintendent Wayman went along to see Dr Edgar Norman Davey, honorary pathologist to the Gloucester Royal Infirmary, into whose hands blood, flesh and bone specimens had been delivered for identification. Unfortunately, Dr Davey had been out of the city when the forensic material arrived late Monday afternoon, so a start on the vital tests was not made until Tuesday. No results were therefore yet available.

Earlier that same Tuesday evening, at about 7.30pm, there had been a caller at the police station at Hartpury, a village five miles to the north of Gloucester. He was Charles Hancock, a lorry driver, who lived at Hasfield, a hamlet situated a mile from Hartpury, and employed by Masters Brothers, hauliers, of Gloucester.

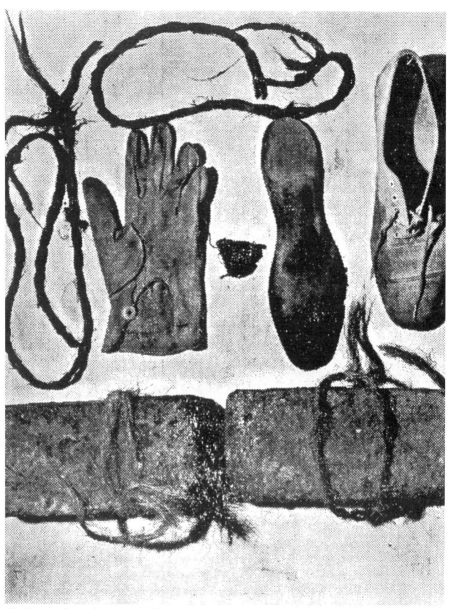

The clues: a glove, a fragment of Irish tweed suiting, a canvas shoe and metatarsal arch support sock which it contained, lengths of rope, and some bricks.

In a statement made to PC Jordan, Mr Hancock said that he had read a report in the local paper of the discovery of bloodstains on Haw Bridge. It so happened that he had been driving his lorry over Haw Bridge towards Cheltenham at about 3am on Monday 10 January, when he had passed a car coming the other way, from the direction of Cheltenham. Although he had repeatedly dipped his lights, the approaching car, travelling at, he estimated, about 15mph, with sidelights full on

10

and headlights blazing, had failed to dim them, dazzling him. Angered, Hancock had switched on his headlights, leant out of his cab and shouted an abusive remark as he passed the car. Peering through his window, he had tried to read the number plate, but it was old and dirty, and all that he could make out was the upper part of the first letter, which had been either a 'P', 'D', or 'B'.

He described the offending car as a dark-coloured Austin, 12 or 20 hp, 1919 - 1929 model tourer, with sidelights on a level with the windscreen, headlamps just above the mudguards, fitted with side screens and corner flaps, and with the hood up. There was a rear index plate of usual oblong pattern, with rear light fixed to the extreme offside.

He had been able to discern the figure of the driver – a man of between 35 and 40 years of age, of medium build, clean-shaven, and wearing a dark overcoat buttoned up to the neck and dark trilby. Sitting next to him had been a man of about the same age, also clean-shaven and wearing a trilby. And, although the interior of the car was unlighted, he could, he said, see something bulky in the rear.

Pulling up on the far end of the bridge and looking back, Hancock saw that the car, which had reached just about midway on the bridge, had drawn over right across the road to its offside and come to a stop by the north side footway; that is to say on the side on which the blood marks were subsequently found. Before he drove on, he saw two dim figures emerge from the Austin, and watched in his mirror as they looked very carefully about them, as if scanning "to check that the coast was clear".

As the results of Dr Davey's tests were eagerly awaited, the police initiated discreet preliminary enquiries. The source of the written mark inside the glove was being assiduously, but so far unsuccessfully, sought. Local garages were visited, seeking possible clues as to the mysteriously behaving Austin tourer. Watermen below the bridge were put on stand-by alert. None knew better that if a body had been thrown into the river, it would rise up after about nine days. And the likeliest spot for its resurrection would be the quay at Gloucester.

In pub and kitchen the air buzzed with theorisings. Someone had done away with a dog and disposed of it in the water. The shoe and glove had fallen by accident out of the car from which the dead animal was thrown. A guilty motorist had thus jettisoned the body of a sheep which he had run over. More gruesomely, a motorist's accidental human victim, being dead, was, to burke an embarrassingly awkward inquiry, consigned to a watery grave, the stains being incurred as the hit-and-run cadaver went over the rail-top.

The later editions of the *Cheltenham and Gloucester Echo* of Wednesday 12 January carried the news that shortly before six o'clock that evening, Dr Davey had gone along to Gloucester Police Station. He had seen Chief Superintendent Wayman and informed him that, after many tests extending over many hours and involving extracts made from the pieces of bone, flesh, and blood scrapings from railings and tarmac submitted to him, and their testing for reaction with antihuman serum in dilution from 1/1 to 1/36,000, no reaction had indicated that the materials were of human origin.

The pathologist had pronounced the blood on the bridge to be animal. The probability was that a motorist had killed a straying sheep and humped the carcass over the railings. Titillatory suspicions of foul play were ruled out. The suggestion that anyone was killed and thrown over the parapet was, said Superintendent Wayman, disposed of. The public interest so rapidly kindled, equally rapidly fizzled disappointedly out. Further police enquiries, it was announced by Wayman, would not be necessary.

He was wrong.

Just how resoundingly, disastrously wrong, it is the purpose of the remainder of this book to recount.

Chapter One

The Butts of Old Bath Road

It was not a happy household. The Captain was bad. His wife was mad. The resident nurse, a highly dubious quantity. They lived, all three of them, in precarious amity, at Number 248 Old Bath Road, on the Leckhampton outskirts of Cheltenham. The fourth member of the establishment was a Manchester terrier whose name may or may not have been Ted.

William Bernard Butt was by any reckoning a strange one, destined for a decidedly chequered career. Albeit, his beginning was conventional enough. Born Tuesday's child, on 1 August 1882, he grew up to defy the old folk rhyme's prophecy about being 'full of grace'. Rather did he mature cruel and gruff.

One of nine – three sons and six daughters – he entered the world at Priors Court, an old timbered mansion and seat in the Worcester parish of Powick. His father, Thomas Butt, a farmer, was a scion of a well known Worcestershire family, who lived at Bransford Court, a splendid country seat on the river Teme, four miles south-west of Worcester. His mother, Hannah, had been a Miss Leech. His grandmother was one of the founders of Stanbrook Abbey. William came, then, from good yeoman farming stock. No academic high-flier, he is said to have joined the army straight from school. Whether this is so or not, he was certainly in South Africa in 1899, when, serving as a private – Number 3798 – in the Cape Mounted Rifles, he saw action in the Boer War, which he came through unscathed, earning entitlement to the Queen's South African Medal, with three clasps.

Back in mufti, he is believed to have remained in South Africa for some years, finding employment in the gold mines. A lady friend of his, Miss Ida Cranswick, in a letter to the police, informed them that Captain Butt was in South Africa when the Boer War started, and that he had joined up. He had mentioned to her that he knew Cape Town, Durban, and Johannesburg. He had also told her that the gold of the signet ring which he always wore on the third finger of his left hand came from the South African mines.

In about 1909, at the age of 27, he returned to England and went to live for a while with his married sister, Gertie – Mrs Gertrude Mary Prew – and her husband, at Upper Farm, Aston-on-Carrant, an east Gloucestershire hamlet, three miles from Tewkesbury.

He did not, however, tax their hospitality long, but took himself off to London. There he met what there is reason to believe that he was in fact looking for: a well-to-do, young widow, 33-year-old Mrs Patience Jane (always known as Lillian) King. There seems small doubt that the widow's not-so-minute mite was the most powerful attraction. As my barrister father used wryly to observe, money is the

The elusive Captian William Bernard Butt.

purist of all motives, and, undeniably, whenever Butt took the plunge into matrimony there was good money at stake.

The couple married in 1913, and went to live in Margate – at 59 Northdown Road. In 1914 the Great War broke out. A year later, on 9 September 1915, his military blood up, the 33-year-old Butt became what was then known as a 'temporary gentleman', obtaining a commission as a second lieutenant in the Worcester Regiment. In the course of the next four years he served with the Worcester colours in India, against the Turks in Mesopotamia, in Persia, and in Russia.

Butt's wartime medical history is socially rather than militarily informative. On 24 November 1916, he was admitted to hospital at Colaba, India, where he remained under treatment for syphilis for 56 days, and the following 24 July was again hospitalised, this time in Poona, where he remained an in-patient until 24 September 1917. The record does not show the cause for those last two months in hospital, but on 22 October 1917, a Medical Board passed him fit for general service.

On 5 November 1919, Butt, now 37 and with the rank of captain, relinquished his commission. His papers make no mention of his ever having sustained any war wounds in the course of his military service, neither, incidentally, do they contain any reference to his bearing any tattoo marks anywhere on his body. This last point is one to bear in mind.

Back in civvy street, Butt joined his wife at 'Elmfield', the home which she had set up during the war years, in the Worcestershire hamlet of Callow End. They were not to remain there long. A year or so later, Lillian's money bought them a farm, Wellington House, at Cooks Mill Green, Writtle, in Essex, a couple of miles west of Chelmsford, where Lillian's brother, Harry Bennett, lived, in Rainsford Road. There, Captain Butt, as he was henceforth to call himself, retaining, not quite properly for he had not been a regular soldier, his wartime commissioned rank, built up a successful dairy produce business, organising the enterprise with military precision. And, indeed, he kept up his army connection as a member of the British Legion – Badge Number 166273. The business-venturesome Lillian Butt's next speculation was the building of the County Hotel in Chelmsford. When it was completed she went to live there, the Captain remaining at the farm, carrying on with the dairy business. In 1925, however, Lillian fell seriously ill. Her husband gave up the farm and moved into the County Hotel to be with her. She died of a heart attack in Chelmsford Hospital on 9 September 1926, and was interred with her father, at Ash, in Surrey.

Footloose once more, still six years on the right side of 50, the bold captain did not long dally in the dales of widowerhood. He had, one shrewdly suspects, adopted the habit of contracting liaisons with ladies of means, which is to say matrimony for money. Anyway, his next adventuring into that holy estate was with another rather well-provided-for marital partner.

After Lillian's death, her widower had taken retrospective steps back to his sister Gertie's at Aston-on-Carrant, whence, it will be remembered, he had set forth to seek fortune in London all those long, pre-war years ago. It must have seemed a strange wheeling of the circle of time that brought him back there now, alone, a life and death's space later. But, as he was soon to discover, things always do appear to be somehow planned, destinies unsought worked out for us.

Back on one of his old stamping grounds, he rediscovered an earlier acquaintance, Miss Edith Florence Tombs Hogg, member of a wealthy local family. This 46-year-old spinster of means lived in the Manor House at Aston-on-Carrant, bequeathed to her, together with the money to reside graciously therein, by a rich relative. With an eye to the main chance, and knowing full well, as his sister was later to testify, that Miss Hogg was far from mentally well, he nonetheless courted her favour assiduously and so successfully that, on 23 February 1927, a mere five months after the loss of Lillian, they were married at the parish church of St Nicholas, Ashchurch – a large village on the high road from Tewkesbury to Evesham. The Captain moved into the Manor House. Eight years they lived there, and it was during this time that the second Mrs Butt began to display increasingly severe symptoms of gross mental affliction.

In April 1928, some 14 months after Edith's marriage to the Captain, a Mrs Lily Ashbee, a 47-year-old woman who had previously lived in a cottage opposite the Manor House, went to help Mrs Butt with the housework. She remained there for nearly seven years.

She testified:

> So far as I saw, Mr and Mrs Butt were quite happy together, and Mr Butt seemed very kind to her. Towards the end of 1934, something appeared to be going wrong with Mrs Butt. She turned against me. She was always strange in her manner, and seemed to think her husband did not want her. But this was untrue. Doctors had been attending Mrs Butt for some time. [She] at last got out of my control, and I advised Mr Butt to get someone else in to look after her, someone who was more used to it, and I left them. A few weeks afterwards, Captain Butt came across and told me he had obtained Mrs Sullivan. She came over once or twice just to have a little chat, but she never at any time mentioned about the Butts' affairs. Mr Butt used to take his wife and Nurse Sullivan out in the car for a drive occasionally. Mrs Sullivan came to the Manor from the Luards of Kemerton, and I had not seen her previous to her coming to the Manor.

It was in March 1935, that the by then unhappy couple left the Manor House and moved, considerably downmarket, to the suburban, pebble-dashed, detached – but only just – little rented house at 248 Old Bath Road, Cheltenham.

The following September the Manor House was let to a Mr AH Chovil, who described himself as an author. Manor Farm, which the Butts also owned, was leased to a Mr Walker.

Shortly before this epochal transference, the Butts had been joined by Nurse Sullivan. The plain but far from simple truth is that Mrs Irene Sullivan had been hired by the Captain on 18 February 1935, to take care of his wife, who, he explained, had latterly developed "some sort of nervous trouble". The fact is that Nurse Sullivan's function seems to have been as much, indeed more, social than medical. Her presence in the house freed the Captain, whose regular, self-indulgent practice it was to disappear without any prior warning for weeks at a time, usually returning, unannounced, as seemingly impetuously as he had left.

The sad truth is that the constitutionally inconstant Captain had long ago wearied of poor Edith. The veil he drew over his private extramarital athletics remains largely unrent, but, as we shall come to see, sundry tantalising chinks are perceptible. There stand revealed, for instance, Ida of Oxford and Winnie and Elsie of Plymouth, as well as certain alleged homosexual capers.

The Butts and Nurse Sullivan had been just one week ensconced at Number 248 when off went the Captain again on one of his solo jaunts – a fortnight in Plymouth.

Upon his return, Nurse Sullivan complained to him of his desertion, abandoning her thus with his ailing wife. Her plaints had no effect. Between 1935 and his final disappearance in 1938, Butt would at frequent intervals vanish, without informing anyone of either his destination or the estimated time of his arrival back, leaving Mrs Butt in Nurse Sullivan's caring but frustrated hands. His longest period of unexplained absence was six weeks. On rare occasions he did actually mention that he was Oxford bound.

The Captain was not, according to Nurse Sullivan, a man to be questioned. He struck her as "strange and preoccupied". In truth, she was instinctively somewhat afraid of him, perceiving the bully lurking just below the polished surface. For had she not indeed observed, with powerless misgivings, the cruelty and callousness of the way in which he behaved towards his mentally troubled wife? The unctuous ritual politeness of courtship and honeymoon period had long since evaporated; all too often now he assumed in his dealings with Edith a bullying, mocking, jibing attitude.

Although sundry of Butt's friends were wont to say that he was an easy-going man, very readily influenced by those with whom he was intimately acquainted, easy-going most certainly did not describe his demeanour towards his wife, his treatment of whom was disgraceful.

Explained Nurse Sullivan:

> It was borne in upon me how Captain Butt would set out deliberately to hurt his wife's feelings. He would address her with pointed sarcasm as "Edith, dear", or "Florence, darling". He would turn his back upon her, and ignore her when she spoke to him, and this would work her up into a state of hysteria, which I would have the utmost difficulty in restraining. There were a hundred and one ways in which he tortured

Mrs Edith Florence Butt. The Captian's unstable wife was prone to bouts of extreme emotion and depression.

his wife, the control of whose property and money he had by this time achieved by means of power of attorney. [This had been granted to him on 4 August 1934].

While on that subject, Nurse Sullivan shrewdly pointed out that, although he allowed his more intimate female acquaintances to believe that he derived his apparent wealth from mining interests in Africa, it was his wife's money that he spent on those trips of his which so upset her.

> Sometimes he would send me out to the pictures, and when I came back I would invariably find Mrs Butt in tears, and she has told me, "That man has been at me again, and made me sign my name away". Once I was told that he had stood over her with an Armenian truncheon and made her sign a paper which gave him a thousand pounds. It was a terribly unhappy household.

Oftentimes he would leave home – always in his car – late at night and return in the early hours of the morning, or, indeed, at 5am or even 9am, with never a word of explanation to his wife or Nurse Sullivan for his absence.

Mrs Butt would often speak of her husband's association with other women – referring to "Hilda" and "Ida", whom, she said, he was always visiting whenever they went to Oxford. She was deeply suspicious of Butt's absences in terms of the presence of "another woman" in his life.

Not bothering to put too fine a point on it, Nurse Sullivan frankly admitted that Captain Butt was a man whom she found it impossible to like. There were those of his friends who said of him, as though it were a virtue, that he was always careful in money matters. Nurse Sullivan expressed it differently. "He was the meanest man I have ever met," and she had, she said, the greatest trouble in extracting even her pound-a-week wages from him. It was, she felt, fortunate that she had no part in the arranging of the supply of food and drink for the household, save, of course, when the master was off on one of those prolonged walkabouts. He had accounts with the local tradesmen to which she could charge necessary commodities.

That first summer of 1935 when Nurse Sullivan was with the Butts at Number 248, the Captain brought a specialist from Gloucester to see his wife. Nurse Sullivan could not remember his name, but thought that he came from either Wootton or the Barnwood Asylum, at Gloucester. Dr Archibald Condor MD, of Eaton Lodge, The Park, Cheltenham, was present at the interview which, although Captain Butt did not say it to Nurse Sullivan in so many words, he had nonetheless contrived to convey to her, had been arranged because he wanted his wife put away. In the event, Mrs Butt was not taken off to a madhouse.

The following January – 1936 – she was removed for a short while to a private nursing home at Shurdington, a village some three miles south-west of

Cheltenham, where the question of having her certified was again broached by her husband. And again, nothing transpired.

During the fortnight that his wife was away, the Captain went to stay at Horton House, Horton Road, Gloucester, the home of his friend, Harold Moffatt, a Gloucester timber merchant, whose wife also happened to be away at the time.

The misfortunate Edith Butt was not without supporters. The Captain's sister, Mrs Gertie Prew, sympathised with her, and said that it was a shame that her brother wanted to have his wife confined to an asylum. Mrs Prew held no exalted opinion of brother William. She disagreed with his constant dalliances with other women. She also found him very mean, and resented a former refusal of his, at a time of crisis, to loan her a modest sum of money.

Judged by any reasonable standard, Captain Butt's life in the Cheltenham of the mid-1930s was leisurely and pleasant, agreeably cushioned by his rich wife's money. This Jekyll and Hyde, Street Angel and House Devil, character, was a member of the highly respectable Glentworth Club, in Hatherley Road, Cheltenham, where, among other recreational amenities, bridge tables were furnished. Indeed, it was especially for the bridge that Butt, a passionate player, had joined.

Slightly down the scale, the Captain was also an enthusiastic member of the Cheltenham Town Football Club, and, not restricting that enthusiasm solely to the terraces of home, he was one of those who, with a few other local stalwarts, travelled up on Saturday 27 November 1937, to Watford to watch his eleven's battle in their memorable first round of the cup-tie away match. They lost – three nil.

Even further down the scale, more or less discreetly concealed, but nonetheless real and disreputable for that, were the temporary gentleman's habitual demi-mondaine sexual adventurings and excursions.

Having, during the earlier part of the summer of 1937, done a five or six-week vanishing trick, that September Butt suddenly whisked his wife and Nurse Sullivan off to Cornwall for a fortnight's holiday at Polperro, where they were put up by Nurse Sullivan's son, Brian, in his cottage there. At the holiday's end, the Captain slipped Brian a couple of pounds to cover their stay.

The Captain made one more solo trip, of merely a single night's duration, to Exeter, in the October or November. On Christmas Eve, 1937, he and Edith set off to spend Christmas and New Year, as they did each year, with his widowed elder sister, Mrs Mary Agnes Hobson, at her home, Hobson's Riding School, 1 Greenview, Green Road, Wolvercote, two and a half miles north of Oxford.

It was, in fact, Mary's late husband, Francis Frederick Hobson, who had left her after five years of marriage and had died at Plymouth in August 1935, who had been exceptionally friendly with his brother-in-law, William Butt, and had often taken him sailing with him on his yacht, *Seacroft*, on which Hobson had for a time lived.

The day before the Butts left Cheltenham for Wolvercote, Mrs Gertie Prew had

Captain Butt's house, 248 Old Bath Road, Cheltenham.

paid them a seasonal good wish visit at Number 248. William and Gertie never met again.

The Yuletide turkey, plum-pudding and mince-pies, the New Year toasts, the whiskies and *Auld Lang Synes* in the melodious parish of the Oxford bells – and the Captain's in season visit to his Oxford belle – behind them, on the afternoon of Monday 3 January 1938, Mr and Mrs Butt drove sedately back in the Daimler through the Oxfordshire lanes and winding Gloucestershire roads to Cheltenham, arriving home in Old Bath Road at about 4pm. Slipping immediately back into cosy domestic routine, the Captain asked Nurse Sullivan to make tea, which the three of them sat down to together.

Neither the Captain nor Mrs Butt went out that night. Brian Sullivan looked in to Number 248, went off for his customary evening walk and drink, and came back later to say goodnight to his mother. He spoke with Mrs Butt, too. But whether or not he saw Captain Butt at the house, Nurse Sullivan could not afterwards say.

The following day, Tuesday 4 January 1938, an historic one in the sequence of the 'Torso Affair', Nurse Sullivan, who had popped briefly out, returned to Number 248 at about 5pm, just in time to encounter the Captain coming down the stairs. He asked her to put the kettle on and get tea.

"I would like you, Nurse," he said, "to take Edith to the pictures, as she seems unhappy after her holiday," adding, "and that's an order!"

"Certainly I'll take her," she replied, although, as she subsequently confessed, she was not really keen on going.

The ill-assorted trio had tea, the two women got suitably attired for their outing, and by half-past six were all ready to sally forth, leaving Captain Butt behind on his own in the house.

Just as they were stepping out of the front-door, Mrs Butt, apparently seething with inward anger at her husband's unwillingness to ferry them down to the cinema in the car, burst out with a nasty remark to him. Foreseeing a row, anxious to avoid tears and trouble, Nurse Sullivan promptly piped up: "Never mind, Edith, we'll go by bus," and with all due speed ushered her down the path, quitting the house without another word to the churlish Captain.

Having departed under bad auspices, they crossed the road to the bus stop, which was in front of the Wheatsheaf public-house, right opposite Number 248, and as they were approaching it, Brian Sullivan hove into sight in his car. He drove up to them,

"Hello, Mother, I was just coming to see you."

Nurse Sullivan gave him a rapid rundown on the home-front situation, and he cheerfully uplifted them to the Gaumont Palace, in Winchcombe Street, down in the centre of town.

The film showing that evening was *Love is News,* a skylarking romance, with Tyrone Power, Loretta Young and Don Ameche.

Emerging out into the night at around 10pm, Irene and Edith caught a bus back from Cheltenham to Old Bath Road. Alighting at the Wheatsheaf, they ran into Mrs Mary Frances Kent, of Number 262, whose daughter had recently undergone an operation. Nurse Sullivan and Mrs Kent were in full spate exchanging medical platitudes, when, once again, who should drive up but Brian, hailing his mother.

"Oh, excuse me," she apologised to Mrs Kent, "there's my son."

Approaching Number 248, Nurse Sullivan noticed that the side gates and the garage doors were open. Neither fact had escaped the outraged, scanning eye of Mrs Butt.

"There,"she spat forth, "that man's gone again!"

Looking at the dead windows and dark, brooding bulk of Number 248, Nurse Sullivan almost involuntarily remarked: "Oh, dear, I hate going into this place in the darkness". Hearing which, Brian accompanied them inside.

When they were all safely settled in the living-room, Mrs Butt turned nasty again, accusing her missing husband of having sent them to the pictures while he went traipsing off out; up to no good. She rambled on about him in such disparaging vein for a while, and then, all of a sudden, demanded beer. There being none in the house, she created a scene, until Brian gallantly volunteered to foray forth to a neighbouring public-house – the Wheatsheaf, no doubt – and bear back a supply.

This he did. Peace was restored to Mrs Butt's ruffled bosom, her ill-humour passed as rapidly as it had arrived, and Brian remained chatting with the alcoholically propitiated ladies in the sitting-room until verging upon midnight.

No mention was made in the course of conversation of the non-reappearance of the wayward Captain. It was, after all, by no means unusual for him to be out with his car until that time of night – and well after.

And when the next day came, still bringing no sign of the Captain's return, nobody was either particularly surprised or especially worried; they thought that he had just gone off on another of those wanderlustings of his.

They did not, could not, know it then, but this time it was to be different. This time he would never return. From that day to this he has never been seen alive again.

It is as if he had vanished into thin air ... or was it deep water?

Chapter Two

The Enigmatic Nurse Sullivan

In order that a little further necessary light be shed upon that *huis clos* household in the Old Bath Road, we must now take a closer look at the third occupant and her background – Nurse Irene Sullivan.

Indeed, did not she herself say: "It is essential you should understand something of the relationship between Brian and me and the Butts so that you will be in a position to better gauge the mystery surrounding the death of Brian and the disappearance of Captain Butt."?

Nurse Irene Sullivan was a self-made artefact. Born Sarah Elizabeth Emma Fribbins, the daughter of a farmer, she re-christened herself Irene, changed her name by marriage to Sullivan, and adopted, without benefit of proper qualificatory training, the 'Nurse' prefix.

Sarah Fribbins, daughter of Sarah Ann and Isaac Fribbins, of Anvilles Farm, Pewsey, Wiltshire, came into the world in 1881 – that is some seven years before the advent of Jack the Ripper – on, it is believed, Thursday 30 June. She had two elder sisters: Fanny, aged nine, and Martha, aged three.

When, on 7 March 1904, at the age of 22, she married a 22-year-old commission agent, John William Lincoln Sullivan, of 79 Saint Thomas Road, in the church of St John of Jerusalem, Lauriston Road, which was the parish church of South Hackney, in north-east London, she gave her address as 9 Albany Terrace, Marlborough, Wiltshire. By that time both her father and mother were dead.

She bore her husband two children, a girl, Violet Eileen, born in 1906, and a son, Brian Johnstone, born on 22 November 1909, at Gothic Cottage, Stroud Road, Gloucester. Violet contracted pulmonary tuberculosis and was sent to Cranham Sanatorium, near Stroud. She was back living with her mother at 1 Andover Terrace, Cheltenham, when she died of the disease on 27 January 1925. She was only 19.

Sullivan was no longer on the scene after five years of marriage. His wife put it about that he had died when Brian was three months old, but was later to admit to Scotland Yard detectives that he had left her around 1909.

Since his desertion, Mrs Sullivan had struggled bravely to earn a living for herself and her brood by private nursing. Patients had come to her by way of recommendation from the Cheltenham doctors, and, despite the fact that she had had no orthodox nursing training, she had, throughout the last 20 years, nursed successfully for nearly all the doctors practising in the district.

Over a period of twelve years, from 1921, she nursed a Miss Daubney, of Northwood, Fairfield Park Road, Cheltenham, who, when she died, left her £500 in her will. This was Irene's second legacy, for her mother had also left her £500 upon her death in 1902.

Following the birth of Brian, Irene Sullivan had, it would appear, moved with her two children to Dowdeswell, a grey village on a green slope of the Cotswolds, some four miles south-east of Cheltenham, and boasting an unrivalled view of that town's rustic reservoir.

Details of the years between 1910 and 1920 are not so much sparse as non-existent, unless, that is, the statement made in 1938 to the Warwickshire Constabulary by Percy Albert Morris, a 53-year-old, unmarried engineering draughtsman of Coventry, is accepted as referring to Irene Sullivan, which, despite her use of the name Evelyn, it almost certainly does.

In the year 1910 or 1911, I was living in North Street, Cheltenham, in lodgings. At that time I knew a young lady about twenty-eight years of age in the name of Evelyn Sullivan. She was an attendant at a cinema then in the street opposite the Promenade. The site I believe now is occupied by a garage. I was on rather friendly terms with her and I was occasionally in her company. Whilst I was in these lodgings, a friend of the family visited them a lot, and I recollect his conversation referring to Evelyn Sullivan. He alleged that she was married to a sailor and he had left her. This may not have been correct and I have never verified it.

Shortly after this, it would be about September 1910 or 1911, I left Cheltenham, and from that day to this I have never seen her. As old friends, she has corresponded with me. In her letters to me she has told me that she was engaged in nursing cases, and I have had letters from her at Bournemouth and Old Bath Road, Cheltenham. This latter place, I knew she was at during Christmas 1937, because I received a letter from her.

She has never confided to me any details of her affairs, and I was not aware that she had a son. From her letters I judged that she was a very lonely woman, and seemed anxious to keep in touch with old friends. She has never approached me for assistance in any shape or form, and the general impression I have is that she has always interested herself in my welfare, asking about my health, whether I was married, and she enquired also, on occasions, about my parents, and whether they were still alive.

Regarding the letter to her last Christmas, I think I addressed it to a three-figure number in Old Bath Road, Cheltenham, and my impression was that this address was a Nurses' Headquarters.

To describe the Sullivans' life between 1919 and 1932 as nomadic is not unreasonable. Six different addresses are known, all in the Cheltenham area, at which, for periods of time unknown, Mrs Sullivan was apparently domiciled. The answer may, of course, have something to do with nursing engagements. Let us in charity postulate professionalism rather than wandering psychopathy.

For the record, those addresses are: 1 Andover Terrace, Ashford Road, Cheltenham (1919); Salt Farm, Charlton Kings, Andoversford (1925); Charmwood, 5 Priory Street, Cheltenham (1927); 6 Keynsham Parade, Cheltenham (1930); Holmewood, Church Road, Leckhampton (1932); Northwood, Fairfield Park Road, Cheltenham (1933).

Whatever the vagaries of her peregrinations, Nurse Sullivan's first concern was to make sure as best she could that her son's schooling was good, sound and systematic. He was sent first to Cheltenham's Launton Park Road Council School, and on from there to the town's Technical School, where he did not, however, continue after reaching the age of 15.

A keen-as-mustard motor-cyclist, he got himself a job as an assistant in Leslie Paynter's motor-bicycle showroom, in Bath Street, Cheltenham. His boss liked him, saying that the lad was of a very cheerful nature, but at the same time he could not help feeling that Brian was obviously unsuited for the work, being far more interested in ball-room dancing than in selling motor-bikes.

Brian quit Paynter's in December 1926, and thereafter, the odd small excursion into business and property aside, devoted the major part of his efforts at earning a living to the professional pursuit of Terpsichore.

It was, claimed Raymond Smith, a friend who had been at the Technical School with him, he who had, after they left school, taught Brian to dance. He found him a both apt and willing pupil, whose declared ambition it was to be taken on as a professional dancer at the Palais de Danse at Cheltenham Winter Gardens. And, indeed, in the fulness of a very short time, having acquired considerable skill on the dance-floor, he was appointed as instructor and demonstrator at the Palais, and began also to run dancing classes at his mother's house in Priory Street, a portion of which he transformed into 'The Priory Studio of Dancing'.

He was now to be seen regularly attending dances at Cheltenham Town Hall, and his reputation grew locally. By the time he was 21, Brian's twinkling feet had carried him off to London.

It was in September 1933, that Nurse Sullivan took over Tower Lodge from Mrs Margaret Elwes, widow of Henry John Elwes, FRS, the celebrated arborist, author of *The Trees of Great Britain and Ireland*, of Colesborne Park, Colesborne, seven miles south of Cheltenham. The lease of her future home was for three years, at a cost of £30 *per annum* exclusive of rates.

She frankly admitted:

> The reason I took Tower Lodge was that I could not afford to continue to pay the rent of the house in Fairfield Park Road, which was £55 a year, exclusive of rates.

Tower Lodge, Leckhampton Hill, Cheltenham. The gothic building which was to become the centre of gossip, intrigue and rumour.

Since it is to play a major rôle in the strange story of the Cheltenham Torso, it is worth taking time here to describe Tower Lodge in some detail.

A small, grey stone, two-storey building with a most distinctive castellated roof, ivy creeping from the front-door upwards over its walls to the machicolated parapet, it stood – still stands, in splendid renovated condition – on Leckhampton Hill, the very steep wooded rise towards the Cotswold escarpment, overlooking the spires and crescents of Regency Cheltenham. Situate some little way up the hill, it is uncluttered by any adjoining or nearby premises on that side of the road.

Nurse Sullivan wrote of it that it was,

> … one of the loveliest old buildings I have ever known. It was built at the same time as Leckhampton Court, which lies below in the hollow … [it] is a squat, square building, built of centuries old Cotswold stone. It is perched on the side of Leckhampton Hill, and stands there alone, maintaining a vigil it has maintained for centuries.*
> It is the oldest lodge of the three attached to Leckhampton Court, and the most picturesque. With its ivy-clad turreted top, it made an appeal to me the very first time I saw it, and as I had always longed to have a permanent home in Cheltenham, when I knew it was available I determined to take it. I felt that it would be a lovely week-end retreat for Brian after the long nights spent in London as a dance host at the Piccadilly Hotel. I felt that it would be somewhere where I could always be happy between my nursing engagements. I lived at Tower Lodge for a year, and Brian came to see me very often.

It was during that year – 1934 – that she was engaged by Mrs Mary Edith Luard, a widow, of Upper Court, Kemerton, in Worcestershire, to look after her ailing mother-in-law. She recalled:

> I believe I was told of Nurse Sullivan through Mr Wiggin's Registry Office, Cheltenham. For a reference I went to two gentlemen who kept dogs at or near Deerhurst. They were dog breeders. I have a faint idea it was Edwards, the name. A sister of these men whom I saw told me she [Nurse Sullivan] was very nice, and had nursed her mother. She eventually came to Upper Court, and stayed temporarily for about a month. During the time she was here, her son, I have since learned, came to tea and supper on several occasions. I only saw him once, and that was in the kitchen. Some little time after, Mrs Sullivan came here again for a few days, during a change of nurses.

---

*This is, perhaps, drawing the romantic bow a shade too long. Tower Lodge was actually built about 1800-01, and later in the century did service as an ale-house for the Leckhampton quarry workers.

Nurse Sullivan herself remembered:

> After a year, I felt I ought to do something to add to the little money I had. I let Tower Lodge for a year to Mr and Mrs Sumner, a newly married couple from London. They took it over in September 1934. I went to London and stayed with Brian at 2 Radlett Place, St John's Wood, until just before Christmas. I looked after an old lady in Abbey Road, Maida Vale. It was mostly daily work.
>
> I returned to Cheltenham shortly before Christmas 1934, and returned to Tower Lodge. When I had let the place to the Sumners, I had, on the advice of Mrs Elwes, retained a bedroom. This was the back bedroom upstairs. I loved the Lodge, and I know that Brian loved it as much as I did.
>
> I did one or two odd jobs of nursing in Cheltenham and district which kept me occupied right up to the February of 1935, when I became nurse to Mrs Butt.
>
> The Sumners left Tower Lodge in September 1935. I then had the place cleaned up, and it remained unoccupied from then until the last week in July 1937. All my life I have been a professional nurse, and it was in a purely professional capacity that I first got to know Captain and Mrs Butt. I had just finished attending a patient at Cheltenham and was staying at an hotel there when Captain Butt rang up one day to ask me whether I would call upon him with a view to looking after Mrs Butt, who is a very highly strung and nervous woman. He told me that he had been recommended to me by somebody who knew me.
>
> I did not know it then, but the beautiful, old-world place where Captain and Mrs Butt were living out at Aston-on-Carrant, called the Manor House, was part of the property which had been left to Mrs Butt by a relative, together with a large fortune. I was not anxious to go out into the country, but I thought I would have the interview and decide then. I accordingly saw Captain and Mrs Butt, and at once felt a great sympathy with Mrs Butt, who eventually I used to call Edith. I decided to take the situation and went to the Manor House.

Her salary was settled at £1 per week, plus food and accommodation.

> It was a huge, rambling building, and I was rather surprised when I found that there were no servants there. There had been a housekeeper, but she had left. I arrived on Monday [18 February 1935]. On Thursday, Captain Butt left the house, telling nobody where he was going or when he would be back, and leaving Mrs Butt and myself entirely alone in the place. He was away a fortnight.
>
> In the months and years to follow I was to learn that this was no new

experience. That was just one of the many occasions that he simply vanished without a word of warning. And it was during that fortnight I learned the torture that Mrs Butt went through during these periods. She would cry for hours, whilst I endeavoured to comfort her. As for myself, there were only one or two houses in the village, and the place was so huge and empty of people that I told Captain Butt on his return that I could not possibly stay there, and whilst I was loth to leave Mrs Butt, I could not stand the strain of the loneliness.

He did not go away for some little time again, but eventually he did so, and was away for several days. I then told him that I was leaving, but he begged me to stay, and said, "If I get a house in the town will you consent to stay on with Edith?" There was obviously only one object in this suggestion. He felt that his wife was in good hands, and he wanted to be able to go off at any time he liked on these mysterious excursions. For they were mysterious. During the time that he was away he never communicated with his wife or with me. He simply passed out of our existence, and returned when he felt inclined, anything from one to six weeks afterwards. He never volunteered any information to his wife where he had been, beyond saying, perhaps, that he had been for a cruise.

It was in this manner that we came – in March 1935 – to live at 248 Old Bath Road, where we were living when Captain Butt finally disappeared. I was not with them continually, for now and again I would leave for a few weeks when Mrs Butt appeared to be a bit better.

An interesting glimpse of Nurse Sullivan and her activities during one of these away periods is chance revealed by a Mrs Elizabeth Kate Barlow, of Corfe Castle, Dorset, who came forward to tell the local police:

One evening in 1935, a Mrs Sullivan was looking for rooms in Corfe Castle. Seeing me at the gate of my house, she asked me if I could accommodate her. She was in a black car, which was being driven by her son. She had two young men with her, aged 19 and 25 respectively – her son and his friend. I put her up for one night, and the two young men slept elsewhere – in the car, according to Mrs Sullivan. They left for Swanage on the following morning, Mrs Sullivan stating that she was going to try and set up a house for old people there. But the same day I saw her returning through Corfe Castle towards Wareham.

The following year Mrs Sullivan came to my house one day, at about lunch-time and had with her an elderly lady who was very funny in her actions, and who appeared to be dominated by, and in fear of, Mrs Sullivan. Mrs Sullivan asked me to put her up for a week, and this I refused to do, as I had taken a great dislike to her. Before leaving on this occasion she asked my husband the time of the trains for Bournemouth.

At that time Nurse Sullivan wanted to raise money for some new clothes, so she let the Lodge for five weeks, which brought her in a very welcome £10 13s. Speaking of her tennancy of Tower Lodge, Nurse Sullivan said:

> Mrs Butt and I visited it from time to time, but now Mrs Butt had a number of very bad mental turns. I took her up there three or four times in the daytime. After I went to the Butts', I let the Captain, who was very keen on gardening, have the garden, and he used to grow lots of vegetables. Captain Butt never stayed at the Lodge overnight to my knowledge, but he might have done. He went up there frequently during the daytime.

In November 1935, she approached Captain Butt, making it clear that she did not consider that she was being paid a sufficient wage. She explained to him that she could not afford to pay the rent and rates of Tower Lodge if he was not only paying her too little, but failing to pay even that little regularly.

To be fair, he saw the point and suggested that it would be a good idea if he were to take over the Lodge and pay the necessary charges on it, which amounted to 14s a week, as it would be a nice place for her to take Mrs Butt sometimes, and he would himself like the garden.

Thinking that he meant that she would receive the 14s a week in addition to her pound-a-week wage – thus making her total income 34s per week – she readily agreed to his take-over bid. But it did not pan out quite like that. He brought his wife up to Tower Lodge, but Mrs Butt had a very bad turn, was most distressed, and he was obliged to take her back to Number 248.

Neither did the arrangement work out satisfactorily from Nurse Sullivan's point of view, because although Butt paid the rent and rates – sometimes by cheque made out to her, and sometimes with cheques made out to the owner and ground landlords respectively – she continued to have trouble in obtaining her wages from him. It was not that he was in any way short of funds. He was simply constitutionally miserly, and found the paying out even of his legitimate dues a cause of very real distress. In fact, when he did his final involuntary vanishing trick in January 1938, according to Nurse Sullivan, he owed her something between a sizeable £40 and £50 for wages unpaid.

Still looking around for ways and means to expand her very slender income, in July 1936 Nurse Sullivan paid a call on Mrs Helen May Hopkins, of Wigwood Farm, Tirley. She told Inspector Large:

> She said she had been sent by the people across the river. She came to ask if Cockbury Hall Cottages were for sale. These cottages are on the river side at Chaceley Stock [opposite side to Deerhurst]. The first time

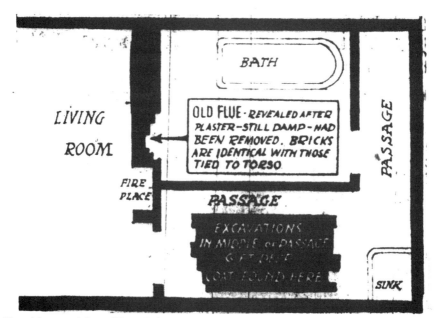

Plan of the ground-floor of Tower Lodge.

The ground-floor living room at Tower Lodge.

she came, Mrs Sullivan had a woman friend with her. She called a few days after with her son, as she wanted him to see the cottages. She told me she belonged to a musical family, and also said, "I'm a widow and I'm taking up nursing again". She said she wanted the cottages for mental patients, just for the summer time, and she could furnish the place and make it look nice. Her chief point was to buy the cottages. I told her they became flooded in the winter months, and she said she would only want them for the summer months. As far as I can remember, Mrs Sullivan's son asked me if I took paying-guests, as he and some friends would like to come and stay in this part. Mrs Sullivan agreed to take the cottages, but cancelled a few days after by letter.

The Sullivans, mother and son, were both keen main-eye-chancers. But it was Tower Lodge of which Nurse Sullivan was obviously most seriously and lastingly enamoured.

It was not a very large place. There was a fair-sized living-room downstairs, with two very low windows looking out on to the roadway. The Lodge, I should explain, stood right on the footway, so that passers-by could look right into the windows. When I first took the Lodge, these downstairs windows were boarded up from the outside. I mention this fact because I was closely questioned as to why the windows had been match-boarded up from the inside. I will tell you why. When I had settled down there, the boarded-up windows looked so ugly that I had the boards removed.

Some little time afterwards one of the new double-decker buses was being taken down to Gloucester when it got out of hand coming down the hill and, in turning the bus into a tree in order to avoid a worse accident, the vehicle nearly struck me. It missed me by only a few inches.

When I told Brian, he was greatly upset, and pointed out that if by any chance a car got out of hand coming down the hill it might easily crash into the Lodge, and if it did so, while it would do no great damage to the sturdy walls of the place, it might easily shatter the low-built windows, and if I were in the room I might easily be injured. "I'll have them boarded up from inside," he said, and, although months went by, he had them done just before Christmas.

That is the whole story of the boarded-up windows, although the most sinister purport was attached to them during the recent inquiries. It was probably conjectured that this was all part of the dark scheme of things to hide what was going on behind those grey walls.

Apart from the living-room downstairs, there was a passageway leading into a kitchenette and bathroom, which had been built on to the older part of the Lodge. Then there was a staircase leading to the upstairs rooms, consisting of the bedroom over the living-room and the smaller back bedroom.

Against the background of the countryside, Tower Lodge has a definite majesty. Against the background of the night, there was something almost eerie about it. Yet even on the pitch-dark nights, when I had to walk up the hill alone, I never felt the least bit nervous of going into the place. There is one thing, too, I have never been able to fathom. Both during the night and day, I have heard ghostly voices and ghostly musicians there. In my bedroom I have lain awake and heard the most beautiful voice singing a sort of lullaby. It sounded to me as though it were in Latin. In the room downstairs I have also heard this voice. On occasions others besides myself have heard these voices, and on one occasion when a friend of mine, Mrs Wray, was there with me, there came the sound of music, which she distinctly heard.

I have never heard of any ghost in connection with the Lodge, and I have never seen anything there. Heard nothing but the voices and the music.

No ghosts, perhaps, but all too soon Tower Lodge was to become the demesne of sheer horror, known throughout the length and breadth of the land as the dark centre of a sensational mystery of death and butchery.

Chapter Three

The Smiling Dancer

Calling himself Byron Smith, his initials remaining conveniently the same, the metamorphosed Brian Sullivan was, by the early 1930s, securely established in London. He earned his daily bread with his prancing feet as a handsomely remunerated dancing partner, or 'Dance Host' as the preferred title had it, on the pay-roll – £2 per week plus extras – of the smart, up-market Piccadilly Hotel, situated within a champagne bottle's fling of Eros at the Circus.

The term 'gigolo' still bears the 'sleazy dago' connotation bestowed upon it by the American dance-hall's 'ten-cents-a-dance' system. But the English dancing partner of the 1930s, such as the romantically named Byron Smith, followed what was then regarded as a perfectly respectable, albeit sometimes slightly effete, occupation. Indeed, most of the big hotels of the *thé dansant* heyday fielded a team of salaried dancers, the dance hosts and hostesses, as a management amenity, so that unaccompanied patrons of either sex were sure to be able to trip the light fantastic, and, into the bargain, be painlessly taught the latest fashionable dance-steps.

The first steps, aside from those on the polished parquet of the dance-floor, which Brian took to consolidate his position in the capital are hidden behind the long unrollings of the mists of time past.

The earliest metropolitan glimpse that we are afforded shows him in full-flowering, settled focus. He is living in a mews flat, Number 2 Radlett Place, lying between Avenue Road and Primrose Hill, in St John's Wood, NW8. He is sharing it with a man named Keith Harold Newman, whom he had met at the Piccadilly Hotel in 1931.

This Newman proved on closer acquaintance to be a distinctly dodgy character. Under the name of Roger Radcliffe, and describing himself as an agent, he was, in February 1933, at the age of 23, charged with obtaining goods by false pretences. He pleaded not guilty – but was unrepresented by counsel.

Newman told the Chairman of the Quarter Sessions that he had made arrangements with a solicitor for his defence and had sent him the money, but it had been stolen in transit, and the solicitor was not present in court. At the suggestion of Mr Frank Phillips, prosecuting, the hearing was put back, and the solicitor referred to was communicated with by telephone.

Later in the day, the case was called on again. The Chairman then said that the solicitor in question stated that he had at one time appeared for the prisoner, but, for reasons which he (the Chairman) need hardly refer to, he was not taking any further steps in regard to the prisoner's defence.

Sullivan, with his dance partner Eileen Sharpe, probably taken at Cheltenham Town Hall. Early in his career as a professional gigolo, Brian was extremely successful and popular.

Newman had thereupon asked whether the case could be adjourned to the next Sessions, in order that he might make arrangements about his defence. The Chairman said that that could not be done, but at his request Mr Hunter Rodwell agreed to defend the prisoner.

It was charged that on 13 December 1932, Newman went into the shop of Messrs Asprey & Co, in Bond Street, and said that he wanted a boy's cheap wristwatch. The shop people were busy with the Christmas rush, and a temporary assistant served him. Newman had selected a watch priced at £3 15s. He had then said that he wanted a gold cigarette case. He selected one, valued at £15 7s 6d. He next thought that he would like a fountain pen and pencil, which cost only £2 12s 6d. The total of the bill was £21 15s.

He asked the assistant for one of the firm's cheque forms, on which customers could fill in the name of their bank. He filled in 'Barclays Bank, London Road, Basingstoke', made the cheque for £21 15s, and signed it 'KH Newman'. Barclays Bank at Basingstoke was in Market Place, and there was no account there in the names of either Newman or Radcliffe. He left, taking with him the articles; shortly afterwards he pawned the cigarette case.

The second charge was that of attempting, on 19 December 1932, to obtain a bicycle by false pretences from Alfred B Chase, proprietor of a cycle shop in the High Street, Epping, Essex.

Counsel said that when the accused had come to deal with the Essex people, "it did not come off". Newman, calling himself Radcliffe, had gone into Mr Chase's shop and ordered a bicycle. He had asked to have various accessories fitted, and, returning later, wrote out a cheque for £7 1s 9d, on a cheque form similar to that which he had used at Asprey's, filling in 'Midland Bank, Main Street, Fleet, Hampshire', and signing it 'R Radcliffe'.

The accused suggested that Mr Chase should telephone the bank to see that the cheque was all right. He did so. There was no Main Street in Fleet, and no branch of the Midland Bank. Consequently, Mr Chase kept the bicycle and the cheque, and got in touch with the police.

Accused, on oath, said that his real name was Keith H Newman. He claimed to have met a man named Jack Moore, and they had decided to start an agency for a cabaret show. He had given Moore £25 to be put to £25 provided by Moore. He used the name of Newman and Radcliffe for the purpose of the cabaret business. Moore had told him that he had opened accounts at the Midland Bank, Fleet, and Barclays Bank, Basingstoke, and he (the accused) signed two bank slips at Moore's request.

Newman declared that he had thought the cheques were genuine when he presented them, and said that he purchased something at Messrs Asprey's the previous Christmas, and paid for it by cheque in exactly the same way. He bought the articles, he said, for Christmas presents. He explained that he pawned the cigarette case because he wanted £3 to pay an artiste some money that was owing, and at the particular time of day he wanted it he could not go to the bank.

The jury, after a brief deliberation, returned a verdict of guilty. Detective Sergeant Carpenter reported that in November 1932, at Feltham, the accused was fined £15 or two months' hard labour on each of two charges of obtaining cigarette cases by means of a trick. The fine was not paid, and two committal warrants were held in respect of those offences. There were three outstanding charges of obtaining money by false pretences, which the accused wished to be taken into consideration.

The Chairman, in sentencing Newman to nine months' hard labour, said that he was a plausible, dangerous swindler, of a particularly mean type.

And this was the man with whom Brian Sullivan was, over the next six or seven years, to share an intimate personal, as well as a disastrous business, relationship.

In 1932, however, before all Newman's malfeasances caught up with him, an asparagus-green – or was he? – Sullivan had approached the landlord, Mr Collier Smithers, of Roland Gardens, South Kensington, for a renewal of the lease on the premises where he and Newman were flat-mates, and for the granting to him of a similar lease on the adjacent flat Number 4. Both leases were duly assigned, and Newman became henceforth Sullivan's tenant.

Soon after his arrival in London, Brian had progressed from motor-bikes to motor-cars, and garaged his new car at the Lord Palmerston Garage, in Palmerston Road, Kilburn. That was where he came into contact with James Ralph, who was actually employed there, and with a rather shady character, Brian Sutherland.

Sutherland, whose given name was not Brian at all, but Todd O'Halloran Devereux Sutherland, was, like Newman, 'other than a good one'. The son of Captain JG Sutherland, RNR, he had, after showing great early promise – being captain of his school and so forth – slithered rapidly into a criminal career.

He was first sentenced in May 1926, when he would have been only 19 or 20, to six months' hard labour for theft. He was to go down again in March 1934, when he was charged at Marlborough Street with obtaining a ticket for the Chelsea Arts Ball by means of a forged cheque, and with, more despicably, robbing his fellow Rugby players. He asked for other cases to be taken into consideration.

Mr J Chesterton, defending, told the Court that a fortnight before his arrest, Sutherland had met and married a 23-year-old girl, who, taking him at face value, had had no idea of the kind of life that he had been living. His downfall, said counsel, might be attributed to lack of home life. When he was a boy his parents were divorced, and he had had a deprivation in his personal circumstances.

His uncle, the Reverend V Lawson, vicar of St Lawrence's Church, Chevening Road, Brondesbury, pleaded on his behalf:

> I believe that in spite of his record, he is now under an influence such
> as he has never had before. He is in love, and his wife loves him in
> spite of everything. She wants to reclaim him, and I think that love is

the only chance a criminal has to be reclaimed. I have great faith that, if you give him a chance, she can reclaim him. She is going to stand by him whatever happens.

The Bench was not impressed. He was sentenced to nine months' hard labour. On hearing this, a girl at the back of the court buried her face in her hands, and was led out, half fainting, by an elderly woman.

It was about the June of 1933, a good nine months before the pronouncement of this sentence, that Sullivan, who had always rather fancied himself as a mechanical engineer, and who seems to have been a most dubious picker of partners, set up, in partnership with Sutherland, an enterprise – Brian's Car Hire – under the impressive sounding banner of 'Messrs Sullivan & Sutherland, Motor Engineers', at 30a Acacia Road, St John's Wood. James Ralph was taken on as a chauffeur, and one Duncan Eric Ward was invited by Brian Sullivan to assist in the running of the business. The venture did not succeed and had, by November 1933, been dissolved.

Nothing daunted, Sullivan had another crack at the motor hire business within twelve months. This time he formed a partnership with Keith Newman. Once again, 30a Acacia Road was the venue of aspirant hope. The new business was christened 'Roadways and Airways Hire Service'. A good deal of its work consisted in arranging the transporting of people to and from Croydon airport. Duncan Eric Ward was introduced to Newman and engaged as manager. Sutherland and Ralph had no part in the venture. Brian Sullivan was a sleeping partner. Ward was afterwards to suggest that it was the constant quarrelling between Sullivan and Newman that brought about the failure of the enterprise. Whatever, within six months Roadways and Airways had also closed down.

The demise of the business had not apparently been fair, square and clean. Newman had left Sullivan saddled with an unpleasantly liberal crop of debts. And the creditors were not of the gentlest.

Ernest Battie testifies that he, a porter at the Piccadilly, having heard that Brian Sullivan was interested in motors and motoring, had, in 1933, introduced himself to him with the request that he would advise him regarding the purchase of a second-hand motor-bike. Brian had fixed him up with a decent machine, cheaply. Ever since they had been firm friends and, in the autumn of 1934, Sullivan – at that time apparently living temporarily on his own in Acacia Road – had invited Ern to share his lodgings.

Battie accepted, and relates how Brian used to bolt and bar every door, warning him how he was on no account to answer any knocks. When asked why, Brian sketchily explained that he had been left with several bad debts.

During the time that Battie and Brian were living together, Nurse Sullivan visited them and volunteered to Ern that she had had to advance Brian £80 – out of her legacy from Miss Daubeny – to get him out of some trouble.

While living with Brian, Battie had gained the impression that he was scared of someone or other, and that that contributed to Nurse Sullivan's anxiety. She had, in fact, actually asked Battie if her son was mixed up with bad companions, and suggested to him that if he knew of any he might perhaps be good enough to write to her at Cheltenham. During this conversation she specifically mentioned the man Brian Sutherland, and indicated that she was aware that he had been to prison.

The duration of Ern Battie's stay at Acacia Road was four weeks precisely. When he told Brian of his intention to leave, the latter was most disturbed, and begged him not to go, even offering for him to remain there rent free if only he would stay. Battie was, however, adamant that he must move on. He described Brian's behaviour as all that might be expected, and had no complaints. And he went on to say that it was evident that he was extremely fond of the opposite sex. This, in view of what we are later to hear of Brian Sullivan's alleged sexual proclivities, is, at the very least, noteworthy. Being on night duty, Battie used to make a point of calling on Brian each morning to check that all was well with him, and they usually had a breakfast cup of tea together.

Physically, Brian was generally described as a weakling, although on one occasion he is said to have astonished Battie and others present at the Piccadilly Hotel, when he completely mastered, with a skilful display of ju-jitsu, a rather big man who had been making fun of him. Battie said that he spoke to Brian about this afterwards, and was told by him that he had had training in the Japanese art. The great surprise occasioned by the incident was on account of Brian's small stature and inoffensive appearance. It may be noted, therefore, that it will not do to underestimate the undersized Brian.

Of unprepossessing appearance, weighing some eight stone eight pounds, standing about five foot seven inches in his dancing pumps, he nonetheless succeeded in presenting a certain vulnerable charm; he had a way with him to please hotel patrons. He was, moreover, regarded as a good conversationalist, ever ready to talk on any subject. He was always in demand as a partner among those women who went regularly to the Piccadilly.

There were, however, as in perhaps all of our cases, perceptive variations. While one employee at the Piccadilly, a male, had Brian down as an affectionate type of person who often, and sentimentally, mentioned his mother, other employees, female, dance hostesses, spoke of him as spiteful, vicious even, given to practising upon them, whenever the chance presented, that nasty twisting of the skin of the arm in diverse directions, dubbed by schoolboys – and Brian – 'Chinese torture'.

Two dance hostesses, Miss Beryl Mary Phillips and Miss Jill Bryan, were exceptionally wary of him. Miss Bryan had indeed good reason to be so, for on one occasion Brian had applied this brutality to her with such sadistic vigour that a ligament was strained and she required medical attention for more than a week. For this injuring of the young woman he was actually threatened with dismissal. According to Miss Bryan, if Brian had been drinking he was inclined to be

Keith Newman's Jaguar DXT 375. Taken at Radlett Place.

"spiteful and ill-tempered", and would commit these assaults for no apparent reason.

Such assertions did not, of course, at all accord with Nurse Sullivan's view of her ewe-lamb, which was merely that he was "always a highly strung boy and rather adventurous". And she added: "We grew up together great pals. Brian would always consult me about things."

Speaking of the time when she had first settled into Tower Lodge, she reminisced:

> After his work at the hotel was finished, late on a Saturday night, he would come down to the Lodge in his car, speeding through the early morning hours. There he would rest, take me out in the car on the Sunday, spend his time happily with me, sometimes bringing a friend

down with him from London. I saw Brian frequently. We were on the most affectionate terms, as one can imagine of a mother and her only son.

One of the friends whom Brian brought to Cheltenham was Ern Battie, but, according to him, he never actually stayed at Tower Lodge. Another was Keith Newman. He first visited Cheltenham about 1935. He did not on that occasion stay at the Lodge, but put up for the night at a local hotel. He was in Cheltenham again later that year, and in the spring of 1936, staying this time for one or two nights at the Lodge. It may be noted, therefore, that Newman would have been reasonably well acquainted with Tower Lodge and its internal and external economies.

Sometimes Brian's visits to Cheltenham would have an essentially practical purpose – for instance, to partner women at dances there, which would earn him as much as £5 for a night's work; a tidy sum in terms of purchasing power in those long ago days.

Sometimes he would bring a young woman down from London with him, ostensibly to attend a ball and practise her dancing steps with him, for, of course, a fee. The word 'ostensibly' is deliberately interposed here, because, as we shall see, other and more sinister reasons for these periodic importations were to be bruited.

Among the young women patrons of the Piccadilly Hotel dances who liked to sway around the floor in the arms of the lithe, horn-rim-bespectacled Byron Smith, was a Miss May Margaret Edwards. She had first met him there late in 1935. A former hotel dance-partner of Brian's opined:

> With Brian and his wife-to-be, it seemed to be a case of love at first sight. After their first meeting, she constantly took a table at the cabaret show. Then, a month or two later, he told us that he was going to marry. He did so, and then left us.

Described as dark and good-looking, Miss Edwards was also a sound businesswoman, who, coming into the firm of Messrs GB Chapman, naturalists, of 24 Tottenham Court Road, St Pancras, London, in 1921, at the age of 17, had risen to become a director of the company. At 32, six years Brian's senior, she was sufficiently charmed, hypnotised perhaps, to make the mistake of marrying him.

On 1 February 1936, something of a blow fell upon Byron Smith. After seven years, his services at the Piccadilly Hotel were suddenly dispensed with, so that when, on 4 April 1936, he and Margaret were married at Hampstead Register Office, the groom had been out of work for two months, and was without prospect of any immediate return to employment. The bride, who gave her address on the marriage certificate as 24 Tottenham Court Road, which was that of her place of employment, was at the time the sole breadwinner. The newly-weds moved into

Brian's flat – Number 4 Radlett Place. Keith Newman was their immediate neighbour, occupying Number 2.

The marriage was not to last. Brian's mother's memory was that:

> It was in the spring of 1936 that Brian came down to me one weekend looking like death. Usually he was bright and cheerful and had abounding energy. But on this occasion his eyes were dull, and he looked terribly ill. I at once said to him: "Why, whatever is the matter, Brian? What on earth have you been doing to yourself? You look terrible."
>
> I had not seen him for about a month, and although I had received letters, they had said nothing about him being ill. Consequently I was very surprised when he suddenly turned to me and said:
>
> "Oh, Mother, I have been awfully ill. I haven't known what to do with myself, and I can't understand it."
>
> "But why on earth didn't you send for me?" I asked him. "You know that I would have dropped everything to come and look after you."
>
> He smiled. It was such a sad smile. "I didn't like to trouble you, Mother. You have got enough to do to look after yourself and your patients."
>
> At the time I wondered if he had taken any sort of drug, and I even questioned him on the point, although I had never heard of him doing anything so stupid. He only laughed and reassured me that his illness was due to nothing of that sort. And that was all. I did not know till afterwards that at that time he was already married, and that the reason why he could not very well send for me to look after him was because he had not told me of his wedding, which he had kept so secret.

Indeed, for some unexplained – inexplicable – reason of his own, Brian had asked his wife to pose as Miss Edwards. She, however, would have none of it, insisting, quite understandably, that his mother must be told of the marriage.

It is, all circumstances being taken into account, hardly surprising perhaps that the 'secret marriage' was turning rapidly sour. It was to addle irreversibly within a gestatory nine months.

According to Margaret, it was she who had paid for the furniture in the marital home. She complained that Brian was lazy in his habits, and said that this soon caused differences between them.

During August 1936, Brian went off to stay for three weeks in Bournemouth with his mother, and during that time he did his level best to induce Margaret to give up her job and come and open up a boarding-house in Bournemouth. She replied that she would do no such thing, and warned him that on his return to London he would find her – and the furniture – missing.

Brian Sullivan and bride. The relationship was a brief and unsettled one, Brian's mother being unaware of his marriage to Margaret Edwards until months after the event.

Brian went back to Radlett Place, stayed about a week, leading a cat-and-dog life, and then, in September, cleared off 'back to mother' in Cheltenham. Whereupon, Margaret Sullivan left Radlett Place and took up residence at 10 Cambridge Gate Mews, Albany Street, NW1.

A few days later, Brian was back from Cheltenham, staying with Keith Newman at Number 2 Radlett Place. He telephoned his wife at her office. But she refused to have anything more to do with him, because, she said, she believed that he was associating with other women.

Undeterred by her refusal, a very determined Brian turned up, waiting outside her work place. When she came out, he pleaded very convincingly that they should let bygones be bygones, try again, make a new start, resume normal relations. After a great deal of hard talking he managed to persuade her, and she took him back with her to her Cambridge Gate Mews flat.

But he was incorrigible, and inevitably differences again arose. The break-up may, it has been suggested, have been due to Brian's continuing frequent visits to Cheltenham in his sports car, accompanied, so it is said, on each occasion by a different young lady in the passenger seat. Certainly Margaret did complain that he was always away in Cheltenham, but, to be fair, considerable doubt exists as to whether such trips were merely adventurous and adulterous. They may have been, as we shall discover, strictly business trips. In any event, Margaret Sullivan tells a different story, sings a different song.

The relationship limped along, with periodic fiery stumblings, until 4 January 1937, on which fateful Monday Margaret firmly and finally told Byron to sling his hook – permanently. He did so, taking her motor-car with him. His last gesture of spiteful defiance.

Her son's nuptials and all their sad train of little tragedies left behind, Nurse Sullivan, not, one feels, without some degree of satisfaction, mused:

> It was while I was staying at the Lodge myself, having left the Butts for a week or two, that I first learned that Brian was married. It came as a terrible shock to me, for it was months after the event had taken place, and when he told me I felt hurt that he had not confided in me regarding this great event in anybody's life.
>
> It came about this way. I had noticed that for some days he appeared to be rather worried about something, and this was so unlike him that I asked him what was the matter. He assured me that he was not worried at all. One day a telegram came for him, and after he had opened it I noticed a frown on his face, and he seemed to have something on his mind.
>
> The following day there were three telegrams, and this time I could tell that he really was worried. I thought he might have got into some sort of scrape in London, and did not care to tell me about it. So I determined to press him, and see if I could not straighten things out.

"Oh, it's about a woman's car," he explained, and when I failed to grasp what he meant, he said he had been driving a woman's car, and she wanted it back.

I did not know then that the woman was his wife, and that she was then bringing an action against him in connection with the car. So I simply said:

"Why, that's nothing to worry about, Brian, you don't need to have any woman's car, you can get one of your own." *

He went to bed.

The next morning he was cleaning his shoes in the garden when suddenly he turned to me and said:

"What would you say, Mother, if I told you I was married?"

I felt a sudden clutching at my heart, but I have always made it a practice to talk over quietly with Brian any little differences I may have had, and so I replied:

"Well, it wouldn't be much good saying anything, would it? Why do you ask me?"

He put his arms around me and said: "I am, Mother. I was married last April."

I walked away, for I did feel terribly hurt, but did not want him to see how much. Later on I told him that he might have let me know, because every mother likes to be present at her only son's wedding. I cannot understand all the secrecy about his marriage. I cannot understand why he should not have told me. It all seems so unnecessary. There was no occasion to keep it from me, for when at length I did know, I was only too eager to meet and welcome his wife. I asked him all about his wife, and later on she came down to see us at the Lodge, and I visited her in town.

Nurse Sullivan stayed a few days with the couple at Cambridge Gate Mews in November 1936. She subsequently came to realise that there was some unhappiness between them.

> I thought maybe they would be happier if they were remarried at Leckhampton Church. It struck me that the Register Office marriage might be more successful if they had the blessing of the Church upon it. So I suggested that they should have a church wedding, but the idea was not taken up.

One day not very long after her visit to Cambridge Gate Mews, Brian came down to Cheltenham to see his mother.

---

*Mrs Margaret Sullivan subsequently duly sued Brian for the return of her car. She obtained judgment, but this was never satisfied.

I was back at the Butts'. He arrived very early in the morning and told me that he had travelled all night. He was in a terrible state of agitation, and I told him he had better go to bed for an hour or two and we would have a talk when he awakened. At tea-time I roused him, and he then told me that he had had a terrible row with Margaret and that she had accused him of living upon her. He said that he had two hundred pounds when he got married, but had only ten pounds left in the bank at that time. I told him not to worry, and so that he should not feel too badly about things I sold two cottages I had at Severnside, Apperley, which we had used as weekend cottages, and gave him the money. I could not bear the thought that people should think that my boy was living on his wife's income. Not long after this they parted.

In the previous November of 1936, Brian, in the adopted persona of Barry Byron-Smith, had approached Mrs Maude Mills, of 68 Aberdare Gardens, London NW8, and arranged to rent from her, for a term of three years, two little white-washed cottages, high up on Hedgey Ditches Hill, known respectively as 'Hedgey Ditches' and 'Sunrise', which she owned at Polperro, in Cornwall. The rental was £32 *per annum*, to be paid quarterly in advance. Nurse Sullivan recalled:

Brian decided to go to Polperro for a time. I helped him to furnish the two cottages. He was anxious to set up a business catering for the needs of tourists. He already had a motor or steam launch and a caravan, and contemplated buying some ponies. The cottages were set in eleven acres of grounds, and there was a pretty little chalet. There were tennis-courts and a garage and everything there to make a good financial enterprise.

About the end of February 1937, Brian went down to live at Hedgey Ditches Hill, in order to prepare the cottages for letting. He did not remain there an absolute eremite though, but would take off every so often, either to see his mother in Cheltenham, or to pay a nostalgic visit to his old haunts in London.

During the summer months, he rented the two cottages out, and was netting a satisfactory £5 a week from them. He also let part of his own garden to a neighbour, Charles Correll.

Captain Charles Edward Correll, a 45-year-old, retired army officer who had fought at Ypres – and been plagued with nightmares ever since – had had a farming business in Worcestershire which had collapsed. In May 1937, he arrived with his wife, Blanche Ella, and 14-year-old son, Philip Marshall, in Polperro, and moved into New House, Talland Hill – which he planned to open as a guest-house – next-door to Brian's cottages. Another, older, son, John Patrick, rising 16, who was partially sighted, was away as a boarder at Worcester College for the Blind.

The Captain met Brian, whom he always knew as Byron Smith, within days of his arrival, when his Armstrong Siddeley skidded on Talland Hill – the road was solid rock in places – and Brian emerged with a rope to help. Thereafter they became quite close friends, Brian nicknaming him 'Baggy', and together they kept a small market-garden under cultivation there.

The Correll boys remembered:

> Byron Smith was the centre of interest because of his intimate knowledge of the leading bands of the day; Sid Kyte, Sid Bright, and the rest.

John recalled:

> He lived in two condemned – or if they were not they jolly well ought to have been – cottages, occupying the more habitable rooms. The rest were damp and very leaky.

He could remember looking through one of the cottages and admiring Byron Smith's London clothes, which, however, were being ruinously penetrated and destroyed by the all-pervading damp.

Came the autumn, the last summer tenants left, the cottages stood forlornly empty. With pockets to match, Byron Smith confided to Baggy that he was very hard up and would need to get a job that winter to see him through until his cottages were let again.

In the event, returning to Polperro in November from one of his forays outwith, a more cheery Byron Smith announced that the state of his affairs had taken an upward turn, and he would not now need to go job hunting.

Before setting forth once more upon his hibernal peripatetics, Sullivan persuaded the good Captain, in consideration of a commission of ten per cent, to receive upon his behalf any rents which might perchance accrue from the cottages in his absence. In acknowledging this fiduciary arrangement, the upright Captain Correll character-sketched Byron Smith as "straightforward, temperate in his habits, and girlish in his outlook," adding that he "had a horror of blood and would not allow rabbits to be trapped, as he considered it cruel."

This last observation is echoed by young Philip Correll, who recollects how, when he and Byron Smith were shrimping together on a jetty at Looe, the latter could not bring himself to "bash a fish on the head". Surely occision is made of stronger stuff?

Byron Smith took off from Cornwall on 7 December 1937, and that was the last time Captain Correll saw him. He did, however, receive a Christmas card from him, and, on or about 10 January 1938, a letter arrived, in which he intimated that he had had a bad cold, had remained in bed since Christmas, and had decided to return to Polperro.

Nurse Sullivan, outside 248 Old Bath Road. Beside her is the beloved spaniel, Bimbo. The blur on the right is Brian, holding a camera and trying to take a photograph of himself simultaneously.

That December, Brian made a swift descent on London in order to collect the Radlett Place rent monies. And that, averred Keith Newman later, was the last time that he saw Brian Sullivan alive.

Just before Christmas, Brian arrived in Cheltenham to spend the festive season with his mother at Number 248 Old Bath Road. He told her that in the New Year he intended to sell his car and get Newman to drive him back to Polperro. He was anticipating a good season, and the prospect of returning to Cornwall seemed to please him.

Between 5 January and 9 January 1938, Brian called at Number 248 nearly every day. He visited at various times. He always appeared happy. Sometimes he stayed in. At other times he went out in the evenings. Where he went to on those occasions his mother had no idea. Neither did she in any way interfere with his business. She did, however, remember that once, between these dates, he went to a ball at Cheltenham Town Hall.

She remembered, too, that one afternoon Brian arrived at Number 248 at 2pm, had a meal, and then drove her into town to see the shops. He had said that he would not accompany her shop-gazing, and had left her to her own devices in Cheltenham. She had returned home by bus at about half-past four. Thinking it over, she had realised that 5 January was a Wednesday, which was early closing day in Cheltenham. The likelihood, therefore, she decided, was that it was on either Thursday 6 January or Friday 7 January that she went on her window-shopping spree.

On 6 January Brian wrote the following letter to a Mrs Rayner:

> *Tower Lodge*
> *Leckhampton Hill*
> *Nr. Cheltenham*
> *Jan: 6th*
>
> *Dear Mrs Rayner,*
> *Thank you so much for your nice letter which was a pleasant*
> *surprise. I haven't been in London much or I should certainly*
> *have visited you, but I shall be up this weekend so if I may, I will*
> *call and see you. I'll ring you first anyway to see if it is convenient.*
> *   With regard to the cottage there is nothing I would like better, but*
> *we will be able to discuss matters when we meet. In the meanwhile,*
> *I hope everyone is well. My best wishes to all.*
> *Yours sincerely,*
> *Brian.*

Nurse Sullivan wrote that:

> *For about a week before January 7th, Brian told me that he was going to*
> *London to stay with his friend, Keith Newman. On the 7th he told me that he*
> *was actually going up the next day, which was a Saturday. On the Saturday*
> *he came to me and said: "I shall not be going up to London after all today,*
> *Mother. I shall not go till Tuesday." I gave him a Swiss roll to take up to the*
> *Lodge.*

That Swiss roll was afterwards found in a cupboard, untouched.

What had happened was that that Saturday morning, 8 January, Brian had received a telegram:

> *Come Tuesday. Away Weekend. Keith.*

On 9 January, Brian came to Number 248 for Sunday lunch, after which he took his mother out for a ride in his car.

> We went along through Church Lane, past Leckhampton Church [St Peter's] in the direction of the Crippetts. We stopped the car and got out and walked along to have a look at a house which had been burned down.* During that drive we talked about the future. Brian was full of his Polperro enterprise. He told me that he did not intend taking out another licence for the car we were in because he thought of selling it or giving it in part exchange for another car which he wanted to stand up to the Cornish roads. On the way back to tea it was just a toss-up whether we went into the Lodge for tea or not. Brian mentioned it to me. "Shall we pop in and have a cup of tea on our own?" he suggested, but knowing Mrs Butt to be alone, I said we had better go back to 248. We returned to Mrs Butt and had tea together. He stayed for a little while, then went out to have a drink, as was his custom. The Wheatsheaf Hotel is only just across the way from the house. He took Bimbo, his old black and grey spaniel, with him. Later on he returned, coming back to say goodnight some time between nine and ten o'clock.

Nurse Sullivan next saw Brian on the Monday 10 January. He arrived at Number 248 shortly after lunch.

> He came down walking and mentioned then that he had not come by car because it had not been taxed. Anyway, it was only a ten minutes' walk from Tower Lodge to 248 Old Bath Road, and a bit of exercise for the dog. He had tea with Mrs Butt and myself, then went out as usual for his drink, coming back to supper about eight o'clock. I know that it was nine o'clock when he rose to go, because I was surprised at his going so early, and remarked: "Are you going so soon, Brian." He put his arms round me and kissed me just as he always did.
> "Yes, Old Girl," he replied, "I'm going up to London tomorrow and I want to get a good night's sleep."

His mother walked up the garden path to the front gate with him. "Goodnight, Mother. I'll give you a ring," he said. A short distance away he turned and waved his hand to her. She watched as his figure faded, walking in the direction of Leckhampton Hill and Tower Lodge.

And that was the last time she ever saw Brian alive.

---

*The house, 'The Bittams', in Crippetts Lane, had burned down on 3 October 1937.

Chapter Four

Death of a Gigolo

As a watched pot is said never to boil, so does a watched letter-box seem never to yield. Day after January day, Nurse Sullivan looked for a letter, a postcard – a telegram even – from Brian. Nothing. And the telephone was no better. No ring. Never a word. Silence.

Albeit she had been wondering rather than worrying. Brian was, after all, and none knew it better than she did, rather erratic.

> He used often to run up to town and stay for a few days. While sometimes he would telephone or write, there were occasions when he was either too busy, or else put it off, as young people will do, and then come back as unexpectedly as he had gone away. There was nothing in his silence to disturb me.

No, she had told herself, she was not seriously worried, not actually perturbed. But, as the days went by, increasingly seriously wondering what had become of Brian, she decided that she would just slip up to the Lodge to see if there were any letters there, and to have a look around the place.

It was between 6pm and 7pm in the winter's darkness of Wednesday 12 January, that she caught a bus from Old Bath Road up Leckhampton Hill to Tower Lodge. More than a week had gone by since she had last been into the Lodge: on Tuesday 4 January, to be exact.

She recalled her previous visit:

> That afternoon Captain Butt was in the house at 248 Old Bath Road with his wife. I took the opportunity, as she was not alone, to slip up to see Brian. I found him lying on the settee in the living-room at the Lodge reading a book.
> "I've got a lovely book, Mother," he said, and lay there reading while I tidied up the place a bit.
> He asked me to have a cup of tea, but I said I would get back, as Mrs Butt always liked me to have tea with her.

On the occasion of that visit, Nurse Sullivan had certainly not noticed anything unusual about the Lodge. She had been into the kitchen and the lavatory, which adjoined the bathroom. For sure there had been no hole in the bathroom wall and no rubble in the bathroom itself then. The floor of the short passageway, covered by a strip of carpet, had seemed as sound and solid as ever.

On the right-hand side of the passage, there was, beneath the stairs, an alcove, covered over by a curtain. Brian kept his travelling trunk tucked away in there. At one time there had been a hole there, caused by rats. It had been filled in in the previous summer (1937) by a builder named Windigate, of Suffolk Street, Cheltenham. About November 1937, the rats had had another go, making a new hole by the side of the old one, repaired by Mr Windigate. Actually, Brian had spoken to Captain Butt about it, and Nurse Sullivan distinctly remembered Brian's buying a small quantity of cement. He definitely filled in another hole that had been caused by rats in the bathroom.

Of this visit – of Wednesday 12 January 1938 – Nurse Sullivan further recalled:

As I entered the drive, as we call it – but which is simply a few yards of rough ground inside the iron gates leading to the door – I was surprised to hear Bimbo barking from inside the car, which was parked just inside the gates. Brian frequently left the car there when he was not using it, but what did surprise me was that Bimbo was inside the car. At first I thought that Brian must just have got home and was opening up the place. But when I tried the front-door I found it was locked. The side gate was also padlocked, as it always was when he was away.

Whenever we left Tower Lodge it was the custom to leave the key to the front-door under the third stone from the door into the little drive. If Brian ever went away without letting me know, he would always leave the key in this spot, so that I could find it and get in. I looked under the stone for the key. It was not there. I thought it was rather stupid of Brian to have gone off with the key. And I could not understand why he had gone off and left Bimbo in the car. Brian loved Bimbo as a child. If he went walking, Bimbo would be waddling by his side. If he went driving, Bimbo would be on the seat beside him. He seldom moved without the dog. If he had wanted to leave Bimbo behind, he could have let him wander down to 248 on his own.

There was no sign of Brian about the place, and no sign of his having returned, so I took Bimbo back with me to the Butts' house. At the time I did not think a great deal about it, although I wondered, but concluded that Brian had thought I would be up at the Lodge, and would thus find Bimbo.

Nurse Sullivan's mind had been full of importunate questions.

Did Brian ever get to London? If not, why? What happened between his leaving me on the night of the 10th [of January] and the morning of the 11th to make him alter his mind? If he did go, where did he go to, and when did he return? Who did he see while he was away, and

Brian the gigolo.

where was he on the 12th? Did he take Bimbo to London with him? How long had Bimbo been in the car when I found him? And who put him there? There were no signs that he had been there for any length of time, such as might have been expected if Brian had placed him in the car early on the morning of the 11th. There was no mess of any kind; nor was the dog ravenous for food, as one would expect it to be after being unfed for nearly two days.

After that, Nurse Sullivan did not in fact go up to the Lodge again for two or three days. When she did, she checked under the stone for the key without success. She still did not really worry:

I thought that Brian would probably be writing any time, or that he would return, and run down to see me as he used to do. It would be the following Monday [17 January] or Tuesday [18 January] I went to the Lodge. A great deal of mystery has been made concerning the finding of certain newspapers in Brian's car. The papers were dated 12th to the 16th of January, the latter being a Sunday. When I went up to Tower Lodge on the seventeenth or eighteenth, I found that there were a number of newspapers stuck through the letter-box. It struck me that if the postman wanted to put any letters through he would have some difficulty, and I consequently removed the newspapers and placed them inside the car.

Nurse Sullivan wended her way to Tower Lodge a couple more times between 19 January and 23 January.

Each time I looked for the key and tried the side gate to see whether I could get in. I always carry a stick when I am out with Bimbo, and on one or two occasions when I went up I tapped on the window with my stick to see whether Brian might have come back and not had time to come down to me. But I knew the place would have been open if he had been there.

So we come to the day of my tragic discovery [24 January 1938]. On that day – the anniversary of the death of my little girl, she died aged seventeen on 24th January.* I thought that I would go up to the Lodge again to see if Brian had returned, and if not bring back some vegetables from the garden.

The gate to the garden was padlocked, and I thought it would be a good idea to take a screwdriver along to unscrew the staples. I also took with me three keys from the Butts' house which I thought might fit the lock. It was rather a nice day, and I suggested to Mrs Butt that she should come up to the Lodge with me. Usually she had a rest in the afternoon, but she went with me on this occasion. Bimbo was also with us.

On our arrival at the Lodge [Brian's] car was still in the drive. I tried the door [of Tower Lodge], but it was still locked. I then went to the back [side] gate and tried to fit the keys into the lock, but they would not work. Then I unscrewed the staple holding the padlock, and we both entered the little walk leading into the garden. The garden is a bit higher than the house, and the earth is retained by means of a stone wall about three feet high, so that one has to walk along a sort of passage with the house on one side and this low wall was [on] the other [side]. In doing so, I had to pass the casement-window, and it was at this point that I received my first surprise. I had sent Mrs Butt on ahead into the garden, which was reached by climbing two or three steps. As I passed the window I noticed that it was open. This was the thing that struck me at first, and sent the blood racing through my veins, because if it had been open when I called upon other occasions I must have noticed it. I had tapped at the window with my stick, and I could not have failed to see it [was] open if it had been.

*Actually, Violet Eileen Sullivan had died aged 19 on 27 January 1925.

55

I looked through the window and there saw Brian's overcoats hanging behind the door, while in the lock I could see the key, which, as I have said, was always left under the stone in the garden. There was a cold clutching at my heart. I felt that there was something wrong, and I ran to the back door and turned the handle. It opened to my touch, and I went in, calling out "Brian, Brian". There was no answer. I called up the stairs. Again there was no answer, and again I felt a strange cold clutching at my heart. It was as though I had sensed something uncanny.

I rushed upstairs. I opened the door ... and there on the bed lay my boy – dead. I remember lifting his hand. It was ice-cold. I remember touching the lock of hair which always fell over his brow when he was asleep. And then the tragedy came upon me in full force. I rushed across to the window and flung it open. It is a low window and I can remember almost falling out. I rushed down the stairs again and into the garden. There was Mrs Butt, a placid, homely-looking figure. It was the sight of her that brought me up with a jerk. It was that which made me do certain things which were afterwards regarded with suspicion.

I spoke to her very gently and quietly, for I knew that if I blurted out the truth to her it might very well have caused her to become a raving lunatic. She was a mental case, poor thing, and that is why, even in the darkest hour of my trouble, my professional instincts came to the fore, and I was able to master my own feelings and tell her: "Follow me home, dear. I am in rather a hurry, but you just come on after me".

First of all, I put Bimbo in the car and shut the door, because he is an old dog and cannot walk very quickly – and also if anybody went to the Lodge he would frighten them off. Then, half running, half walking, down the hill, I made my way as quickly as possible to 248 Old Bath Road. On the way I was trying to think what was best to do. I knew that the police must be told, and I knew that a doctor ought to be called, and then the thought of Mr Thompson, who was a friend of my son as well as his solicitor, flashed into my mind. I said to myself: "He will know the best thing to do – he is a solicitor, he will know just the right people to tell ..."*

The thought was a relief to me, for I still had to think of Mrs Butt as well as of my own grief, and it was good to be able to shelve some of the responsibility on to shoulders capable of bearing it.

Why did I go all the way back to 248 when I could have rung up from the call-box at the bottom of Leckhampton Hill? In the first place, I had no money with me, and I was too distracted to think that I could ring up the police for nothing. In the second place, the distance from the

* Mr Thompson had formerly acted for Brian Sullivan in respect of lease of properties and in the law suit brought by Mrs Margaret Sullivan against her husband.

call-box to the house was only a few minutes' difference, and I should have had to cross the wide road at the bus terminus to get to the call-box. I might have called at the big house opposite [to Tower Lodge], but again, it was a terrible story to have to tell to strangers, and my one thought was to get Mr Thompson as quickly as possible.

It was 3pm when at last Nurse Sullivan spoke to the solicitor in his Cheltenham office.

She told him: "Oh! Mr Thompson, something awful has happened. Brian has killed himself."

He asked her if she had telephoned the police.

She replied: "No. I have just run all the way from Tower Lodge. I couldn't think of anyone else whom to 'phone."

Mr Thompson told her that he would contact the police immediately and then join her at Number 248. Accordingly, he promptly put a call through to the Cheltenham Central Police Station, and was told that Police Constable George Llewellyn Merry, of Charlton Kings police station, would deal with the matter.

Thompson at once drove over to Charlton Kings, picked up PC Merry, and they made their way across to 248 Old Bath Road, where they found Nurse Sullivan waiting for them in the front garden. All three then drove up to Tower Lodge.

PC Merry entered the house alone. At Nurse Sullivan's request, Mr Thompson collected Bimbo from the car in which she had left him, and brought him along to his own. Then, also at her request, he followed Merry into Tower Lodge, went into the sitting-room, and took possession of an attaché-case which was lying on a table there. It had belonged to Brian, and contained his correspondence.

Meanwhile, upstairs Merry had entered the dead man's bedroom. Brian was in bed, covered as far as his chest by the bedclothes. He was wearing a pyjama jacket. He was lying partly on his right side. His face was very dark, and blood had been oozing from his mouth on the side on which he was lying. One of his hands was hanging over the edge of the bed. Merry noticed that a length of floor-board had been ripped up and the gas-pipe that ran underneath had been severed.

Apropos, Nurse Sullivan stated:

> It was the custom of Brian when he went to bed to turn off the gas at the meter. There was a reason for this. On one occasion the rats had gnawed through a length of piping under the floor-boards, and we had to send to the gas company to come and repair it, because there was a leakage. Ever after this Brian always turned the gas off at the meter.

PC Merry opened the front bedroom window and beckoned to Mr Thompson. He asked him to go upstairs. Thompson was reluctant to do so. He saw a body covered up on the bed. He did not see the face. It had, at his instigation, been covered, because he thought that the sight would – and here comes a fine piece of diplomatic circumlocution – "react unfavourably upon his temperamental nature". Merry showed him where the gas-pipe had been cut.

Downstairs, Thompson told Merry of Nurse Sullivan's request that he should take possession of Brian's attaché-case, and, opening it, said, "You see that it only contains papers relating to Sullivan's business matters and correspondence".

At that stage no proper search was made either inside or outside the Lodge. Nurse Sullivan was in the sitting-room for only few minutes. The rest of the time she sat outside with Bimbo in Mr Thompson's car.

Two letters were abstracted from the letter-box. Both were bills. One, addressed to Nurse Sullivan from Mrs Elwes, contained an account for the rent of Tower Lodge. The other, addressed to Brian Sullivan, enclosed an account soliciting payment from Mr Thompson's firm.

The three, plus Bimbo, then returned to Old Bath Road, where Nurse Sullivan, displaying considerable distress, said: "Oh, dear, what shall I do, and now that man has cleared off again".

When asked what she meant, she replied: "Mrs Butt's husband, he was talking of going on a cruise".

As we shall see, indeed he had … right out of this world.

Chapter Five

The Burial of the Dead

One of the first things that Nurse Sullivan did once she had got over the shock of her discovery of Brian's dead body was to send a telegram to Keith Newman, at 2 Radlett Place, St John's Wood. Not only was he the sole person she could think of to tell of Brian's death, but he was also her son's close – perhaps closest – friend. She asked him if he could come to Cheltenham.

Newman wired back that he was 'stunned' by the news, and gave her a number – Primrose 3265 – of a Mr Frost, at which to telephone him.

PC Merry got through for her on the Wednesday, when she spoke to both Newman and a Mrs Frost, living at Number 4 Radlett Place. Newman said that he would come down and Mrs Frost offered to accompany him.

They arrived at Cheltenham the following day – Thursday 27 January – and stayed the night at Number 248. They had the house to themselves, for Nurse Sullivan, who, said Newman, was prostrate and under the care of a doctor, was not there. She was staying overnight with friends, the Gerrishes, and Mrs Butt had been temporarily placed in a nursing home. Keith Newman and Mrs Frost attended both the inquest and the funeral, and afterwards left that same day for London.

Life must suddenly have seemed dreadfully insecure for Nurse Sullivan, but there were those charitable mortals who came to her aid.

> Naturally, after my discovery of Brian's body I got in a terrible condition. I rang up a cousin of Mrs Butts' [Mr EA Hogg], and told him of my trouble. He was extremely sympathetic, and said that we could not talk over the telephone, but he would come over to see me and discuss matters. It was he who suggested that, in the circumstances, it would be better if Mrs Butt went to a nursing home for the time being, a course to which I was only too grateful to agree. He also realised that it would not do for me to go up to the Lodge, and very kindly said, "You must use this house [Number 248] as your own for the time being."

It was between 24 January and 28 January that Nurse Sullivan asked PC Merry if he would fetch her silver watch for her from the Lodge.

> [It was] a tiny watch in the shape of a locket, and also Brian's cigarette case and lighter. The watch I was going to keep for myself, but the

cigarette case and lighter I meant to give to a friend of Brian's. PC Merry could not find the watch – which was afterwards found in the attaché-case taken away by Brian's solicitor [Mr Thompson] – but he came back with the other articles.

I also asked him to look around and see if he could find a biggish attaché-case, and, if so, would he bring that also to 248 …

"If there's anything in it," I told him, "will you empty it out, and bring it down to me?" It was my intention to go away to Bournemouth for a few days to get over the shock of my son's death. How thankful I am in view of what has since transpired that I did not go after all! Can you imagine what would have been hinted at had I done so? Can you imagine the construction which would have been placed on this going away, when Tower Lodge was entered?

There was a dark blue attaché-case which Brian always kept under his bed at Tower Lodge, and it was that one to which I referred. When PC Merry came back, he told me that he had looked but could not find any attaché-case, except a small brown one – he indicated the length of it with his hands – "About so big," he said, measuring about 12 to 14 inches, and then added: "There were some papers in it, but I did not think it would be any good bringing that."

So there was no attaché-case there of the 'biggish' kind I had asked for at the time I asked Mr Merry to look for it. This would be a day or so before the funeral on the 28th. And I would mention here that from the day I found Brian on the 24th, the key to Tower Lodge was out of my possession, and I never entered the place again until I went there with Chief Inspector Worth, at his request, to see if I could help them in any way.

On Thursday 27 January 1938, Merry called on Nurse Sullivan to inform her officially that the inquest on her son would take place the following day, before Mr John Dunn Lane, the Cheltenham Coroner.

Nurse Sullivan had another caller that Thursday. It was Mrs Gerrish, the wife of George Gerrish, the manager of Colesbourne Garage. The Gerrishes had known Nurse Sullivan about four years previously, but had lost touch. When, however, they read in the paper about Brian's death, Mrs Gerrish had hurried round to Old Bath Road to offer her condolences. Mrs Sullivan had asked if she could stay with the Gerrishes that night, and she did so.

The next day, Mr Gerrish drove Irene Sullivan back to Number 248, and, later, to St Peter's Church for the funeral service. After that, he took her back to Colesbourne for lunch, and she remained with Mr and Mrs Gerrish until eight o'clock that evening, when she was driven back by Mr Gerrish to Old Bath Road.

Mr Gerrish said that Nurse Sullivan had not so much as mentioned Captain Butt's name to him. Neither had she made any reference to the death of Brian, except at the graveside, when she had said, "This can't be Brian lying here," or words to that effect. On 3 February, at Nurse Sullivan's request, he had towed Brian's car from Tower Lodge to the garage at 248.

On the morning of 28 February, Mrs Irene Sullivan, represented by Mr J Eric Green, was the first witness called at the Coronor's Court. She took the oath in a whisper. As the coroner began to question her, she burst into tears, and it was some time before she recovered sufficiently to be able to reply.

She told the coroner that her son was a married man, but living apart from his wife.

"I hold that woman responsible for this trouble," she said.

This accusation was absolute rubbish. There remained nothing between Brian and Margaret Sullivan. *And Nurse Sullivan knew it.*

She told the coroner of her discovery of her son's corpse. When, on 24 January, she had found the back door of Tower Lodge shut but unlocked,

"I had a very queer feeling, and I rushed into the room and called out to my son, but there was no reply. I rushed upstairs to his bedroom then… "

At this point Nurse Sullivan broke down and had great difficulty in controlling her grief. Covering her face with her hands, she asked for water, which was brought to her in a glass by a woman police constable. Then, recovering her composure somewhat, she went on to say how she had discovered her son dead. The door of his bedroom was closed, but it had not been locked. She opened it, but did not detect the smell of gas. She realised that he was dead, but it did not occur to her how his death had been brought about.

"I went into the bedroom and saw my son lying on the bed, apparently dead. The sight was terrible – please, please don't ask me about it. I saw him lying there and I rushed to the window. Had this been open, I should have thrown myself through it. I threw one part of the window open and rushed out of the house."

The coroner asked her whether she had enquired of her son's bankers as to his financial position, but she said she had been far too distressed to go into the matter.

The coroner observed: "You told me that he had had domestic troubles, and that he and his wife were living apart."

Nurse Sullivan replied: "Yes, he had. He once went home to their flat to find that she had taken everything out. It was a terrible shock to him. He's never really been the same since."

She went on to say that he had had no financial worries so far as she was aware. "If he wanted money, he knew he always had me to come to, and he always had a home."

She was unable to say whether her son was earning anything. He was not one to burden her with his troubles, but she knew that his marriage worried him – as, indeed, it did her.

"Why did I take Mrs Butt to Tower Lodge on January 24th, the day I found my boy dead? Even the fact that I took Mrs Butt to sleep at the Lodge on three or four occasions was a matter of suspicion, although, as I explained, she was a mental case, and though on occasions she became almost unmanageable in the presence of her husband, when she was alone with me she would quieten down, and so I took her along to the Lodge."

She did have a recollection that the floor-boards in her son's bedroom were somehow disarranged, but she had not noticed the note on the chair beside the bed – she was so horrified.

Before she left Tower Lodge that afternoon of 24 January, PC Merry had shown her a half-sheet of note-paper from which he had read something out to her. She had in fact recognised Brian's handwriting on it, but her condition had been such that she could not remember what he had read. It was the note that had been left at Brian's bedside.

The coroner said that he did not intend to read out the contents of the note, but remarked that it had indicated her son's hope that she would be looked after by friends.

Nurse Sullivan thereupon interjected: "There's nothing terrible in it, is there? What does it say about me? The policeman did tell me, but I forget what it was."

Coroner: "You don't mind it being made public here and now?"

Nurse Sullivan: "I have nothing to be ashamed of and neither had my son."

Describing afterwards this passage in the Inquest Court proceedings, she wrote:

> When the coroner remarked that he did not propose to read it – with the view of sparing my feelings, I suppose – I felt a sudden urge to have it read, because I had only had a brief glimpse of it when Police Constable Merry showed it to me, and I had forgotten all about it, and what it said. So I asked the coroner to read it, and I am very glad I did now, because I hold that that note is not the note that Brian would have left behind if he were going to take his life.

Here is what Brian had allegedly written:

> Please help my Darling mother, who has always done her best for me. I have not supported her as I should have done. I leave everything I possess to her absolutely, except my clothes, which I bequeath to K. Newman.

Nurse Sullivan continues in her written account:

> In the first place, who was he asking to help me? We neither of us had a relation in the world. Why, then, should he ask some unknown persons to look after me? I did not require help. He knew that better than anybody else in the world. He knew that I had brought him up,

and helped him financially when it happened to be necessary. Brian had never 'supported' me in any way at all. It had never been necessary. And above all, why leave his clothes to anybody? The clothes which Brian had worn were not the sort of clothes which anybody else would want to wear. Why, then, should he take such pains as to make out this document, couched in this strange, meaningless language, and yet leave no word of farewell for me? That is why I say now that Brian did not take his own life, and that behind the tragedy of his death there lies a deeper mystery than has yet been revealed.

If Brian had been about to take his own life, instead of the futile message which appears above, do you not think he would have written something more human to his 'darling mother' who had always 'done her best' for him? No matter what sort of trouble he was in, I know that my boy would have come to me, and if he had contemplated taking his life he would never have left me without some word telling me why he had done so. It is absolutely unthinkable that he would have done this thing at Tower Lodge and not left a line of love for me. Instead of the forced, unnatural message that was found, it would have been more on these lines: 'I am in a spot of trouble, old girl, and I do not intend you shall have the worry of helping me out, so I am taking this way out.' There would have been an admission of what the trouble was, and some explanation, ending with a plea for forgiveness from me. I know Brian, and I know what he would have written. That is why I should very much like to have another look at that note to see whether or not it is in Brian's handwriting. It looked so to me by the glimpse I got of it at the inquest on Brian, but I was agitated and distressed and could easily have been mistaken. One does not look for little differences under the stress of great trouble, and I was in such a condition at that time that I may have overlooked anything in my sorrow.

Constable Merry provided further and better details at the inquest. He did not usually, he said, act as coroner's officer for the district, only performing that duty on rare occasions, but it so happened that he was thus engaged on the date in question.

He said that when he opened up Tower Lodge with the key given to him by Mrs Sullivan, he had found, just inside the front-door, a pint bottle of milk, and on a table in the sitting-room was another pint bottle of milk, partly used. A cup and saucer and an empty soda siphon were also on the table. On the mantelshelf was a used glass.

Describing his discovery of the body in the back bedroom, Merry said that the position of the deceased's body was perfectly natural. It was covered by two sheets, five blankets, a counterpane and an eiderdown, all of which were turned back exposing the head and shoulders. It was lying on a horse-hair mattress on top of which was a flock-bed covered with a sheet. The two upper sheets were bloodstained near the top, and these stains appeared to have been caused by bleeding from the nose and mouth of the deceased. Two top blankets were bloodstained in a corresponding spot to the sheets. The underneath sheet and the flock mattress were also bloodstained. The bedclothes were slightly disarranged, and there was a faint smell of gas in the room.

The body, which was clad in pyjamas and socks, was black from coal-gas poisoning. Carbon monoxide poisoning classically turns the skin pink and the blood a brightish cherry-red. One can only suppose that the reported blackness was due to putrefaction.

Merry had found a brownish-grey suit of clothes – jacket, waistcoat and trousers – just thrown across a chair at the foot of the bed. He searched the pockets. In the trouser-pockets he had found 7s 71/2d in silver and coppers. In the bottom right-hand waistcoat pocket there was the ignition key of a motor-car. There was a fountain pen in the outside breast pocket of the jacket and in the inside breast pocket he found a black leather wallet. It contained no money.There was a blank cheque of the Midland Bank, several small snapshots, and a piece of pale blue paper bearing the name 'Regent Motors', filled in in pencil and relating to a Daimler motor-car, KV4595.

He had taken possession of the property found in the clothing of the deceased, and had later that same evening gone round to Number 248, and handed the cash to Nurse Sullivan.

The following morning he called again at Number 248 and delivered the wallet and its contents to Mrs Sullivan. She opened the wallet in his presence, and pulled out the contents. The snapshots, she said, had been taken at Polperro, when they were on holiday there the previous summer. On seeing the blank cheque she remarked: "I think he had enough to meet it, had he gone to London". Taking out the remaining papers from the wallet, including the receipt for the Daimler KV4595, she looked at them, made no comment, and put the wallet down on a table nearby.

Merry testified that in a corner of the room – which, incidentally, measured: height: seven feet six inches, width: eight feet, length: twelve feet – the linoleum had been turned back and a piece of floorboard about a yard in length, had been removed, and this exposed the main gas-pipe, which had been severed. A screwdriver lay on the floor near the ripped-up board. The room's ventilator had been blocked, jammed up with clothing and pieces of brown paper, and the window was tight-shut. He had, he also said, seen a large brown suit-case with the initials 'FFH' on it. He opened it and there was therein what he referred to as "gent's wearing apparel", but he did not examine this in any detail or search the case.

Later that day, the undertakers arrived to remove the body, and he had assisted them to place it in a coffin. One of the undertaker's assistants had had to remove the large brown suit-case from the bedroom to the sitting-room below, as it was in the way of carrying the coffin from the bedroom.

Merry told the Court that he had known Brian Sullivan personally for about two years.

When, at 10.30am on Tuesday 25 January, he had called at 248 Old Bath Road, he had asked Nurse Sullivan if there was anything she needed at Tower Lodge, as he was holding the key.

She had replied: "Yes, Brian has had my silver watch. It is out of order. If it is there, will you bring it down? Also bring down the silver cigarette lighter."

He had told her that he had not noticed a lighter, but that he would make a search for it. He had duly found the cigarette lighter, but was unable to find the watch. He had, however, found the key of the letter-box.

Returning to Tower Lodge, he had registered the fact that an Austin motor-car, Index OX 1010, which, from local knowledge, he knew to have belonged to Brian Sullivan, was parked in a disused drive at the side of the premises. On the ground, between the car and the front-door of the Lodge, he had found the return half of a railway ticket – Number 876, dated 15 January 1938 – the portion found being valid for a journey from Cheltenham to Gloucester.

Merry had also noticed that a portion of the bathroom wall at the Lodge had been recently cemented, and that a quantity of bricks and rubble was on the floor nearby. When he referred to this in conversation with Mrs Sullivan, she had told him: "Oh, I expect Brian had got that there to put under the staircase to keep out the rats. We have put down poison, but that has had no effect."

Dr Thomas Bones Hamilton-Haslett told the Court that he had made a *post mortem* examination of the body and that death had been due to carbon monoxide poisoning. It had taken place several days before the *post mortem*. He had found no evidence of any internal or external injury.

The coroner said that he was quite satisfied that Brian Sullivan took his own life. He had had some domestic troubles, it did not appear that he was actually in employment at the date of his death, although there was no apparent reason for him to become anxious on the score of finance. (His mother had testified that he had an interest in properties in London from which he drew rents.) Mrs Sullivan had clearly taken her son's domestic troubles to heart, and this in turn may have affected him even more than she thought. The note left behind was an indication that he intended to do what he did, and death would be recorded as due to carbon monoxide poisoning and that the deceased took his own life while the balance of his mind was disturbed. The date of death could not be fixed, and he would record only that the body was found on 24 January 1938.

The coroner expressed sympathy with Mrs Sullivan. Mr Green associated himself with that expression. Mrs Sullivan, said Mr Green, wished PC Merry to be thanked for his kindness and assistance.

Nurse Sullivan left the court leaning heavily on the arms of two companions – Keith Newman and Mrs Frost.

A suicide's grave. The burial place of Brian Sullivan in the churchyard of St Peter's, Leckhampton Lane, Cheltenham.

The kindly Mr Gerrish's car conveyed the pathetically small parcel of mourners to the Church of St Peter, in Leckhampton Lane, where Brian's unmarked suicide's grave had been dug beneath a cypress near to the west wall of the churchyard, Plot A 301 (Burial Number 766).

The brief funeral ritual, conducted by the assistant curate, the Reverend FT Newth, concluded, two of the trio of mourners left at once to speed back to London.

Only one remained – Nurse Sullivan, facing alone now the handful of years left to her.

Chapter Six

The Salmon Fishers' Catch

Brian Sullivan had been dead and buried precisely a week when, on 3 February 1938, the three salmon fishers made their grim discovery.

That Thursday dawned cold and grey, and around 8am when the fishermen began netting, wispy wraiths of mist were still curling low over the surface of the Severn at Haw Bridge.

The fishers were local men – Hubert Jack Dudfield, (that same Dudfield who, three weeks before, had cast aside the shoe and glove on the bridge), aged 23, of Fairview, Tirley, and John Bevan, aged 30, of Tirley, and Sidney Enos Church, of Apperley. He, along with I Roberts, who was not out with them that morning, had rented the riparian rights from a point on the Severn two meadows above Wainlode Hill, for a distance of some quarter of a mile upstream towards Haw Bridge, which crosses the Severn on the main Tewkesbury-Ledbury Road, about nine miles from Cheltenham.

The water was high that day – sixteen feet instead of the normal twelve. That was why they had decided to put their net only half-way across the river. Having travelled downstream from Haw Bridge in their boat, they took the net to the limit of their stretch of water, and then, at a point about one mile downstream from Haw Bridge and rather less from Wainlode Hill on the Cheltenham side of the river, drew the whole of the net into the landing place. This was a bay on the left bank, landmarked by two haystacks, and where they had a hut. It was actually situated in the parish of Deerhurst.

It was then that they found that they had netted a great chunk of something fish-belly white, hideously bloated, and so disgusting that one of them was violently sick on the spot.

Entangled in the criss-cross meshes of the salmon net was a human torso, male, from which the head, arms, and legs had all been hacked away. Tied tightly around it, passing under the armpits, was a length of stout cord to which a large white brick was attached by another piece of cord, eight to nine inches long. A second length of cord, from which depended a similar white brick, was tied around the body's waist.

This 'catch' had been trawled up from the narrow, fish-bearing trench on the river-bed in which it had been lying, and the chances of its having dropped into the river just there, where it was vulnerable to being dredged up, were, opined expert rivermen who had spent their working lives around the Severn and who knew every hole in the river-bed and the vagaries of every current, thousands to one against. But at exactly which part of the river the net had picked up the body it was impossible to say.

The Salmon Fishers at the spot on the Severn where the torso was found. Sidney Enos Church and Hubert Jack Dudfield are in the boat, trawling for any other remains.

A telephone call was promptly made from the local pub, the White Lion Inn, to Corse police station, and at 8.45am PC Frederick Thomas Knight, accompanied by PC Greenhall, drove down to the bay on the left bank, two meadows up from Wainlode Hill.

The torso still lay in the water, deep-snared in the net, but drawn up to the bank. No one had touched it. Assisted by the three fishermen, Knight and Greenhall dragged the body on to the bank.

At 11.45am Detective Sergeant Philip Franklin, from Gloucester, arrived on the scene, to be followed by Chief Superintendent Albert James Wayman, also from Gloucester. Higher ranking officers of the force were informed and motored to the spot straightaway. Among them was the Deputy Chief Constable of Gloucestershire, Superintendent JWP Goulder, and, from HQ, Lansdown Road, Cheltenham, Detective Inspector Albert Victor Hancock.

Police photographs were taken of the torso, after which it was carried across the fields to the road. It was then taken by car by Wayman and Franklin to the mortuary at Cheltenham Hospital, where, at 2.30pm, it was handed over to the hospital's pathologist, Dr Hamilton-Haslett.

The *Cheltenham and Gloucestershire Echo* reported:

> At the moment the police say they do not connect the discovery with
> the Haw Bridge bloodstains mystery of January 10 in view of the

pathologist's report that the blood taken from the bridge was not human, and also because the body did not appear to have been in the water for any length of time.

Superintendent Wayman enlarged. He said of the missing arms that one seemed to have been properly dissected from the shoulder cavity with a saw; perhaps by someone with a limited knowledge of anatomy. But the other arm cavity was ragged, as though the limb had been hacked off with a chopper or axe. Both legs had been sawn off close to the hip joint, and the head close to the hollow of the neck. The skin of the torso struck him as being in a healthy condition, and not such as one would expect had it been in water since 10 January. It was the torso of a man of quite mature age, well nourished, plump, muscular, and in good physical condition.

That same afternoon Wayman and Inspector Charles J Large from Tewkesbury revisited the scene of the fishermen's discovery, and Mr Lane, the coroner for North Gloucestershire, went along to inspect it, too.

By 3.15pm, the decision had been taken by the top brass to call in Scotland Yard. It was decided, too, that although it had originally been intended that a local pathologist should carry out the necessary *post mortem*, Sir Bernard Spilsbury, the Home Office expert, and at that time the country's foremost forensic pathologist, should be summoned.

On the instructions of Superintendent Arthur Askew of the Yard, Chief Detective Inspector Percy Worth and Detective Sergeant James Shewry caught the 7.30am train from Paddington on Friday 4 February. They reached Cheltenham at 10.55am, and were met at St James' Station, where a small posse of pressmen was awaiting their arrival, by Superintendent Hopkins, who was in charge of the Cheltenham Division. Worth, having told the press representatives that he would provide them with authoritative information just as soon as he had any to give them, was whisked straight off in a police car to Cheltenham Central Police Station.

The Scotland Yard men remained there for about 15 minutes before being escorted to Gloucestershire Police Headquarters, in Lansdown Road, where a two-hour conference, headed by Deputy Chief Constable Goulder, and with Superintendent Hopkins, Detective Inspector Hancock, and Detective Sergeant Franklin present, was held to review all the known circumstances of the case and to decide upon the immediate line of action to be taken.

At 1.40pm, the conference, which had commenced at shortly after 11.20am, ended, and Worth and Shewry were conducted into town by Superintendent Hopkins for lunch.

Around half-past two, Sergeant Franklin arrived at Haw Bridge, bringing with him Hubert Price, the man who first discovered the blood on the bridge. An hour later, lunch over, a police car swept up and disgorged Worth, Goulder, Hancock and Shewry.

Chief Detective Inspector Percy Worth, of Scotland Yard, in charge of the murder investigation. An arrogant and secretive man.

The bridge was crammed with cars and spectators. They were peremptorily ordered off while the four police officers carried out a close scrutiny. Bottles and other articles were thrown into the river to test its flow towards the Bristol Channel. Worth, busily viewing the scene and acquainting himself with local conditions, called Price over to hear his description of exactly how and where he had found the stains. The police party then examined the river-bank on both sides of the bridge. They also took a good look at a ruined cottage which stood hard by Haw Bridge.

One of the main lines of enquiry at this stage was being directed to trying to establish whether or not the torso in the Severn was in any way linked with the mystery of the bloodstains on Haw Bridge. The present official inclination was to the belief that the crime had been committed in some part of the country many miles distant from Haw Bridge.

Already the police had addressed themselves most industriously to preliminary investigations. A list of all persons missing throughout the country had been assembled. Widespread efforts were under way to trace the car alleged to have been seen to stop on Haw Bridge in the small hours of 10 January.

Sir Bernard Spilsbury; at the time the country's foremost forensic pathologist. He carried out the post-mortem on the torso.

Scotland Yard detectives in London and police forces all over Britain had embarked upon an intensive search of railway station cloak-rooms and left-luggage offices for any parcels, packages, or suit-cases which might contain the missing arms, legs, or head. Searching inquiries were being carried out among bargees and other river folk in the hope that one of them might be able to come up with something of significance.

Particular attention was being directed to the two bricks weighting the torso. Sometimes individual bricks can be identified as to their manufacturer, or be traced to have originated from a specific locality. Brick experts were being duly consulted. What had so far emerged was that the bricks were of some considerable age and appeared to have been taken from a wall or house upon which creepers grew.

All became quiet on the river. The fishermen were back at work – albeit keeping very sharp eyes on their nets. The possibility of dragging operations being undertaken in the hope of perhaps recovering the missing head and limbs, was, though unconfirmed, understood to be likely – at least according to the journalists covering the story.

Three theories had been tentatively formulated: The first was that they were looking at a case of murder. The second, less likely, was that the man had been accidentally killed on the road and his corpse had thus, in panic, been disposed of. The third, and least likely of all, was that the whole thing was a practical joke perpetrated by medical students.

However, there was also a fourth and most sensational theory that animal flesh and bone, together with other misdirecting articles, had been planted on the bridge, and the parapet smeared with animal blood, to put the police off the scent after the weighted body had been thrown into the river.

There was a general feeling that Spilsbury's *post mortem* might reveal some disease from which the dismembered man had been suffering, or certainly provide evidence as to the cause of his death. Such data would narrow considerably the search for identity.

Sir Bernard Spilsbury, having been engaged for the greater part of the day on a case in London, boarded the five o'clock train from Paddington and reached Cheltenham at 7.27pm that Friday (4 February). He was met at St James' Station by Worth, Shewry, and several of the local officers, and driven to Cheltenham General Hospital in a police car.

The hospital mortuary, which served also as the general Cheltenham Mortuary, was located in the hospital's kitchen garden, some 50 or 60 yards behind the main building. Carrying his case of instruments, Sir Bernard was conducted by torchlight along the narrow concrete paths that led between the cabbages and beans to the mortuary. And there, at 8pm, behind locked doors and windows heavily curtained, Spilsbury, rubber aproned and gloved, assisted by the Cheltenham Hospital's pathologist, Dr Thomas Bones Hamilton-Haslett, watched in total silence by Dr Davey, Worth, Shewry and leading local police officers, went at once to work.

Powerful electric lamps blazed down on the mud-caked torso. After a thorough cleansing with hosed water, it was examined exteriorly by Sir Bernard, literally inch by inch. Before slicing into it with his autopsy knife, he took exact measurements and made careful calculations which would enable him to state the approximate height and weight of the whole man. Valuable data when checking the statistics of missing persons.

It was nearly 11pm when at last Sir Bernard had finished. Too late to catch a train from Cheltenham back to London, he was sped by police car to Gloucester in time to get aboard the 12.15am, due in at Paddington at 2.50am. He bore away with him various specimens in sealed jars – pieces of flesh, bits of organs, samples of body fluids, and so forth – which would undergo sophisticated forensic testing in London.

Back at the mortuary, while other officers waited outside, a private conference lasting more than half an hour took place between Chief Detective Inspector Worth and Dr Davey, the Gloucester pathologist who had pronounced the blood on Haw Bridge to be non-human.

Huge crowds gathered on and around Haw Bridge after the shocking discovery of the torso. The unusual case quickly became a national obsession.

It had been confidently anticipated that on Saturday morning (5 February) police activities at Haw Bridge would be humming from an early hour, and that by 9am further dragging would undoubtedly have begun.

In fact, bridge and river were reported as presenting a scene of spring-like tranquillity as late as 10.30am. Within half an hour or so, however, things began to change drastically. A police car arrived with drags, and local fishermen were somewhat imperiously informed that their services would be henceforth required.

It was shortly after eleven o'clock that dragging accordingly began. PC Greenhall, the patrol constable who brought the drags, and PC Knight, lowered two sets of drag-hooks from the bridge to a boat in which were the original torso-finders, Dudfield, Bevan and Church, who immediately began to drag underneath the bridge, upon which a crowd of sightseers soon gathered.

At noon, a lorry loaded with full diving equipment arrived from Gloucester. With it came Joseph Lane, a diver employed by the Gloucester Dock Company.

At 12.55pm, Inspector Worth, Sergeant Shewry, and Inspector Hancock left Cheltenham Central Police Station, where for the last two hours they had been holding a conference with other officers, including Superintendent Hopkins, and were driven out to Haw Bridge. There, the diving apparatus – diving-suit, windlass, and oxygen tank – had been set out on the bank, about 100 yards from the bridge on the Tirley side of the river.

Meanwhile, another boat was putting out. This meant that there were now two of them hopefully dragging, and while throngs watched from every vantage point, a determinedly acrobatic Sergeant Shewry, dangling perilously from the bridge, over the side of which he had been slung in an improvised cradle, compacted of sundry pieces of wood and rope, and himself further tied to the bridge rails for insurance, was scraping away with a razor-blade at some remaining bloodstaining which he had detected on the parapet. The scrapings were being carefully caught in a tumbler which Superintendent Wayman was holding out to him.

Suddenly, at ten minutes to two, there was a shout. It came from a boat which had drifted under the bridge. Spectators, police, and pressmen, galvanised, ran over to the far side of the bridge. They saw the boat being rapidly rowed to the bank. In it, a man was holding a drag. Attached to the drag was what was obviously a limb with a brick tied to it. Alfred Charles Chamberlain, a 48-year-old farm labourer, of Tirley Cross, and his oarsman, Jack Dudfield, had hooked a prize – the right arm of the Cheltenham Torso.

The spot at which they had found it was on the Gloucester side of Haw Bridge, about 14 yards from the bridge. It was a success for a new method of dragging, using a sixteen-pronged farm harrow. But the high hopes of the triumphant police were soon dashed. The hand had been chopped off. There could be no identification by fingerprints.

Superintendent Hopkins had the boatmen carry the arm into the cowshed beside the Haw Bridge Inn. Then he and Inspector Worth went in, firmly shutting the door behind them. The skin of the arm was white – the same fish-belly white as the torso. The brick was tied with binder cord around the elbow joint.

The day's excitements were not yet over. At 3.20pm, watched by the eager crowds, the diver made his descent by means of a short ladder. He was down for about six minutes, working by touch alone in the dark water, where it was only possible for him to work lying flat on his stomach. He brought nothing up. Not even later, when a 30-rung ladder was substituted.

At 7pm that evening, Superintendent Hopkins delivered the severed arm into the safekeeping of the duty house surgeon at Cheltenham Hospital, Dr Vivian Barlow, for Dr Hamilton-Haslett's subsequent attention.

And at 10am the following day, Inspector Hancock made his way to the mortuary, where Dr Hamilton-Haslett cut the twine and removed the brick from the arm. Twine and brick were then carried off to be stored along with the other exhibits at Cheltenham Central Police Station.

Throughout Sunday (6 February) the body-part hunt went on. Thousands of people came from all parts of the Midlands and the West of England to watch. Despite a bitter wind and frequent squalls of rain, they lined the bridge and swarmed over the right bank of the river. Journalists estimated a 5,000 presence.

Dragging and diving operations began bright and early at 9am. The smart, white-hulled motor-launch chugged businesslike upstream from Wainlode with Joseph, the diver, aboard. With flourish and flurry, a flotilla of local watermen launched their flat-bottomed boats and pushed swiftly and purposefully out from the Tirley bank.

During the afternoon police activity peaked. They had decided not only to intensify dragging operations, but also to extend them beyond the immediate vicinity of the bridge and carry them on along the whole stretch of the Severn as far as the bay where the mutilated cadaver had been recovered by the salmon fishers.

Disappointingly, the sole result of the day's draggings and divings was the uplifting by Lane, the diver, on his sixth descent made just after 2pm, of a single barrel rifle of small bore; the type used in shooting booths at fairs.

Chief Superintendent Albert James Wayman (in charge of the Gloucester City Division) and Inspector DM Wagstaff (in charge of dragging operations) discuss their options on the river-bank.

In contrast to the thousands who had flooded the bridge and river-banks on the Sunday, only a handful were gathered by the rails on the bridge when operations were resumed on Monday (7 February), but the number increased to about 50 as the morning wore on. The work of the dragmen and the diver was frequently interrupted by the passage of lines of barges, which used the river in large numbers.

Just a few minutes before eleven o'clock on Tuesday 8 February, George Poole, a 71-year-old army pensioner from Ashleworth Quay, dragging 250 yards below Haw Bridge on the Gloucester side, brought up with the drag a right leg, complete with foot, brick attached. It was handed over to Inspector Wagstaff, who, in turn, handed it on to Chief Superintendent Wayman.

A couple of hours later, coming up to a quarter to three, John Bevan hauled out of the Severn a left leg, also complete with foot and brick. The legs were, at 3pm and 6.30pm respectively, carried off by Superintendent Wayman to Cheltenham Hospital mortuary, where they joined the arm, already immersed in a jar of formalin.

Now, headpiece and left arm apart, the Cheltenham Torso was restored, made *almost* whole again. Perhaps, just perhaps, it might be possible to wrest from it the secret of its identity. Chief Detective Inspector Percy Worth certainly hoped – and truly believed – so.

Chapter Seven

Only Connect

I can connect
Nothing with nothing
TS Eliot *The Wasteland.*

Only connect!
EM Forster *Howards End.*

The vital connection between the missing Captain and the dead Gigolo was made on Sunday 6 February 1938. That was when the information was first officially received that Captain William Bernard Butt had been absent, unaccounted for, from his home at 248 Old Bath Road, Cheltenham, since 4 January, and that Brian Sullivan, the son of the nurse who looked after Captain Butt's mentally sick wife, had committed suicide at his residence, Tower Lodge, where he had been found dead on 24 January.

Inspector Worth learned that the Captain was said to have gone off on a cruise, and might therefore be reasonably expected to be away for some weeks. The inspector also learned that no tangible reason for Brian Sullivan's suicide had emerged at the inquest and, taking the two however disparate seeming circumstances together, he felt immediate further enquiry to be necessary.

So it was that on Monday 7 February, along with Superintendent Hopkins and other local officers, Worth and Shewry paid a call on Nurse Sullivan at Number 248, and obtained from her the key to Tower Lodge.

The first suspicious thing that the officers encountered on entering the Lodge was an irregular patch, roughly four feet six inches, by two feet, of freshly cemented area on the otherwise unblemished inside wall of the bathroom. Worth at once gave orders for it to be removed and the wall opened up. This was duly done, but nothing to justify suspicion was revealed.

Moving through the short passageway leading from the scullery to the sitting-room, the inspector spotted a good half-inch gap between the strip of carpet on the floor and the brickwork at the side of the passage. He had the carpet taken up, and saw two loose boards. It was evident that bricks had been removed at some time and replaced by these boards. He had the boards lifted, and in a hole below them – about 50 inches long, 18 inches wide, and 18 inches deep – was found, buried, a man's tweed overcoat.

The cloth was a brown and white mixture with an overcheck, and a tab sewn inside showed that it had been purchased at Cavendish House, Cheltenham. In

The only known photograph of Captain Butt and Brian Sullivan together – seen here eating al fresco with a friend.

the right outside pocket, was a small bottle, labelled 'Boots', and half-filled with Aspirin tablets. In the opposite, left-hand, pocket, were two full boxes of Bryant & May's safety matches. The coat was wrapped in a parcel and despatched at once by car for microscopical examination at the London police laboratory, at Hendon.

Examining an alcove under the stairs, situated immediately adjacent to the hole in the passageway, Worth and Shewry noticed brickwork flooring that had been tampered with, many bricks having been ripped out of place and the earth below disturbed. But, once again, further investigation revealed nothing of any significance.

In one corner of the Lodge's fairly large garden there was a long shed. Poking about in there, Shewry came upon a length of string and a piece of rope. The rope, together with the displaced bricks which he had seen in the stair alcove, struck him as being strikingly similar to the rope and brick attachments to the torso, and the string seemed very like that which had been used to attach the brick to the recovered right arm.

On the ground near this garden shed was a big heap of ashes. Worth observed another ash-pile in the sitting-room grate, which also bore evidence of there having been a fierce fire lit there. Clearly, there had recently been big burnings at the Tower.

Casting a professional eye round the sitting-room, he noticed a solitary bloodstain, about the size of a sixpence, on the arm of a settee. He saw, too, evidence of some social drinking – a number of quart and pint beer bottles on the floor under a table, and on another table a soda siphon and a tumbler.

Continuing the search upstairs, Shewry found in the dressing-table in the back bedroom, which had been occupied by Brian Sullivan, a key-ring on which there were nine keys. Among them was one, marked 'AA792017', which proved to have been issued by the Automobile Association in Bristol in 1934 to Captain Butt.

Further disconcerting traces of the whilom presence at Tower Lodge of the missing Captain Butt were provided by the contents of a suit-case which was in the sitting-room. This case, which bore the initials 'FHH', had belonged to Francis Frederick Hobson, Butt's brother-in-law, who had died in 1935, and of whose will the Captain was co-executor. In that case Worth discovered a pair of purple-striped pyjamas, a pair of white woollen trunks, a distinctively patterned pocket-handkerchief, a hat-brush, a tin of Artifrice (an artificial tooth cleansing proprietary preparation), and an electric razor (Schick Dry Shaver), all identified as similar to articles possessed by Captain Butt. And mixed in with them in that same case were two pairs of grey flannel trousers, a pair of hogskin gloves, and two scarves, the known property of Brian Sullivan.

In consequence of the various finds made at Tower Lodge, Worth telephoned Dr Roche Lynch, the Home Office analyst, and asked him to come to Cheltenham the following day. He also sent a message to the Yard requesting the attendance at Cheltenham of Chief Inspector Fred Cherrill, the fingerprint expert. Arrangements were made for them to travel together by police car from London.

All that afternoon, and right up to eight o'clock that night, police were digging in Tower Lodge. Early on, a police car had driven swiftly back into Cheltenham, to return with picks, spades and dungarees. A plumber was summoned and, to quote an *Echo* reporter:

> for several hours the thud of hammering and the scraping of shovels could be heard through the thick walls of Cotswold stone. ... The officers, including Worth, donned the dungarees and it appeared by the noise made by the picks and shovels that they were working in the small bathroom. As the light faded and the glow from the street lamps of Cheltenham spread into the night sky, the tense atmosphere of the drama being enacted in the Lodge was increased. The thud, thud of the constant hammering on stone echoed through the empty cottage.

Before leaving the premises, Worth had the gas-meter opened by the Cheltenham Gas Company. It was one of the shilling-in-the-slot type. It was found to contain 9s.

Throughout all these operations uniformed police officers had stood on guard at the gate and the door of Tower Lodge. Later, its doors locked, it would be left under the close guard of two constables, who were to remain on duty there all night.

From Tower Lodge, Chief Inspector Worth, Sergeant Shewry, and Superintendent Hopkins were driven to Number 248, where they stayed until just

The fingerprint expert brought into the case, Superintendent Frederick Cherrill, of the Yard.

after 9.15pm, when they were most politely seen off at the gate by Nurse Sullivan. They left behind a plain clothes officer who was to remain outside the house that night.

Returning to Cheltenham Central Police Station, Worth interviewed PC Merry regarding the conditions which he had found at Tower Lodge on the occasion of his last visit there, round about 25 January.

It was from Merry that Worth learnt that Captain Butt was the owner of a 1933 model 15hp, blue Daimler saloon, KV4594, and that the vehicle was not in the garage at the side of Number 248. Enquiries were put in train around local garages and information was received that the car in question was garaged at the Regent Motors Service Garage, in Regent Street, Cheltenham.

Worth made his way there forthwith and saw a garage attendant, George Griffiths.

Griffiths told him that at 10.40pm on 4 January, a man had brought the Daimler in saying that he wanted to garage the car for about three nights.*

Griffiths had made out the usual garage ticket in triplicate – one, the white copy, he handed to the customer, the pink copy he placed under the wiper on the windscreen of the car, and the third, yellow, copy, he handed in to the garage office.

He had then asked, "Private or commercial?"

"Commercial, it's cheaper," the man had replied.

He was given a ticket marked 'Com'. When asked how long the car would be in, the man had said: "About three nights".

Griffiths took no payment from him, as it was customary to pay when the car was removed from the garage. The car was never collected.

By about the end of January, when the Daimler was still standing there unreclaimed, Griffiths had rummaged through its pockets and found, in the offside front door pocket a 'Tecalemit' greasing record card, on which was the name and address: 'Captain Butt. 248 Old Bath Road'.

Griffiths said that he had never seen the man who brought the Daimler in before. He described him as between five foot seven inches, and five foot eight inches tall, 50-55 years of age, with a small grizzly moustache turning grey, of medium build, with a cultured voice. He was very smart in appearance, wearing a dark overcoat and dark trilby hat. As he left the garage, he took an umbrella from the back seat of the car.

Shown a recent photograph of Captain Butt, Griffiths thought that that was the person who had left the Daimler there. This opinion he based chiefly upon the man's protruding ears, which, incidentally, was a most distinctive feature of Butt's description.

At ten minutes past ten on the previous Monday evening (7 February), the solicitor, Theodore Thompson, turned up at Cheltenham Central Police Station, bringing with him Brian Sullivan's attaché-case. In it was the log book of Captain Butt's Daimler. And in a wallet of Sullivan's, which Thompson produced, was the Regent Garage's receipt for Butt's Daimler.

The following morning – Tuesday 8 February – at the Cheltenham Police Station, the coroner, Mr JD Lane, opened the inquest on "the trunk of the body of a male person found in the River Severn".

He told the jury:

"The remains have been examined by Sir Bernard Spilsbury, the Home Office pathologist, assisted by Dr Haslett. Sir Bernard's report has not yet been received, and the police are still investigating matters and pursuing inquiries, so that the only evidence today will be of a formal nature – the findings of the remains and the formal examination of Dr Haslett."

Hubert Jack Dudfield gave evidence of the finding of the torso. John Edgar Bevan gave confirmatory evidence. Detective Sergeant Philip Benjamin Grocey Franklin testified to having seen the body as described, later assisted in its

---

*Griffiths described the car as black.

removal, and being present when Chief Superintendent Wayman handed it over to Dr Haslett at the mortuary attached to Cheltenham General Hospital. PC Frederick Thomas Knight told the Court of how he had been summoned from Corse Police Station to the banks of the Severn, seen the torso in the net, and helped to lift it out of the water.

Dr Thomas Bones Hamilton-Haslett, MD, MRCP, BSc, DPh, pathologist at Cheltenham General Hospital, said that he made an external examination of the body. The trunk was that of a well-developed male, whose age was probably over 25 years and probably under 50 years. Death could have taken place up to four weeks before his examination. It was probable that the body had been submerged in the water shortly after death, and had remained there. He found there was not sufficient evidence to arrive at the cause of death. He had, at the suggestion of the coroner, been present and assisted Sir Bernard Spilsbury at a later date.

The coroner then told the jury: "That is as far as I propose to take this inquiry today. I will adjourn the inquest to this day week at eleven thirty. If the police inquiries are not then complete, and if I deem it desirable, I will adjourn again from week to week." He then warned the jury: "This case appears to be attracting considerable publicity, and I must ask you to pay no attention to what you may read or hear out of this court, but give your consideration only to the evidence you will hear in the course of this inquiry."

That first sitting of the inquest concluded at 12.25pm.

It wanted a minute or two to 3.30pm, when Dr Roche Lynch and Chief Inspector Cherrill's car drew up at Cheltenham's Central Police Station. Without even setting foot outside the car, the pair were whisked straight off to Number 248, Worth, Shewry, Hopkins, and Hancock accompanying them.

First port of call was the garage, in a sort of alley at the right-hand side of the house, where torches and tape measures were produced, along with the specialist apparatus of dactyloscopy and other tools of close-focus forensic examination, and Brian Sullivan's car was subjected to a minute and expert scrutiny. On the back seat lay a dirty old mackintosh coat, heavy, and lined with a wide check material. On the floor of the car was a sad scattering of dead beech leaves, importing a strange moribund air of neglect and melancholy. The area around Tower Lodge was noted for its beech trees. And beside the front seat, poignant, was a stained and dog-eared map of Cornwall.

The whirr of an electric sweeper could be heard coming from the garage, and in the gathering dusk, a crowd, sensing interesting activity, quickly gathered beyond the garden wall in front of the nondescript little semi-detached house, and as Nurse Sullivan, who usually sat behind the closely-curtained drawing-room windows to shield her from the gaze of the inquisitive, appeared at the window of the downstairs room facing the road, an officious constable moved the loiterers on.

Roche, Lynch and Cherrill proceeded then to Tower Lodge, where they carried out their respective examinations. Having performed certain tests, and examined stains found on various items of furniture and carpets, Dr Lynch confided to

Worth his opinion that, whatever else might have happened there, the dismemberment of the body had not taken place at Tower Lodge.

A decisive step was taken that evening when, at 5.45pm, Scotland Yard forwarded the text of a description of Captain Butt, supplied by Chief Inspector Worth, to the BBC. It was put out in the 6.15pm and 9pm news bulletins.

> The police are anxious to trace the whereabouts of Captain William Bernard Butt, retired from the Worcester Regiment in 1919. His description is: Aged 52, height five foot nine inches, hair brown, turning grey, thick, believed parted left side. Long face, complexion pale. Eyes grey, rather large nose, full military grey moustache, probably artificial teeth, slim build, sloping shoulders, cultured voice. When last seen at 10.40pm, on the fourth of January, at Cheltenham, he was wearing a light coloured tweed suit, brown Trilby hat with flat brim. Will anybody who has seen him since the fourth of January, or who can give any information, please communicate Chief Constable Gloucestershire. Telephone: Cheltenham 2028.

At the same time, arrangements were made for a photograph of the missing Captain to be reproduced in the following day's newspapers. Things were beginning to settle into a definite shape. The hunt was now on in earnest.

Chapter Eight

Suspects and Suspicions

Secretly, in the dark hours of 7 – 8 February 1938, the two Yard men, Worth and Shewry, left Cheltenham and made a midnight dash by police car to London.

This rapidly taken decision of theirs followed upon the receipt of the news that Brian Sullivan's intimate friend, Keith Harold Newman, had been located and brought into Scotland Yard for interrogation.

Newman, 28 years old, a self-styled 'motor car agent', of Number 2 Radlett Place, NW8, was unquestionably an odd bird. He was, he said, a married man, but had been separated from his wife for the past couple of years. His wife was Celia Greally.

This was a most interesting, not to say potentially significant, fact, for it turned out that Celia Greally was the young woman who had been interviewed with regard to the glove that had been found on Haw Bridge. The laundry mark, CLR 614, written in that glove had been reported by Mrs Beatrice Baldwin, manageress of the branch office – at 81 Great Titchfield Street, W1 – of the Castle Laundry, Frogmore, Wandsworth, as being that laundry's dry cleaning mark. Checking her books, she had been able to tell the police that that particular mark had, in 1934, been allotted to a Miss Greally, of Vandyck Mansions, 27 Langham Street, W1. The customer had informed the laundry that she was moving, and had instructed them not to call again.

Miss Greally had been traced by the police to Number 36 Glasshouse Street, Piccadilly, and was discovered to have a criminal record – 28 convictions for prostitution between October 1932 and February 1938.

Newman first got to know Greally in 1931, when she was in charge of the café at the Forum Theatre, in Fulham Road. They had married on 18 January 1934.

Greally stated that she could not remember having included any "gent's gloves" in her laundry, but said frankly that this could have happened. It was perfectly conceivable that by a mistake, either Keith or his friend Brian might have left their gloves at her flat, and it was actually her custom to have her maid forward to her laundry any articles of clothing accidentally left behind by visitors to her flat, so that if called for, they could be restored to their owner in good, clean condition.

Newman admitted that he had visited her in the past, and still did so occasionally, for sexual intercourse, and Brian used at times to accompany him. Sullivan, he said, was fond of the opposite sex and was not, in his opinion, the type to engage in acts of immorality with men. This is worth noting, for, as we shall see later, there were suggestions that Brian and Captain Butt had a homosexual relationship.

On separating from his wife, Newman took over the flat at Number 2 Radlett Place from Brian Sullivan, who was the lessee. He and Brian first met about 1930-31, during Sullivan's dance host days at the Piccadilly Hotel. He knew that Brian visited his mother in Cheltenham, and he knew that he used to go to Polperro, where he had two cottages. Brian had from time to time stayed with him at Radlett Place.

Newman had visited Cheltenham on a number of occasions. The first time was about 1935. Brian and his mother were then living at Tower Lodge, and he had stayed the night at a local hotel. On that first visit Nurse Sullivan had introduced him to the owner of 248 Old Bath Road, and to his wife, whom she was nursing. The owner was referred to simply as 'The Captain', and no other name was mentioned.

There was a second visit in 1935, and he had been in Cheltenham again in the spring of 1936, when he stayed one or two nights with Brian at Tower Lodge. There was also a one night stay at the Lodge in August 1937. Whenever he stayed at Tower Lodge with Brian Sullivan, there was never any other person present during the night.

He was not in Cheltenham again until he drove down from London in his hire-purchase SS Jaguar DXT375 to attend Brian's funeral. That time he was taken up to Tower Lodge by PC Merry, who gruesomely retailed to him there all the details of how Brian had committed suicide. Newman was shown some brownish stains on the bedclothes, and Merry told him that they were caused by the body having been kept so long.

Asked to furnish names and addresses of persons who could prove that he was in London from 1 – 10 January 1938, Newman supplied:

1. David Frost, a musical director, of Flat 360, The White House, Albany Street, London, NW.
2. Marjorie Irene Frost, separated wife of David Frost, living at Number 4 Radlett Place, NW8.
3. Mrs Jean Keates, of 50 Endymion Road, Harringay, who had worked as a maid for Mrs Frost for more than four years.
4. Mr & Mrs Featherstone, of Number 1 Radlett Place, NW8.
5. Mr & Mrs Wedge, of Number 5 Radlett Place, NW8.
6. Frederick Player, a chauffeur, whose employer's car was garaged at Number 3 Radlett Place.
7. Douglas Ell, of the Great Eastern Rubber Co, 31 Norton Folgate, Bishopsgate.

David Frost stated that he and his wife had been living apart since November 1937, and that she had a divorce suit pending. They took over Number 4 Radlett Place from Brian Sullivan in October 1936. Keith Newman lived at Number 2 Radlett Place, and they became very friendly. Newman had possessed the SS

Jaguar car since July 1937, and Frost with his wife and Newman went on a tour to the continent in it. He, Frost, had never been to Cheltenham. From the time that he took over the flat until December 1937, he did not see Brian Sullivan. On that occasion Brian was outside the flat in a car, but Frost did not speak to him. He remembered Newman saying that Sullivan was a bit of a nuisance in asking him to go to Cheltenham and giving the impression that he [Newman] was not anxious to see him. He was able to testify that Newman was definitely in London on 13 January 1938, for on that date he signed a promissory note in respect of a loan of £85 by Frost against his Jaguar car as security.

Marjorie Irene Frost said that on her taking over Number 4 Radlett Place, Newman became a regular visitor to the flat, and he eventually came to know of the difference between her and her husband. Newman remained on friendly terms with them both. Since November 1937, she had been leading a quiet life, and whenever she was away from the flat it had been in the company of Newman. She chose to go with him as an established friend, as she feared that association with former male friends might have rendered her divorce proceedings more difficult. Since her husband left the flat in November, she had seen Newman every day, and he could not have made any long distance journeys without her knowledge.

On 17 January 1938, she and Newman left in his car for a tour of the West of England, visiting Exeter, Falmouth, Torquay, Newquay, St Ives, and Truro, and returned to London on Wednesday 26 January, by way of Minehead and Salisbury.

Brian Sullivan visited her flat in the company of Newman some time before Christmas 1937, and she had not seen him since. She went to his funeral at the request of Mrs Sullivan, as she understood that Mrs Brian Sullivan had declined to attend. When the news of Brian's death arrived, Newman said that he felt bad about it, and that it was a pity that he had put off the visit.

She had last seen Newman at midnight on 6 February. He had picked her up in the West End in his car. He told her that he had been approached by newspaper reporters and the police in connection with Brian Sullivan's death, and she understood him to say that he was going to Cheltenham on the matter. He told her that he had been into the room in which Brian had died and that he had seen some blood on the bed. He had thought that in the circumstances that was rather curious. Mention was also made of a letter written by Brian Sullivan in which he had left his clothing to Newman.

Mrs Jean Keates simply confirmed that she remembered Mrs Frost and Newman leaving together for a holiday tour. She had no knowledge of where they went, but verified the date of their departure as 17 January and their date of return as 26 January 1938.

Neither Mr or Mrs Featherstone could speak as to Newman's presence in London on the material dates.

Mrs Alice Wedge, on the other hand, who had known Newman since she came to reside at Radlett Place in 1936, clearly recalled his being away from London in company with Mrs Frost for just over a week, and returning during the last week in January. Prior to his going off on that holiday, she was, she said, practically certain that she had seen Newman in Radlett Place every day since the New Year.

Frederick Theodore Player told of cleaning Newman's car on several occasions. The last time that he saw him was on 29 January 1938, and he believed that it was in the final week of that month that he last cleaned his car. He had then noticed slight damage to its spotlight. This was doubtless the repair that was carried out at Moon's Garage on 13 January.

Apropos of this, Newman had told Inspector Worth that another car had run into his while it was standing stationary outside the Post Office in St John's Wood Terrace. Enquiry at Moon's Garage elicited that DXT375 had indeed been in for repairs on 13 January, and that they had consisted of the straightening of the front nearside horn and beating out the rim of the spotlight. Worth examined the car, saw that the damage had undoubtedly been slight, and was certainly not consistent with its having been caused by a collision with a pedestrian or any accident of that kind.

Douglas Ell said that he had known Newman for 25 years. As near as he could remember, Newman visited him on or about 7 or 8 January 1938, and on 12 January they had dined together in the West End. He last saw him between 13 and 16 January, when they talked about a short holiday in the West of England that Newman was contemplating taking with Mrs Frost. Ell produced a letter which he had received from Newman. It was post-marked 'Truro. 24 January 1938'.

Inspector Worth decided that the investigation did not – thus far, at least – indicate that Newman was implicated in the disposal of the human remains at Cheltenham, and at 7.45am on 8 February, he was released. Worth accompanied him back to his flat in Radlett Place, where the detective examined some clothing, including a pair of old wash leather gloves. They bore no laundry mark and were not, he registered, of the same quality as the glove found on Haw Bridge.

On the Wednesday – 9 February – having despatched sundry exhibits to London for forensic evaluation, Worth went up to Tower Lodge again and made arrangements there for organised digging and a minute examination of the entire interior of the place.

At Number 248 Old Bath Road he made an effort to question Mrs Butt, but in view of her mental state found it a hopeless task. A thorough search of the house was conducted, paying particular attention to Captain Butt's correspondence and personal belongings.

Late that evening, Worth made his way over to the Black Bear, a public-house in Tewkesbury, to interview John Edwin Beck, the son of the licensee and a young man who had been an acquaintance of Brian Sullivan's, having previously lived near Old Bath Road in Cheltenham.

Beck told the inspector that at about 8.45pm on either the 3 or 4 January 1938, he had seen Sullivan come into the pub accompanied by a man whom Beck did not know. He described him as being aged 30 to 35, five foot nine inches tall, of slight build, with a thin face, dark hair, pale to sallow complexion, dressed in dark or black clothes, and wearing, he thought, a black trilby hat. Young Beck was serving customers at the time and had no occasion to take any special notice of Brian's companion, but he did see that Sullivan was doing most of the talking. The pair left at about 9pm, after drinking two bottles of beer apiece.

Beck saw Sullivan come in again at around 9pm on either 7 or 8 January. This time he was alone. He remained for about a quarter of an hour, standing drinking in the passage at the back of the bar. Beck said that he recalled this particularly because it was rather unusual for Sullivan to come in twice in one week.

Anxious to get a look at the old Austin Tourer, PD4786, formerly owned by Brian Sullivan, who, on 8 November 1937, had sold it to a Mr James Fruin, who sold it on to Percival Millard, a builder, of 23 St Luke's Road, Cheltenham, Worth went with his sergeant to the Paragon Garage, Bath Road, Cheltenham, owned by Mr Fruin. The detectives were quick to recognise that the car answered the description of the one mentioned by Hancock, the lorry driver. Moreover, the peculiarity of the index letter, as seen by him in passing, appeared to correspond with that on this car.

Millard used the car for his business as well as for private purposes. The back seat was regularly removed so that he could carry paints and other building and decorating material on a wooden platform which he had installed. The car was seldom cleaned and the interior was much stained by the builder's materials. Of considerable interest to Worth and Shewry was the fact that the car was garaged in an open stall to which anyone could have free access.

Throughout all of the exhaustive enquiries which were made to trace the car seen by Hancock, none was found which seemed to be as likely as this one to have been used in the transportation and disposal of the Haw Bridge human remains. A most careful examination by Dr Roche Lynch failed, however, to disclose any evidence of such usage.

During the course of conversation, Mr Fruin told Inspector Worth that shortly after Brian Sullivan had sold his car to Mr Millard, he brought to the garage his own Austin saloon, OX 1010, for repair. He had wanted it done immediately, as he had to go to London. Mr Fruin had regretted that it would not be possible to complete the necessary work as quickly as that. Brian thereupon said that he absolutely must leave for town, and if the work could not be done he would borrow Mr Millard's car. Fruin objected that he could not do that without permission, but Sullivan said that Millard would understand. In the event, Fruin managed by dint of calling in extra help to complete the repair in time for Sullivan to take his own car to London.

Mr Millard, when questioned, was quite emphatic that he had no knowledge of any person's having used his car without his permission. He did, however, admit that it would have been a simple matter for anyone to do so. When the car was purchased from Mr Fruin, it was grey in colour, but on 25 January it had been washed down and painted blue.

In company with Superintendent Hopkins, Inspector Worth called, on 10 February, at the private residence of Colonel Henn, the Chief Constable of Gloucester. They gave him a full account of the results of all their enquiries to date, and Worth said that he was anxious to put into immediate operation a really thorough search of the surrounding district of Cheltenham, including woods, quarries, rubbish heaps, stretches of water, derelict buildings, outhouses, and all likely places where the head might have been secreted, and to find the scene where the dismemberment had been carried out.

To these ends, the Chief Constable placed at Worth's disposal a party of recruits under the supervision of their instructor, Sergeant Willmott, and arrangements were made by Superintendent Hopkins for the area to be searched.

The Times, on Thursday 10 February, printed the following Press Association Report:

> Mr Keith Newman, of 2 Radlett Mews, Avenue Road, St. John's Wood, after consultation with his solicitors [Messrs Lawrence, Collett and Fearnley-Whittingstall] wishes to make the following statement: 'My relationship with Brian Sullivan was that of landlord and tenant living in neighbouring flats. Such discussions as I had with him and such visits as I paid to him were purely on business matters arising out of that relationship. I have been described, not by Sullivan but by a member of his family (with whom I have not the slightest acquaintance) as "Sullivan's best friend". I have never regarded myself in this light. My only concern is to give what assistance I may still be able to furnish to the police authorities and to withdraw from this publicity, which I do not seek, and which has accorded me most acute distress.'

The coroner having released the body, the torso was, on 10 February, buried in a four foot by eight inches, unvarnished, elm coffin at the Cheltenham Graveyard, Bouncers Lane, Prestbury, at the expense of the Public Assistance Committee. Section A1, Plot 87. The coffin was followed by only one mourner – the keeper of Cheltenham Graveyard.

The arms and legs were buried three months later, 2 May 1938, in the same grave.

Then ... just quietly slipped into two consecutive issues of the *Echo* were two distinctly disquieting paragraphs.

The *Echo*, 11 February:

> Another mystifying feature that has come to light is the size of the coffin in which Sullivan was buried. Sullivan was a small man, no

more than 5ft. 3ins. in height and of slight build, but the coffin in which he was buried is stated to have been 6ft. 6ins. long.

The *Echo*, 12 February:

> Another astonishing theory being advanced is that the man who lies buried in Leckhampton Churchyard is not Brian Sullivan. These sensational rumours were based on the fact, confirmed by the undertaker, that although Sullivan was only about 5ft. 4ins. in height, the body when measured in the mortuary was 5ft. 111/2 ins. It is well known that physical changes take place after death, but could they have been so drastic as to have added about seven inches to the length of the corpse? In view of this amazing theory there is all the more reason to believe that eventually the police may find it necessary to exhume the coffin from the grave at Leckhampton. It is understood that the corpse removed from Tower Lodge was much distorted, as is usual following death from gas poisoning.

These are indeed muddied waters, into which it will be necessary for us to wade uncomfortably deeply.

Chapter Nine

Head-Hunters

The hunt for the torso's missing head was on with a vengeance. No nook, no cranny, the police decided, should go unscrutinised, no stone remain unturned, no waterway unplumbed, for, apart from the solving of the overwhelming riddle of identity, the head was essential in order for the doctors to be able to assign a cause of death.

And so the barren, scrub-strewn slopes of hills, the fields and hedgerows, ponds, pools, streams – even the water in cattle troughs was stirred and inspected – were meticulously scanned. Water diviners came dutifully forward with offers of help.

Initially, a painstaking search of all the land at the rear of Tower Lodge was mounted. A ploughed field adjoining the garden was minutely examined foot by foot for any sign of the earth's having been disturbed since ploughing. Policemen poked hedges, ditches and undergrowth with sticks, dug down into places where they thought it possible that the surface of the ground had been previously broken. One policeman climbed a hollow tree in a field above the Lodge and peered deep into its dark interior.

Inspector Hancock led members of the Gloucestershire CID a quarter of a mile across the fields from Tower Lodge to Leckhampton Reservoir, to search all around its perimeter for footprints or any other tell-tale marks that might betray the former presence there of one with an unwelcome burden for the watery jettisoning. Another search-party ransacked the small copse known as Dog Kennel Wood.

Under the direction of their instructor, Sergeant James Willmott, of the Cheltenham Police, a party of ten police recruits spent twelve days between 11 and 25 February picking their way over the stones and boulders of the Leckhampton Hill Quarries; probing the crevices of the cliff face and the cavities close to the celebrated local landmark, the isolated pillar of rock, the Devil's Chimney, probably left by quarrymen who worked the hill 200 years ago. The Tower Lodge outbuildings were excavated, its ground quartered, and a vast sweep of the surrounding countryside combed.

A further possibility that was being considered was that the head had been thrown from a car over the Mythe Bridge at Tewkesbury. This bridge carried the main Tewkesbury-Ledbury road across the Severn, and was one of the chief routes from Tewkesbury to Haw Bridge. The sand-pits in the vicinity of Tewkesbury were also earmarked for police attention.

And whatever the weather, the search went doggedly on – as witness a newspaper report of 14 February: 'In a heavy snow-storm scores of police officers continued their search for the head in outlying places near Cheltenham today'.

Volunteer parties of schoolboys and adult civilians also took part in the mammoth head-hunt, but, unfortunately, it all came to nothing.

There were, however, interesting discoveries in certain other directions. The search at 248 Old Bath Road disclosed, for instance, the fact that Captain Butt's financial state was far from healthy. For some time past he had been living well beyond his means.

An interview – on 13 February – with Nurse Sullivan's neighbours, the Prices, at Number 246, furnished some extremely interesting, and rather worrying, information. Mrs Ida Price told Inspector Worth that Nurse Sullivan had spoken to her of the unsociability and meanness of Captain Butt, and many times, both before and after the Captain's disappearance, she had disclosed to her that she was afraid of him and often locked her bedroom door at night.

At about 9.30pm on 24 January 1938, Nurse Sullivan had called upon Mrs Price. She was very distressed and asked: "May I come in a minute? My poor boy is dead. He has killed himself". She had then gone on to relate all the dreadful details of how she had found her son's body. She had, she said, telephoned her doctor, Dr Condor, and he was sending her some sleeping tablets (Soneryl). At about 10.30pm Mr and Mrs Price had accompanied her back next-door, and Mrs Price had seen her safely into bed.

Nurse Sullivan was most concerned that her daughter-in-law should, as she saw it, fulfil her duty as a wife, and attend Brian's funeral. But Mrs Margaret Sullivan had absolutely no intention of doing anything of the kind and, indeed, did not put in any appearance at Cheltenham.

At 7.45am on the day before the inquest on Brian Sullivan, that is on 27 January 1938, while he was dressing in the back bedroom at Number 246 Old Bath Road, Mr Cyril Price was somewhat startled to hear loud screaming. Looking out of the window, he saw Nurse Sullivan, clad in nightdress, dressing-jacket, and bedroom slippers, pacing wildly about the garden of Number 248, emitting piercing shrieks. In some consternation he told his wife what was happening, and she, like a good neighbour, went next-door to see what was wrong.

Nurse Sullivan was hysterical. As soon as she saw Mrs Price she shouted: "My dear! My dear! That awful man has come back in the night".

Mrs Price led her gently into the house, sat her down on a couch in the sitting-room, and invited her to tell her all about what was troubling her. Wringing her hands, Nurse Sullivan said:

"I shall go mad. That awful man came back in the night and bent over me with a most awful distorted face."

Mrs Price, having done her not very successful best to calm her distraught neighbour, telephoned Dr Condor, who advised another sleeping tablet.

At half-past eight, Mrs Price's husband looked in, and Nurse Sullivan repeated to him her story about the "terrible man". She told him: "I could see his terrible leering face standing over me".

Mr Price asked, "What terrible face?"

"Captain Butt's," she replied.

At his wife's request, Mr Price went up to the Captain's bedroom – "Just to check". Returning, he assured Nurse Sullivan that no one was there.

During her ravings Nurse Sullivan made the enigmatic remark: "I think perhaps I may have made a mistake. It may not have been my boy".

In a statement which he made, Dr Archibald Condor said that he recollected Nurse Sullivan's mentioning the idea that the body at Tower Lodge might not have been that of her son. He added that "this statement was obviously made by her in view of the considerable alteration due to *post mortem* changes."

On the day after the inquest – 29 January – Mrs Price again visited Nurse Sullivan, who, when asked what kind of a night she had had, replied:

"Oh, dreadful, dreadful. I'll never take any of those tablets again. I had an awful dream last night. I dreamt that I was in a dissecting theatre seeing bodies dissected."

Mrs Price advised her to discontinue the tablets!

There are those who might think to see shadows, at least, of sinister or guilty knowledge manifesting themselves in Irene Sullivan's uneasy dreams. Of this, more anon.

The *Echo*, of 12 February, contained a tantalising paragraph:

> Inquiries are being made following a statement to the police by the proprietors of a shop that an article of woman's underclothing was sent to Tower Lodge and received by a man on 14 January.

It will be recalled that on 12 January, Nurse Sullivan had been up to the Lodge, found the place locked and deserted, and Bimbo, the spaniel, in Brian's parked car.

After that, she did not go up to the Lodge again, she said, for two or three days – 13, 14 and 15 January. In fact, according to her statement, it was on the 17 or 18 January that she next went there, finding a number of newspapers sticking out of the front-door letter-box, but still no sign of life.

The question was, then, who had been in occupation and received the package said to have been delivered to Tower Lodge on the afternoon of Friday 14 January?

The tale as told to the police was intriguing.

It was Miss Susan Shill, the proprietress of Shill's, the draper's, of Bath Road, Cheltenham, who brought the matter to their attention. She had known Nurse Sullivan for ten years, and throughout that period she had had an account at the shop. The lady assistants employed at Shill's all knew her, too. For the last few years an account had also been current in the name of Captain Butt.

In the early afternoon of 14 January 1938, 20-year-old John Bubb, normally an assistant in the furniture side of the business but standing in that day for young John Collier, the 16-year-old delivery boy who had the day off to help his parents move house, went over to the drapery department to sort out the parcels which were ready for delivery. Among them was one addressed in ink to: 'Nurse Sullivan. Tower Lodge'. Bubb did not register whose handwriting it was on the package, but from the peculiar way the label was stuck on he guessed that the parcel had been put together by the assistant, Miss Birt.

The parcel was very light in weight, and from its size and appearance he guessed – correctly – that it contained sanitary towels. Observing that it had been marked 'Urgent,' he took the parcel to Mr Shill and told him that, in view of its apparent urgency, he proposed to deliver it. Mr Shill pointed out that it was raining hard, and suggested that Bubb should enquire from the assistant who had made the sale just how urgent it was, and whether delivery could be delayed for a while.

Bubb accordingly went to one of the lower counters in the drapery department and spoke to an assistant who told him that the parcel could definitely not be delayed. Unfortunately, Bubb could not afterwards be sure who the assistant concerned had been, but said that he had the impression that it was Miss Birt. He placed the parcel on the carrier of a trade bicycle and pedalled off through the incessant rain to Tower Lodge.

It was between 3.30pm and 4pm when he arrived there. He leant the bicycle against the outside wall. It slipped, fell down sideways, and the parcel shot out of the carrier, landing on the wet ground. As he picked it up, Bubb saw that the brown paper wrapping had got torn, and he could see underneath it the characteristic blue colour of the cardboard box, confirming that the contents of the parcel was, as he had thought, a box of sanitary towels. And, as he was afterwards to say, it had struck him at the time as rather odd that Nurse Sullivan, whom he knew well, should, in view of her age, require such articles.

The padlock hanging on a chain on the Lodge gates seemed to be locked, so he went round to the side-door, which was actually situated on the main road, and knocked. There was no reply. He therefore returned to the main gates, opened them by lifting the chain, made his way to the front-door, and knocked. No reply.

As he stood there on the door-step, he noticed a motor-car – dark brown, he thought, with a hooded top – parked in the drive.

Several times more he knocked on the door. He could hear a dog barking inside and a man's voice telling it to be quiet. After about five minutes – he actually waited so long because it was still pouring with rain and he was taking advantage of the shelter – the door opened a little way and a man put his head out. He was about 30 years of age, clean-shaven, pasty-faced, with almost black tortoise-shell rimmed glasses, and wore a dark trilby hat, probably turned down in front. He did not appear to be a big-built man. Bubb did not then, and said that he would not again in the future be able to, recognise him.

He told the man that he had called from Shill's and had a parcel for Nurse Sullivan. The man put out his hand, took the parcel without speaking, and closed the door. He seemed agitated and surprised, and Bubb got the distinct feeling that the call had been unexpected. He knew Captain Butt, and he was not the man who took in the parcel. He knew Nurse Sullivan too, but he did not know her son.

None of the lady assistants at Shill's was able to throw any light on the mysterious order for sanitary towels. Two of them, Miss Alice Powell and Miss Phyllis Weeds, felt sure that they had seen Nurse Sullivan in the shop by Miss Birt's counter some time after Christmas, but neither was able to give even an approximate date, nor could they in any way connect Nurse Sullivan with the order for sanitary towels.

Miss Birt clearly remembered serving Nurse Sullivan at Christmas-time (1937), and could even recall the articles that she purchased as well as booking them to her account. But that, she said, was definitely the last occasion upon which she had served her. Indeed, it was also the last time she recollected seeing her in the shop.

It was the practice at Shill's on receiving an order from an account customer who did not make payment at the time, to write out a bill, upon which was shown the customer's name and address, the goods taken, and the value thereof. Later, the goods would be despatched, particulars of the transaction being entered in the customers' accounts ledger by another assistant.

In the event that the account customer pays for the goods at the time of giving the order, the articles would be made up into a parcel, and labelled for despatch. In the case of such a transaction, a bill would be made out, but the particulars would not be entered in the ledger, so that the only record kept would be the duplicate bill.

Miss Birt went so far as to say that in the case of a cash transaction by an account customer asking for the purchased goods to be delivered, there would be nothing unusual in the goods being prepared and labelled ready for despatch and the bill to be made out omitting the customer's name and address. Indeed, Miss Birt admitted to having done this on many occasions.

An examination of Shill's books showed that the last purchase or order given there by Nurse Sullivan was just before Christmas 1937, when she bought pocket-handkerchiefs and cloths. The duplicate bills relating to the records of cash sales did not reveal any purchase since that time by Nurse Sullivan.

But what they did reveal was that three boxes of sanitary towels, any of which might have been of the type delivered to Tower Lodge, had been sold on 13 January – two boxes by Miss Birt and one by Miss Powell. They were both closely questioned, but neither was able to recall by whom the purchases were made, and neither could in any way connect Nurse Sullivan with those sales.

Nurse Sullivan herself, referring to the curious affair of the sanitary towels, had this to say:

I have been questioned and questioned again on [the] incident which happened on the 14th January. On that day – which was a Friday – somebody entered a draper's shop in Cheltenham and bought some articles which only a woman would require. That person, whoever it was, asked that the articles should be delivered at Tower Lodge. Now I have dealt at this particular shop for some time, and when the purchase of these articles was put to me I at once stated that I did not go into the shop that day or purchase any such articles. I have not been into that shop since before Christmas.

The articles were delivered to the Lodge that day, and were taken in by a man. The assistant who delivered them also heard a dog there. At this time Bimbo was with me at 248. I had taken him away on the 12th.

Who then was the man who took the parcel in, and whose was the dog at the Lodge on the 14th? If Brian was then dead, what were they doing there? If he was not dead, where was he? What had happened within Tower Lodge between the 10th January, when Brian returned there with Bimbo from 248 Old Bath Road, and the 14th of January when this package was delivered?

I have been asked whether I was quite sure that I had not ordered the articles, and was not at Tower Lodge when they were delivered. And I told the police … that I know nothing whatever about the matter. On the last two occasions when I was interviewed by the police on the subject I asked them that I be confronted with the assistant from whom the articles had been ordered so that I could prove it was not I who ordered them.

As a matter of fact, an exhaustive enquiry at Shill's had failed to discover any assistant who was prepared to say that she had served her.

Inspector Worth, having noted that Nurse Sullivan could offer no explanation, also noted that there was in fact nothing to connect the incident with any act of hers. He accepted that the last time that she was in Shill's was at Christmas 1937, "when she bought handkerchiefs and other little things for which she paid about ten shillings cash. She was short of money at the time, and one or two articles were entered in the account. She owes Shill's probably £1 to £2. The last goods sent from Shill's to Tower Lodge were two deck-chairs, in July or August, 1937."

The inspector felt that he could not accept the view that the sanitary towels had been ordered to be used in removing traces of blood derived from the torso, for, as he firmly pointed out, there was positively no evidence whatsoever that dismemberment had been carried out at the Lodge. It might, he suggested, be that a young woman was concerned in the affair, and that she had had personal need of them that day. He could not totally dismiss the possibility that, all her denials notwithstanding, Nurse Sullivan might have been at Tower Lodge with Bimbo on 14 January, when the messenger heard the barking of a dog. What he did feel most strongly was that, going on the description given by John Bubb, the man who took in the parcel was Brian Sullivan.

Pelion upon Ossa, the puzzles mounted!

Chapter Ten

The Sexual Politics of Captain Butt

It was on 9 February 1938, that a reporter for the *Daily Mail* wrote:

> I understand that letters illustrating the close friendship between
> Captain Butt and Sullivan were found today by the police, as well as
> evidence that more than once they went away together.

A nod being, as they say, as good as a wink to an optically disadvantaged horse,
those readers who were not interlinearly blind were quick to pick up the
'insinuendo' that Butt and Brian enjoyed a homosexual relationship. The actual
evidence on this score seems a shade flimsy.

Of the so-significant letter said to have passed between Butt and Brian, there is
no trace to be found. It is not among the documents deposited in the
Gloucestershire Record Office by the Chief Constable between 1962 and 1985, no
copy of it is to be found in the Scotland Yard documentation of the case, and the
police disclaim any knowledge of its surviving whereabouts. It seems, like so
many missing documents from the official Jack the Ripper files, to be a case of lost,
stolen, or strayed.

One is, therefore, chary about labelling either Brian or Will homosexual. On the
other hand, there were those who came forward to testify to the Captain's sexual
peccadillos in the then fraught arena of sodomy.

A certain Gloucester greengrocer, Nelson Gardner of Southgate Street,
convicted of that offence – and to two years' hard labour – a decade earlier,
interviewed on 15 February 1938, stated that he had first met the upright Captain
in October 1927. They had both been sitting on a seat near the Winter Gardens, in
Cheltenham, at the time. They fell into casual conversation, and then into less
casual activity in a nearby public lavatory; and there was a repeat performance
later that same day in a shop doorway in the town.

The pair kept a rendezvous a few days later at Cheltenham's Great Western
Railway Station. Gardner said that he was seen on that occasion by George
Compton, a railway booking-clerk who knew Captain Butt well. The greengrocer
had been out with Butt about six times in all, the last adventuring together being
back in 1927. He recalled Butt paying him £8 when he [Gardner] was going to
London for a weekend.

He last saw the Captain about January 1937. Butt had then admitted that
Compton had told him that he (Gardner) had been in prison, and in consequence
there had been no further dalliance between them. Gardner was, however, able to

Captain William Bernard Butt.

reveal that Butt had also committed sodomy with a tobacconist, Bernard Belcher, of Montpellier, Cheltenham, as well as acts of indecency with a number of other men whom he named.

But, despite an exhaustive enquiry and the interviewing of persons cited by the garrulous greengrocer, Inspector Worth was unable to discover the slightest evidence that Captain Butt harboured desire for, or indulged himself in, such immoral practices with males. Neither could he find the smallest evidential indication that Brian Sullivan was 'that way' disposed.

What was both discoverable and discovered was the noble Captain's susceptibility to the ladies. For several years past he had been having fleshly association with 'Idey', as he called Miss Ida Cranswick, of Oxford, who reciprocally christened him 'Billy'.

She was, by 1938, a 46-year-old spinster, living in Polstead Road, where she and her mother kept a boarding-house. It was the Captain's younger brother, John, who had introduced them. That was in May 1935, when John Butt was living with his married sister, Mrs Mary Agnes Hobson, at Wolvercote. John had moved away in August 1937. Billy and Idey had become exceedingly friendly, and it was his wont, or want, to visit her whenever he came to Oxford.

Worth paid her a call. He found her to be completely frank and honest. The Captain had, she said, told her all about Mrs Butt's mental state and the incapacity which it implied. She had supplied that lack, intimacy taking place regularly between them, although he never stayed the night. They used to go on outings together, visiting road houses and the like. On a number of occasions they went to the country or the seaside, staying in hotels as man and wife. In between meetings they kept up a regular correspondence with each other, exchanging on average two letters a week. There was, however, no question of, in the event of anything happening to the legitimate Mrs Butt, their getting married to each other, although Miss Cranswick had reserved her favours totally for the Captain, for whom she declared her affection. She had not been intimate with any other man.

She went on to say that always after his visits Captain Butt would write her a letter, but she had neither seen nor heard from him since 2 January 1938, although he had called on her during Christmas-time, when he and his wife were staying with his sister at Wolvercote. When she had last seen him he appeared to be in good health and good spirits, but what was decidedly odd was that, although throughout the entire period of their friendship Captain Butt had always told her when and where he was going away, this time there had been never a word from him.

In the first year of their friendship, he went to Plymouth for six weeks, and wrote to her from there. In September 1937, he was in Polperro, and wrote. During October or November 1937, he spent, she knew, a single night in Exeter, but she did not know why, or where he stayed.

Shown the overcoat recovered from the hole in the passage at Tower Lodge, she felt positive that it was Captain Butt's. She also examined the fragment of cloth found on Haw Bridge, and clearly remembered his wearing a suit made of similar material in the summer of 1937.

At Worth's request the Exeter police went along to see a Miss Hilda Holland-Hobson, aka Whitfield, of Number 4 The Quadrant, Mount Radford, Walford Road, Exeter. Francis Frederick Hobson, whose sister or step-sister she purported to be, tacking his name on to her own, had married Captain Butt's eldest sister, Mary Agnes, but left her five years after the marriage. Miss Holland-Hobson first met Captain Butt in 1910, and from time to time she, Francis Hobson, and Butt lived together on a yacht in Southampton Water. Later, she and Hobson shared a yacht at Totnes, Devon, where Butt was a frequent visitor. She was not, she most emphatically stated, Butt's mistress. He, with a Mr Hazelwood, a solicitor, of Temple Chambers, Temple Avenue, London, EC, was a joint-trustee under Francis Frederick Hobson's will.

Since Hobson's death, at Plymouth in 1935, Butt had visited her on the yacht, *Seacroft*, which Hobson had left to her, on two occasions. The first time, he spent two or three days aboard with her at Plymouth. The second time, he was about a week on the yacht, after which he took her back with him to 248 Old Bath Road, where she stayed for some three weeks. She had not, she said, actually seen the Captain since October 1935, but they had kept up a correspondence.

Reports from Plymouth City Police provided the information that the yacht, *Seacroft*, had – with the exception of short periods – been berthed at the Great Western Railway Docks, Millbay, Plymouth, from 20 May 1934, until 20 April 1936. On 9 October 1936, ownership of the vessel was transferred to a Mr Harry Edgell, of Cleasdy, Braywoodside, Maidenhead.

It was Miss Holland-Hobson who revealed the Captain's friendship with a woman named Winnie, along with the fact that he was paying for the education of her child. Although, by one of life's strange coincidences, that information also reached the police from a totally different source – a conversation overheard in Harry Blight's ship chandler's shop hard by the Plymouth docks.

Charles Henry Wood, a 28-year-old mechanic, employed by the Albert Garage, in Albert Road, Margate, happened to be in Plymouth on 11 February 1938, picking up a passenger and luggage from a boat at the docks. Needing a rope with which to make fast the luggage on the car, he called in at Blight's, and it was there that he heard the woman who served him talking to another male customer.

The shop assistant, a woman of about fifty – actually Mrs Blight – was saying how particularly interested she was in the Cheltenham Torso case, because she had known Captain Butt personally. He had, she said, at one time a yacht at Plymouth, and used to call on her for different tackle. She went on to say how he had married into money, and how he used to flaunt around with women. She knew where two of his women were in Plymouth at the present time.

Investigation disclosed that one of them was a Mrs Winifred Braven, of Amherst Road, Pennycomequick, Plymouth, who was separated from her husband. She had been introduced to Hobson and Butt by a woman named Thomson, in 1934. She became friendly with Butt and paid visits to the *Seacroft*. Those visits were, she claimed, purely platonic. No misconduct had taken place at any time.

Elsie Thomson, barmaid, tracked down at Cotchele Avenue, Prince Rock, Plymouth, stated that she had been employed in that capacity at the Lockyer Hotel, Plymouth, from 1924 to 1934, and thereafter, until August 1937, at Plymouth's Royal Hotel. She confirmed that yes, she knew Mrs Braven. Yes, she knew Mr Hobson and Captain Butt, and had introduced Mrs Braven to them. Butt frequently stayed on the yacht at Plymouth, and she frequently visited the vessel, sometimes spending the night aboard. She said that no sexual intercourse had ever taken place between her and Hobson, but pointedly made no reference to the relationship obtaining between her and the Captain.

Both women had been known to the Plymouth City Police for some years, and their moral characters had always been recognised as good.

Another of Captain Butt's sisters, Mrs Gertrude Mary Prew, living apart from her husband at 28 Heathfield Road, Gloucester, admitted that Mrs Butt had accused her and the Captain of immoral relations – but this had been in the course of one of Mrs Butt's bad mental turns.

Mrs Prew's daughter, 24-year-old Miranda (Judy), said that on 3 February 1938, Nurse Sullivan had told her mother that Captain Butt had said to Brian that he should not have anything to do with her (Judy). She knew of no reason why he should have said such a thing.

She had first met Brian Sullivan at 248 Old Bath Road, in 1935, when he was home on holiday from his job at the Piccadilly Hotel. She went with him to a couple of dances that year, one of them at Cheltenham, when he told her that he had just come back from Cornwall, but had not been with him to any since. She had also gone out for the odd car ride with him and his mother.

Brian never spoke to her of his friends. Their relationship was nothing more than a formal friendship. There was never any sexual intimacy between them. She naturally, therefore, strongly resented her Uncle Will's implication, and told Nurse Sullivan, who "was behaving like a raving lunatic all the time, and appeared to be in a vile temper because Captain Butt had not returned home," so. She could not remember all that was said, but claimed that Nurse Sullivan had given her the impression that the Captain had other women, and that this was possibly the reason for his absence.

Nurse Sullivan later commented:

> A great deal has been said regarding Butt's association with Brian. There have been stories of their meetings up in London and elsewhere. I do not know anything about this. But judging from their behaviour when they met, they were simply on the casual terms of acquaintanceship which one might expect through Brian's relationship with me. Captain Butt certainly used to go up to Tower Lodge fairly often, because I had previously said that he could have the garden, as he was very fond of gardening. But I have not discovered anybody who ever saw him and Brian about together, and no evidence was produced at the inquest of any association.

Captain Butt was, it has been said, an established patron of the hotel where 'Byron Smith' danced professionally, and is rumoured to have visited the Piccadilly often while Brian was working there. There was also a rumour that Butt and Brian visited dances together in Bristol. Here, the emphasis is on the word rumours.

Less flattering was the light thrown on to Brian Sullivan by research into his London life carried out by *Daily Mail* reporter Ralph Hewins.

A friend – if that is quite the right term for him – of Brian's told of the great success which he scored at the Piccadilly Hotel, where businessmen and their wives would go along to the grill-room and welcome the polite, charming, smiling – always smiling – young man to their tables as an old friend. He was an able conversationalist, a subtle flatterer, and always projected a persona of utter sincerity and frank reliability. Married men unhesitatingly permitted him to waltz their pretty, bejewelled wives off on to the dance-floor without misgivings.

What was more – and more important to Brian – they used to pay him well. Some weeks he would clock up as much as £20 to £30 extra. If he had only made a tenner, he would consider that he had done badly. It was a black week. Then there were always 'presents' – cigarette cases, lighters, boxes of expensive cigars – which could, of course, be sold.

Wealthy, unescorted women were wont to make a bee (for Byron)-line for the suave, twinkle-toed, youthful Lothario, who was not the usual smoothly professional gigolo, but a cheery, vivacious, slightly naïve-seeming young man.

Such was the Brian of his early years at the Piccadilly. Everything changes. And with the passage of time romantic Byron Smith underwent a metamorphosis – for the worse.

It was noticed that gradually his success went to his head. He lost his naïve ways, and was noticed eyeing women's furs and jewels, and sizing up the length of men's purses. He went whole hog on 'the make' – remorselessly. Instead of getting up and dancing, he lingered at rich men's tables, drinking more and more champagne and brandy, and making less and less carefully veiled passes at the married women. In fact, he became an out-and-out gigolo.

Brian Sullivan's fall from grace came about catastrophically. There was a wealthy, 70-year-old usurer who toddled in regularly night after night to the grill. It was his habit to order a large table for one, sit himself down at it, and let it be known that he was happy to stand drinks for everybody. Any strangers were welcome to partake of his bibulous hospitality. And one of the first to sit down was always sweetly smiling, amiably prattling Byron Smith. Thus seduced, the old moneylender came to regard Sullivan as his good and faithful friend.

Now Brian, no slouch, was well aware that the old man always had his pockets stuffed with bundles of five-pound notes on these nights out of his, so that he was well-primed for whatever adventures might present. And Brian had evolved a plan to rob him. He used to take the gamy old gentleman off with him to a night club. There, he would wait until his victim-elect, well-wined, dozed off, before slipping a hand inside his pocket and helping himself. Alternatively, Sullivan and a girl confederate would persuade the aged moneylender into her house, where he would be duly fleeced.

This thievery was performed once too often. Having been robbed in all six or seven times, to the tune of about £150, the worm finally turned. The next day the old man went straight to the Piccadilly Hotel management, and Sullivan was sacked on the spot.

Hewins also claimed to have discovered that, during his season of metropolitan prosperity, Sullivan had acquired a 5hp, two-bunked motor-boat, which he kept at Gloucester and used for week-long orgies, during trips to Tewkesbury and Weston-super-Mare. He bought this vessel when he left London in 1936, to replace one which he had kept moored at the Chelsea Yacht and Boat Company wharf, near Albert Bridge, Battersea. This motor-boat was actually an old black crock, and before he sold it he took it to Whitstable with two girls and a man, and returned without them. The story, according to one of the staff of the Yacht and Boat Company, goes that they left him because he had robbed them. Sullivan was seen throwing bottle after empty bottle over the side when he returned to the Albert Bridge wharf.

He subsequently sold this boat, and, after doing so, removed its stove and a 20 foot by 20 foot black tarpaulin, presumably to equip his new boat.

Most interestingly, Hewins asserts that he has been able to verify that Captain Butt was in the habit of going off on river jaunts with Sullivan.

But there is, I repeat, not the faintest shadow of evidence to substantiate the idea that Butt and Brian were gay. That they were both adventurously heterosexual would seem to be beyond doubt. That they were bisexual is, of course, a very distinct, and significant, possibility, which most certainly cannot be dismissed.

Chapter Eleven

Visions and Revisions

Active as well as the police – pro-active, indeed – were the members of the press, Crime Reporters Ubiquitous, pushing, shoving, prying, peeping, and peering conscientiously under stones.

The press, in the shape of a *Daily Mail* reporter, was there on 9 February 1938, to log up the two and a half hours spent by detectives and local police at Number 248 in the company of Nurse Sullivan. The officers had brought with them bundles of clothes found at Tower Lodge which they believed to be those of Captain Butt.

Detectives in dungarees were observed at dusk carrying forth from the Lodge a heavy basket containing water-pipes which were to be examined for any traces of blood which might have been poured down a sink.

While Chief Inspector Worth was constrained ultimately to report a most disappointing lack of assistance of any kind from Mrs Butt, the Captain's widow, who, mentally unwell, displayed total apathy, an alert pressman claimed a satisfactorily different result.

He wrote in the *Daily Mail*, of 10 February:

> The grey-haired wife of Captain Butt [who] had throughout the investigation remained unseen, a semi-invalid ... tonight [Wednesday 9 February], despondent, smoking a cigarette, and seeming not to notice the watching crowd ... left her house while Chief Inspector Worth and other detectives were inside.
> "I don't understand – it's all too terrible to believe," she said to me, tears in her eyes as we walked along Old Bath Road.
> "Are those horrible relics in the Severn really the remains of my poor husband? Did Brian Sullivan kill him? I cannot think that 'Yes' is the answer. Yet we have had no word from Will since he left home to go into the town on January 4th, and Brian has died by his own hand. Will and I came back from a happy Christmas holiday with friends at Wolvercote on January 3rd. We spent that evening and a good part of the next day quietly at home. After we had all had tea on January 4th, Will said he was going to his club for the evening, quite a regular thing for him. He went, taking his car, and Mrs Sullivan and I went to the pictures. I never saw Will again. What happened to him after he left his club and put his car in a Cheltenham garage at about 10.45 p.m. I do not know. Heaven knows if he has been murdered. There seems no

earthly reason why anybody should wish him ill."

Mrs Butt's face cleared momentarily as she paid tribute to her husband.

"He was wonderfully affectionate, kind and sympathetic,' she said. 'He was strong-willed, too, and not a man with whom anybody could trifle. This was particularly true as far as money was concerned. He was most careful in his financial dealings."

One cannot help suspecting that the pressman, Edwin Tetlow, has drawn the long bow somewhat in his ascription of such words of tender compliment to Mrs Butt, for ample other evidence exists to show that her husband was not the sort of husband to inspire even such lip-service laudation from his ground-down spouse. It is well always to take such 'exclusive' and startling press tales and revelations strictly *cum grano salis*.

The meticulous quartering of the countryside was still going on apace. Particular attention being paid to the rough land in the neighbourhood of the lime-kilns near Bentham, Cranham Woods, Ullenwood Estates, the country to the right towards the Air Balloon public-house, and the vicinity of Salterley Grange Sanatorium.

On Friday 18 February, Frank Hawker was ploughing a field belonging to Abbots Court Farm, which was next to two adjoining cottages at Deerhurst (two and a half miles south-west of Tewkesbury), which Nurse Sullivan had bought in 1933, and sold again at the end of 1936.

The cottages were situated across a marshy common, well back from the roadway, and a few hundred yards from the river Severn, at the point where the White Lion Inn stands. The one of the pair used by Nurse Sullivan and her son – sometimes staying there together, sometimes separately – was 'Byways', a small, brick-built dwelling, with one room up, one room down. The other cottage, older and much larger, used to be let out by Nurse Sullivan to different people.

It was near these cottages that young Hawker found a bloodstained rug. It was folded up and lying on the ground. It was like a horse rug, very thick and almost waterproof. Despite the staining and having been cut, it was in fairly good condition, and the youth took it home. An ex-policeman, Oliver Mince, heard about the find, and insisted on taking it along to the police station. In the event it turned out to be of no evidential value: simply another of the blind-alley 'clues' with which the case seems to have been especially beset.

Just six days previously – 12 February, a Saturday – another promising clue had surfaced; a glove, clotted with blood, and a roll of banknotes were found on desolate Cleeve Common, at Prestbury, Cheltenham, where it was reported that two men with a flashlight had been seen on the night of 4 January. But this clue, too, had just petered out, and things ground on more or less unspectacularly for another week.

Then, on Saturday 19 February, came a real find. At 4.45pm a human left arm, minus the hand, with a piece of binder twine tied around it at the elbow joint, was hauled up out of the Severn, about 250 yards south of Haw Bridge, by Alfred Chamberlain, for whom it was second time lucky, he having been the one who had netted the right arm of the torso on 5 February. The fact that this time no brick was attached to the limb strongly suggested that the binder twine had been severed during dragging operations. It so happened that Superintendent Wayman had just recently obtained a farmer's harrow, which had the effect of raking the river-bed and removing from it anything that had become slightly embedded in the mud. The harrow also had strong, sharp edges to it, which could easily have cut through the twine and freed the brick. This harrow was manipulated from a motor-launch, which had two boats operating drags following immediately behind it. The arm was carried off in triumph by Wayman to the Cheltenham Hospital mortuary.

The following day Worth met Sir Bernard Spilsbury at 11.30am at Kemble railway station and took him to Tower Lodge, where Chief Constable Colonel Henn was waiting to greet him. Spilsbury was shown over the Lodge and its grounds, Worth accompanying him and detailing his findings and views on the case generally.

Later on, Spilsbury was escorted to the Cheltenham Hospital mortuary, where, in company with Dr Hamilton-Haslett, he spent more than two hours examining the four recovered limbs, and, according to the *Daily Mail*, arranged for plaster casts to be taken to help to give the police some idea of the stature and appearance of the victim.

First of all, Sir Bernard fitted fragments of bone attached to the severed limbs to the portions of the bones which remained in the torso, and clearly established that the limbs belonged to the torso.

A pair of Captain Butt's shoes were tried on the feet of the severed legs, and proved a good fit. Both knee joints were found to exhibit slight indications of arthritis.

From measurements made of the femur and tibia bones of the leg, and the humerus and radius bones of the arm, Spilsbury, using Karl Pearson's formulae, calculated the deceased man's height as having been between five foot seven inches and five foot nine inches. The muscular development of the limbs indicated that he had been vigorous and active in life.

He found present a degree of bruising. On the back of the right leg, about four inches above the heel, there was a bruise about one and a quarter inches long. On the inner side of the right ankle there was another bruise about two inches long. Beneath these bruises there was bruising of the muscle. On the front of the left shin-bone, the tibia, just below the knee, there was a bruise about one and a half inches long, which extended down to the bone.

Sir Bernard was also able to say that dismemberment, effected very roughly and displaying scant skill, had involved cutting through the soft tissues and the use of such an instrument as a hatchet on the bones. It was, moreover, most probably carried out shortly after death and before putrefaction had developed. In any case, dismembered limbs placed in a rapidly flowing river in winter time before putrefaction had set in would have little tendency to undergo putrefaction, however long they remained immersed in the water.

The following Wednesday, 23 February, Mrs Butt left Number 248, being taken off by her cousin, Mr EA Hogg, to stay with him at his house, The Nook, in Abbots Road, Tewkesbury. She was never to return to Old Bath Road, her tenancy being surrendered on 25 March following. In the meantime, Nurse Sullivan was permitted to remain there. In addition to a plain clothes policeman on permanent duty outside the house, a plain clothes policewoman was posted in the house, day and night, until Nurse Sullivan's final departure on 11 March.

An interesting result ensued from the detectives' investigation into the circumstances surrounding the issue of the cheap day return ticket from Gloucester to Cheltenham, dated 15 January 1938, which it will be recalled PC Merry found lying on the ground of the short drive-in area at Tower Lodge.

Enquiries at the Great Western railway station at Gloucester elicited from the booking clerk, Leo Collier, that this particular ticket was actually the first of 14 issued for the 8.23am train that Saturday.

A ticket collector, James Yeates, said that the 8.23am Gloucester to Cheltenham was chiefly used by season ticket holders. He had been on duty from 3.15am to 11.50am each day from 10 to 15 January. It was at about 8.15am on either the 13th, 14th, or 15th, that a young man of 25-30 years came to the gate with a ticket. He was five foot six or seven inches tall, clean-shaven, with round features, dark hair, and horn-rimmed glasses, wearing a dark jacket and a dark pork-pie hat. He was carrying either an attaché-case with two fasteners, or what might have been a gramophone record case, and he walked with what was a noticeably effeminate gait.

Yeates' attention was called to this young man because he appeared to be a stranger. After he had punched his ticket and directed him to the appropriate platform, which was over the bridge, the young man came back and asked him, "Which do you call the other side?" Having duly redirected him, Yeates observed to a guard standing by, "There's a cissy for you!" And when, subsequently, he saw Brian Sullivan's photograph in the paper, it struck him forcibly as being similar to the effeminate young man whom he had seen that day.

Significantly, Brian Sullivan did possess a portable wireless and gramophone set. However, it did seem unlikely that he would be unfamiliar with Gloucester station and have to ask his way to the platform for the Cheltenham train. The police were in no doubt that Sullivan knew Gloucester well, but, rather oddly, in spite of making exhaustive enquiries, it proved impossible to trace a single person in that city who knew him.

Painstakingly the police plodded conscientiously on, checking every angle in what the papers were calling 'The Case of the Sawn-up Man'. And from time to time the old black magic of the press emerged rampant, stirring things up. Thus, in the *Daily Mail* of 14 February, Edwin Tetlow wrote:

Captain Butt was in the hands of blackmailers. That is the belief which his younger brother, John Butt, of Newtown, St Boswells, Roxburghshire, expressed yesterday. "What was at the bottom of it all, I don't know," he said. "I merely suspect, that is all. I have not seen very much of my brother since the war, but I should say these blackmailers are of the very worst type. My brother knew how to look after himself. But he was unlucky."

A writer in the previous day's *Sunday Dispatch* had provided his two-penn'orth of 'revelation':

An acquaintance of Sullivan revealed today that months ago he was already preoccupied with death. Remarkable notes on life and death were written by Sullivan in a book which is now in the possession of Mrs N Oliver, owner of a dairy at Polperro, where the dead dancer spent most of last year [1937]. Butt stayed with Sullivan at Polperro during last August. The book which Sullivan lent to Mrs Oliver's husband is *The Pleasures of Life* by Sir John Lubbock. When giving it to Mr Oliver he said: "It is the most wonderful book I have ever read. I feel a different man". Sullivan told Mr Oliver his thoughts were even then concerned with death. Among quotations underlined were: 'Peace, peace, he is not dead, he doth but sleep,' and 'There is no death. What seems so is transition.' Villagers say Sullivan seemed so timid that he turned away from a rabbit lying maimed in a trap.

And in another popular Sunday paper, the *People*, there appeared on 27 February, an exclusive – 'Girl With Secret of Torso Crime'. It was herein propounded that a young English woman, Annie Norman, from Cheltenham, who had committed suicide by overdosing with veronal in her apartment at Les Andelys, near Paris, might well be connected with the Haw Bridge affair. She had, it was suggested, gone to Les Andelys to escape being questioned by the police about Brian Sullivan, with whom she had been on friendly terms for a number of years. English newspapers were sent to her daily from Paris, and it was noticed that she was only interested in the items relating to the 'Torso Mystery'. It was alleged that it was after reading an article in one of these papers in which it was stated that the police were on a new trail, that she retired to the room in which she was found dead next morning. She was said to have made a telephone call to Cheltenham the night before, and to have spoken to someone there for about ten minutes. The detectives made enquiries at Cheltenham. They failed to trace any such telephone call from Les Andelys, or any connection of a woman named Annie Norman with that town. It eventually transpired that the whole thing had been a fictitious concoction.

Ralph Hewins, of the *Daily Mail*, tracked down and interviewed Keith Newman. He described him as a 27-year-old, small, fair, bespectacled man-about-town. Newman said that he thought Brian Sullivan had been crazy, and told the reporter:

> I first met Sullivan two years ago when he sub-let my present flat to me, and I have seen him only five or six times since. Last time I saw him was just before Christmas [1937], when he came up from Cheltenham and spent a few nights in my flat. He kept an old dinner-jacket there, and used it when he made one of his rare returns to London. I never knew him very well socially or went dancing with him. We had not got much in common.
>
> The first time I got to know him was when the furniture was removed from his other flat next to mine, shortly after my arrival in Radlett Place. Early one morning I found him settling himself in a car for want of somewhere better to go. I took him in, and afterwards often gave him a bed. He was always smiling, and seemed so incapable of meaning harm to anybody that I was glad to help him. In some ways he was excitable and easily carried away, but I was astonished to hear of his suicide. I can only suppose he left his old clothes to me out of gratitude for the small kindnesses I was able to render him. On the other hand, he was a bit crazy, and his bequest may simply have been a stupid whim. I never heard him mention Captain William Bernard Butt.*

This account which Newman gave Hewins of his so-casual relationship with Brian Sullivan does not accord with the true facts. Newman seems, for whatever reason, to have adopted a deliberate policy of playing down their undoubtedly fairly close connection.

Elsewhere, Newman is reported as having ungraciously remarked with reference to the clothes bequeathed to him by Brian: "I would not touch them with a barge pole"**

Titillating was the *News of the World's* 'exclusive disclosure' of:

> One curious story told of Sullivan concerning the film *Night Must Fall*. "For days he could talk of nothing else," said a woman friend, "and he was always whistling or humming *Mighty like a Rose*, the tune of which the murderer in the film was so fond." *Night Must Fall* is a grim, fascinating, psychological study of a murderer. In the film the torso of a body is buried in a wood, but the murderer is disturbed before he has time to dispose of the head, which, for the remainder of the film, remains hidden in a hat-box under his bed.

* The *Daily Mail*, 9 February 1938.
** The *Daily Express*, 12 February 1938.

The police plodded on, meticulously checking every possible angle, cross-checking every conceivable clue, carefully inching over every vacant property within a ten-mile radius of Cheltenham, scalpel-sharp for the slightest sign of an anatomical exercise of any kind having taken place there.

In London, too, the sleuthing, official and unofficial, continued tirelessly, and over-excited newsmen metamorphosed Brian's, admittedly boisterous, small hours Radlett Place parties into full-blown orgies.

From all corners of the compass people who claimed to be vital witnesses and long-lost intimates surfaced in droves. Well-meaning folk around Cheltenham and those parts came forward to say that they had seen Butt, or Brian, or sometimes both together, in strange, unexpected localities, sometimes on foot, sometimes in cars of varying makes. There were the usual shoals of red herring and cacophonies of false alarms.

The papers rustled up the mysterious 'Bull Neck', and set a tremendous manhunt in motion. This five-star suspect was a man of about 56 years and massive build, standing a solid six foot in his socks. He had put up on the night of 2 January 1938, at the Prince of Wales Hotel, in Portland Street, Cheltenham, and departed at 1.30pm the following day without notice, and neglecting the small nicety of settling his five-shilling bill. He left several articles of underclothing behind him, and it was from the laundry mark on an injudiciously abandoned vest that the identity of this refugee, whose absence was beginning to loom increasingly large and important in the Haw Bridge hunt, was eventually established. He was Gordon Wilson aka William Smith Alexander, a man with a criminal record, currently sought in connection with fraud, larceny and forgery. There proved, however, to be no connection between Bull Neck and Butt.

The newspaper phrase-makers were now calling it 'The Case of a Thousand Clues'. The only trouble was that none of those clues was good enough. They petered out, melted away, every last one of them.

Chapter Twelve

Reconstructions

Seven weeks into the Cheltenham mysteries. No daylight. Time to take stock. Time to look back. Time for reconstructions.

The detectives, at a dead-end, began to pull files, leaf through them. January 1938. Tuesday 4 was, at first glance, a day of twin potential significances.

The first incident occurred at between 11.30am and noon at the Hop Pole Hotel, Tewkesbury – that same hostelry celebrated by Charles Dickens as the inn at which Mr Pickwick stopped to dine.

It was Frederick Charles French, a waiter at the Hop Pole, who first noticed the three agitated men. They went into the back lounge, which they had to themselves. One of the men was very stout, about 50 years of age. He was wearing a dark coat and a bowler hat. The other two were both wearing sandy brown tweed suits and caps – a kind of golfing get-up. One of the trio was very tall. The second was a little shorter, the third about five foot six inches tall. French brought them the drinks that they ordered – a whisky and two beers. He noticed that whenever he entered the lounge they abruptly, and very obviously, ceased speaking.

As he watched the men leave, French instructed another waiter, John Aichinger, an American over here as a hotel pupil, to take the number of their car – an old four-seater tourer, the hood of which was drawn down – which drove off in the direction of Gloucester.

French made his first statement to the police on 7 February. Unfortunately, he had, he said, mislaid the note which Aichinger had made of the car's number. However, he was back on 24 February. He had found the missing envelope on which the number had been jotted down. It was KV4595. By a curious coincidence that was the same number as had appeared in that day's newspaper. It was, indeed, the one allocated to Captain Butt's Daimler.

Inspector Worth had French in a couple of days later to be closely re-interrogated. He now admitted that he was unable to say whether KV4595 had been the number of the car which belonged to the three strange men at the Hop Pole. He had assumed that it was because Aichinger told him so.

And that, commented Worth, is yet another instance of a person giving 'information' he has actually read in the newspapers.

The second potentially significant incident also proved, upon closer investigation, to lose its potency.

According to the statement of George Jenkins, a 50-year-old labourer – described in some newspapers as an ex-jockey – of Grove Street, Cheltenham, it was shortly after 4pm on 9 January 1938, that he and his female companion, a widow, whom, for personal, delicate reasons, he refused to produce or identify, saw a four-seater saloon car parked at the end of New Barn Lane, Prestbury, at which point a stile gave access to fields bordering on the Cheltenham Racecourse.

Jenkins and his woman friend crossed a field and reached a spot which, although a good distance off, was immediately opposite the stile. They remained there for some time, Jenkins standing in such a position that he was facing in the direction of the stile. After some 20 minutes, he saw, in a corner of the field to his extreme right, someone moving about with a light held near to the ground.

It would have been at around 5.40pm that Jenkins and his companion made their way back to New Barn Lane, where, on reaching the stationary car, Jenkins noticed that there was no one in it. He also noticed that there was a brown canvas bundle – he thought it was an army officer's hold-all – on the back seat.

He and the widow walked on, and just as they were reaching a small bridge in a nearby road, a car, which had come from the direction of New Barn Lane, pulled up on the opposite side of the road. In it were two men. One, who Jenkins thought might have been Brian Sullivan, got out of the car with a black dog, and walked off down a neighbouring lane. Shortly afterwards, dog and man returned and both got into the car, which reversed and then drove off.

Inspector Worth was none too happy with the tale that Jenkins had to tell, remarking that he was a man with an imaginative mind, and noting that when he was brought to the police station to have his statement taken down, he was recognised by officers of the local CID as an informant who on former occasions had supplied them with false information.

Jenkins' tale was all too vague and evidentially insubstantial. He was unable to describe the men, and the solitary slightly persuasive factor was the presence of the black dog, which *might* have been Bimbo. The car, however, "a four-seater saloon", could have been Sullivan's Austin (OX1010).

Rather more rewarding seemed the file containing the crossing-keeper's story. William Bowden was the railway crossing-keeper at Marle Hill Crossing, near Swindon, a village two miles north-west of Cheltenham, and some nine miles from Haw Bridge. At about ten minutes past midnight on 10 January 1938, he had opened the crossing gates for a car travelling in the direction of the Tewkesbury Road, in which there were two men. He described the car, which he was sure that he had never seen before, as being of an old type, rather dirty looking, a four-seater, with a hood and side screens. He saw no rear light or index plate, but remembered that there were two headlights.

The driver was a man aged between 40 and 50, well set up, with a big, round face and a small moustache. He had on a dark overcoat with the collar turned up. The other man, beyond the fact that he was smaller than his companion, Bowden was unable to describe. The men sat still in their vehicle, and he heard no words spoken. He had had only a very short time in which to observe anything, but by the light of the flash-lamp he was carrying he had seen on the back seat of the car

Tower Lodge, Leckhampton Hill, Cheltenham. The locals were fascinated by the mystery.

what appeared to him to be a heap of rugs. He was suspicious of the car on two counts: owing to the lateness of the hour, and because the driver said nothing in the way of thanks, which was unusual.

On returning to the railway crossing house, Bowden had mentioned his suspicion to his wife. He had also, later, on 21 February, actually reported the matter to the station master at Cheltenham, wondering if there might perhaps be some connection between this car and the one referred to in the newspapers as having been seen by the lorry driver on Haw Bridge.

Worth noted the marked similarity in the descriptions of the two cars, but also the marked difference between the times – 12.10am at Marle Hill Crossing, *circa* 3am at Haw Bridge. The inspector felt that the value of this witness' statement might be lessened by his reputation as a busybody, together with the fact that, despite repeated appeals in the press for information, it was getting on for three weeks before Bowden came forward.

However, hypothesising that 9 January could have been the date of the death of the man whose torso was found, and that the scene of the dismemberment could possibly have been in the vicinity of the route between the railway crossing and the bridge, Worth surveyed the district personally, and also directed a further search of the whole area by Sergeant Willmott and his officers. It produced no results.

And that was the trouble. Everything was feasible. In each case the feeling was that the information supplied could be, might be, possibly was, correct – but never, so far at any rate, was there a single instance where one could feel a resounding conviction that this was good, solid, dependable evidence. The car described by Mr Bowden certainly resembled Sullivan's Austin open-top tourer (PD4786).

Of interest was a statement taken from a Mr Donald Brookes, of Churchill Road, Cheltenham, describing himself as a motor demonstrator, and claiming that he knew Brian Sullivan well. They had, he said, attended the same school, and used also to go together to dances in Cheltenham.

It had been on a Wednesday, either 5 or 12 January 1938, he could not remember which, that he had bumped into Sullivan at about 8.30pm in the Pheasant public-house, in Gloucester Road, Cheltenham. He had not seen Brian Sullivan since the previous summer. Now Brian had appeared agitated, nervous. He was unshaven and dressed in a dark grey overcoat with a belt at the back, black tie and white collar. He was hatless and wearing horn-rimmed glasses and dirty chamois gloves.

They had a drink together and Brian told him that he had given up dancing in London, and that he was awaiting an opportunity to take up a career in surveying and land property. He recalled that Sullivan took a drink out to someone sitting in a car outside. Brookes did not see who that person was, nor had he made any enquiry of Brian regarding his or her identity. He had asked Brian if he was going back to London. "No, I've got a date in Gloucester," was the reply.

Unfortunately, any potential value to this was cancelled out by Brookes' total inability to fix the date of the meeting. If it had been on 5 January that the chance meeting had taken place it would have been of little importance, since Brian was known to have been in and around Cheltenham at that time. But if it had been on 12 January, that was a different matter, for Brian, according to the witness of his mother, was supposed to have departed for London on 11 January, and his continuing presence in the area a couple of days later would be a clue of distinct importance.

But here, yet again, one was faced with that critical element of dubiety – the impossibility of firming up the date, the vagueness about 'someone' sitting in a car outside. The whole story was totally unsatisfactory.

There was a clutch of statements from witnesses who, quite unconnected with the case, had observations to offer of things connected with Tower Lodge which had come to their attention quite by chance.

Frederick Broad, a schoolmaster, of Grosvenor Street, Cheltenham, for instance. He had come forward to say that he had been walking past Tower Lodge between 10am and 11am on either 6 or 7 January 1938, and had heard screams and shouting coming from the place. He took it that a domestic brawl was in progress. He had not been able to make out any words, but the shouting was certainly that of a man and the screaming, which was high-pitched, seemed to him to be that of a woman.

The house had every appearance of being shut up, and he did not see any motor-car anywhere about the place.

Inspector Worth noted that every enquiry had been made of persons residing both opposite and near to Tower Lodge, but it had proved impossible to obtain any corroboration of Mr Broad's statement.

With a similarly disappointing degree of vagueness or imprecision, Edward Berry, a retired veterinary surgeon, of Leckhampton Hill, remembered that it was on either 6 or 7 January that he posted a letter, by either the 7.30pm or 8.45pm collection, from the pillar-box at the foot of Leckhampton Hill, and in order to do so he had, on his way down, to pass Tower Lodge.

The Lodge gates had been closed, but the front-door was open and he could see that a light was burning inside. Two cars were standing in the drive. Both were of the covered type, but whether hooded or saloon, he could not say. Neither of the cars had any light on. One of them was close to the door of the Lodge and its off-side door was hanging open. Mr Berry had then suddenly become aware of the presence of a short man in the space between the two cars. He was dressed in a dark overcoat and was wearing a trilby hat. This man seemed to be lifting and pushing some heavy object from one car to the other, towards the door of the Lodge. What it was, Berry could not see. What he could see, was the head and shoulders of another person – between the Lodge door and the side and rear of the car nearest to him.

When he passed the Lodge again some 15 minutes later, on his way back from the pillar-box, he saw a four-seater car stationary at the near-side of the road, about 20 yards below the Lodge, facing downhill, that is to say in the direction of Cheltenham. The Lodge gates were closed. The house was in darkness. There was now no car or person in the drive.

A veterinary surgeon, an essentially acute professional person, may be expected to provide reliable witness, and it is interesting to speculate as to what the weighty object that was being transferred from one car to the other may have been. Since the date of this sighting was at least two or three days before the generally accepted time of the jettisoning of the torso, it may seem a little early for its being transported around thus. But perhaps not.

The next witness' observation related to 9 January, and a strange smell of burning. Kate Townsend, of Yew Tree Cottage, Crickley Hill, Badgeworth, near Cheltenham, said that at about three o'clock that afternoon she was walking down Leckhampton Hill with her cousin, Miss Annie Wiggall, head housemaid employed by Sir Lionel Darell, of Saul Lodge, Saul, Gloucestershire, with the object of catching the 3.05pm bus into Cheltenham. As they were hurrying past Tower Lodge they smelt what she described as a horrible odour – "Like the burning of some rubbish, old bones and rubber". It was coming from the Lodge, and was a very obnoxious smell. She was, in fact, obliged to place her handkerchief over her mouth and nose.

"I thought at the time that someone was burning the remains of their Christmas dinner. It was vile, " she recalled.

She passed the Lodge again at around 4.40pm. She then noticed in the drive an old saloon car which she had seen there several times previously. She saw no one about the building.

The following day, 10 January, Miss Constance Parker, a general maid, aged 30, when passing Tower Lodge at 6.10pm, saw an old greyish-fawn tourer car parked in the roadway outside the gates, and facing up Leckhampton Hill. It had no light showing, the hood and side screens were up. To her, the vehicle appeared to be standing in a dangerous position. There was not a soul about and Tower Lodge was in pitch-darkness.

The car thus described would unquestionably have been Sullivan's Austin tourer (PD4786), which he had traded in in November 1937, in part exchange, when he bought the Austin saloon (OX1010) from Mr Fruin, of the Paragon Garage, Bath Road, Cheltenham. And 9 – 10 January, it will be recalled, was the night of the Haw Bridge incident.

This informant had actually known Brian Sullivan during and immediately after her schooldays, but she had lost touch with him about 1928, when, she believed, he had gone off to London. It was, she said, about two years ago that she became aware that he was back in Cheltenham, living at Tower Lodge, and she had seen him on several occasions, sometimes alone, sometimes with a middle-aged woman whom she assumed to be his mother. The last time that she actually saw him was in the autumn of 1937.

She had passed by Tower Lodge again between 2pm and 3pm on Wednesday 19 January 1938, before Brian Sullivan was found dead, and she had then been conscious of a strong smell of gas. She had paid no heed to it, and most certainly had not connected it with Tower Lodge, where, incidentally, all the curtains had been drawn.

Once more, Inspector Worth was a bit uneasy about the witness, his professional hackles rising. She had already, some days previously, set off a wild goose chase by bringing information to the police that while exercising her dog on Cleeve Hill she had seen a bloodstained sack. True enough, a piece of sacking had been found at the spot which she indicated, but it was not bloodstained, and it had no connection with the present case. Miss Parker turned out to be a Christian Science worker and, in her own words, was "inclined to be psychic". Inspector Worth had a hunch of his own: to attach no importance to her statement.

He was much more impressed with what Mrs Eleanor Mustoe had to tell. A widow, aged 48, she worked as a daily at a house on Leckhampton Hill called 'Coney Gree'. She had started her job there on 17 January 1938. That first day of her new job she had finished work at 3.25pm, and was walking down the hill, back to her home in Cheltenham, on the same side of the road as Tower Lodge. She was about 100 yards from the Lodge when she spotted the stationary car standing in the road outside its entrance gates. The car was facing up the hill, the off-side door was swinging open and a man was sitting in the driver's seat. As

Mrs Mustoe drew level, another man, of about 30 years of age, hatless, wearing a heavy coat, which probably made him look bigger than he actually was, came out of the Lodge gates and got into the car. As he did so, the man in the car moved across into the front passenger seat, and the big man slithered into the driving seat.

The car then moved rapidly off up the hill. As it passed her, Mrs Mustoe saw that it was a dark-coloured, two-seater with a dickey seat at the back, and, she thought, a black canvas hood. She was unable to say whether or not there was at the time any other car parked in the Tower Lodge drive.

The following Monday (24 January), again passing the Lodge on her way home from Coney Gree at 3.30pm, she noticed a big, dark, saloon car of some old type of model, she could not say which, parked in the drive with its back towards the main road. Going by her description of it, that car was almost certainly Brian Sullivan's Austin saloon (OX1010).

Not only had Worth been taken with Mrs Mustoe's demeanour and the way she told her story, but he also happened to know that Brian Sullivan had possessed a heavy 'teddy bear' coat, and he felt that her, admittedly rather vague, description of the man who had come out of the Lodge and clambered into the driving seat might well have applied to him. Indeed, if so, here was the first bit of evidence to indicate that Brian Sullivan was alive on 17 January.

Another interesting titbit of information, although it is difficult to know quite what to make of it, had been supplied by Mr RE Ritchings, a quarryman, of Church Road, Cheltenham. At half-past six on the morning of 22 January 1938, he had passed Tower Lodge on his way to work. And, as he had afterwards told the detectives, he had seen someone in the garden flash a light on the side of the building furthest away from the road. He also saw Brian Sullivan's car parked at the side of the house.

It is difficult to know what to make of this. One has to wonder for what conceivable reason, either innocent or guilty, anybody would be wandering around the outside of the house with a flash-light at 6.30am. The parked car will have been the Austin saloon (OX1010).

Looking for evidence supplying some degree of continuity with regard to the apparent state of affairs at Tower Lodge from the time of Brian Sullivan's supposed disappearance to the time of the discovery of his dead body, Worth re-examined the testimony of those regular trade visitants to the Lodge – the milkman and the newspaper delivery boys.

To begin with was the evidence of what may be designated 'the Milk Saga'. The supplier of milk to Tower Lodge, at the request of Brian's mother, was Arthur Millard, milkman, of Bath Road, Cheltenham. He employed a delivery boy, 13-year-old Geoffrey Webb.

The first significant date was Tuesday 11 January 1938. The milk was delivered as usual that day – by Geoffrey Webb – from Millard's car. The next day, 12 January, Millard himself made the delivery. He was somewhat surprised to find

Tuesday's bottle still standing on the door-step. Looking about him, Millard saw that the curtains at the upstairs windows were drawn together. Rather more disturbing was the fact that a dark saloon car – OX1010 – parked in the driveway, had a dog inside it. He was perfectly certain that neither car nor dog had been there yesterday. He would without doubt have seen them. All day Arthur Millard kept worrying about the dog; so much so that he returned to the Lodge at seven o'clock that evening. To his immense relief, although the car was still there, the dog had gone.

On Thursday 13 January, young Webb went to the Lodge with a bottle of milk and instructions not to leave it if yesterday's delivery was still there. It was – on the door-step, untouched. So the boy returned that day's new delivery bottle to Mr Millard.

At one o'clock on Friday afternoon, Millard popped along to take another look at the Tower Lodge milk situation. This time there was no milk bottle on the step.

On Saturday 15 January, when Geoffrey Webb went to the Lodge, he saw no sign of any milk there. He knocked at the door. There was no reply, so he decided not to leave any milk. As he was about to depart, he noticed that the daily newspapers, which up to then had been left accumulating in the letter-box, had been taken out and put into the car on the drive. Millard, on his visit of 17 or 18 January, observed that the upstairs window curtains had now been drawn apart.

The evidence of the sharp eyes of the newspaper lads sheds some further light. White's, newsagents, of Church Road, Cheltenham, supplied Tower Lodge with the *Daily Express*, which was delivered at 7.45am each day by one or other of White's two delivery boys, Stanley Joynes or Leonard Luscott. It was Joynes who had made the deliveries up to 11 January. On 12, 13, and 14 January, it was Luscott who delivered the newspaper, putting it in the letter-box on the outside gate. On 14 January, he spotted the two previous days' deliveries still there, sticking out of the letter-box. Returning to the shop, he told Mr White, who accordingly decided to discontinue the delivery for the moment. Neither Joynes nor Luscott had at any time during the course of their deliveries seen or heard anyone at Tower Lodge.

Much of the accumulated evidence was, and remained, useless. Worth cast his eye over the record of the odd trophies received by Superintendent Wayman back on 11 January.

There was a piece of red braid, about two and a half feet long, looped in the centre. It had been picked up on 10 January, by Hubert Charles Price, about 30 yards from the spot on the other side of Haw Bridge where the blood was found. There was a brown button, about half an inch in diameter, picked up on 11 January, on the Tirley side of Haw Bridge. Attached to it were strands of purplish fabric. Finally, there was a girl's tweed belt found by Wayman and Sergeant Franklin on the grass verge on the left-hand side of the road going towards Apperly, about 400 yards from Haw Bridge. The fabric of the belt was similar to that attached to the brown button.

Neither of these putative 'clues' ever proved to have the slightest value.

The *Daily Mail* of 11 February contained a report from Edwin Tetlow. It related to 10 February, when, said Tetlow, Mr Harold Draper, a Cheltenham farmer, gave information to Inspector Worth.

> I was driving home up Prestbury Hill at about 10.30pm, on January 4th, when I saw a car without lights parked at the roadside. Two men were moving about near the car. As I passed they flashed a torch in my direction. I drove on without taking any further notice. I knew Brian Sullivan, but I cannot say for certain he was one of the two men concerned. The car, however, was an open tourer of the kind which has been mentioned in connection with the Haw Bridge Mystery.

This was the second report relating to the presence of "two strange men" parked at the roadside in an open tourer, such as Sullivan's previous Austin open-top tourer (PD4786), in the Prestbury area. As we have already seen, five days before, George Jenkins had encountered two men and a dog and a parked four-seater saloon, such as Sullivan's Austin saloon (OX1010), in Prestbury. It is puzzling to know just what importance, if indeed any, to allot to this distinctly odd pair of sightings.

According to the *Daily Mail*, the police received 'important information'. It indicated that Brian Sullivan was seen, with a mysterious friend who kept well in the background, on or about 14 January 1938, at the King's Arms, the inn at Prestbury, where William Archer, the famous jockey who won the Grand National on Little Charlie in 1858, and father of the even more celebrated jockey, Fred Archer, was once the landlord.

Sullivan's visit had impressed itself upon the landlady because of the unusual drink taken by himself and a friend who did not put in an appearance in the bar, but had his – or her – refreshment carried by Brian to a car outside. Said the landlady:

"Brian Sullivan ordered two double whiskies to be poured into two glasses of port. Mixed whisky and port is a strange drink. That is why I remember him so well."

If the estimate of the date of Sullivan's visit is correct, this was the last time he was seen alive. Previous police records of his movements took them only to 9 January – unless, that is, the young man seen by the ticket collector at Gloucester railway station on 15 January, is accepted to have been Brian Sullivan.

An especially interesting day proved to be 7 February. That was when Worth had paid another personal visit to Tower Lodge. In an alcove under the stairs he had found a hatchet among a quantity of tools in a tool box. He was not saying that it was, but it could well have been, one of the instruments employed in the dismemberment of the body.

Evidence from the sitting-room also struck him as being of significance. He had found there a number of beer bottles. They had contained bitter ale brewed by H &

G Simonds, of Old Market Street, Bristol, and bore labels in that name together with the perforated date, *3.1.38*. There were also discovered in the house two four-bottle crates. This, Worth thought, constituted a possible indication of the presence of strangers in Tower Lodge.

Subsequent enquiries at Simonds' revealed that the beer was bottled on 1 January 1938, and had been supplied on 4 January to Messrs Buton's Stores, 188 Bath Road, Cheltenham, and to Messrs Martin Bros, 318 High Street, Cheltenham, these being the only two firms in the town to which Messrs Simonds supplied such bottled beer. Enquiries were made of the two firms, and although Brian Sullivan was known at Messrs Buton's, which was the shop nearest to Tower Lodge, and had occasionally purchased a bottle of beer there, he could in no way be connected with the purchase of the Simonds' beer referred to. Neither could the sale of this particular brand and quantity to any particular person be recalled by any of the staff, and there was no order recorded in regard to any such sale. The result of similar enquiries of Messrs Martin Bros brought about a similar negative result.

On 8 February, Inspector Cherrill found finger-marks on three quart beer bottles, a siphon, and a tumbler, in the Tower Lodge sitting-room, and on a fourth quart, and two pint, beer bottles in the scullery. The articles concerned were taken to Scotland Yard, together with a list of persons with criminal records whose names had turned up in the course of the enquiry, including that of Keith Newman. The fingerprints of all persons having legitimate access to Tower Lodge were also taken for comparison and elimination purposes. An imprint on the tumbler and another on one of the bottles proved identical with those of PC Merry. None of the other marks were matched by any of those submitted for comparison. Neither were marks which Cherrill had found on the steering-wheel of Captain Butt's Daimler at the Regent Garage identical with any of those on the bottles, siphon, and tumbler.

In the early-setting-in darkness of the night of Saturday 12 February, using Hancock's lorry and the Austin Tourer (PD4786) previously owned by Brian Sullivan, Worth scrupulously reconstructed the conditions surrounding the reported incident on Haw Bridge on the dark night of 9 – 10 January. He was thus able to confirm that it had been perfectly possible for Hancock to have seen all that he claimed to have seen with the headlights of the two vehicles full on.

Later, Worth also interviewed Mr Masters, Hancock's employer, at Gloucester, and took statements from a number of people living in the vicinity of Haw Bridge, who clearly recalled hearing the noise of the stopping and starting of a motor engine in the silence of the wee small hours of 10 January.

During the investigating detectives' searching of the Lodge, literally hundreds of names and addresses were obtained from Brian Sullivan's correspondence and that of his mother. These were collated and circular letters appertaining to them were compiled and despatched to the many different police forces involved. They drew a blank.

But one letter, written on 2 February 1938, in complete ignorance of the befallen tragedy, was, in its way, especially poignant.

New House,
Polperro,
Cornwall.
2/2/38

Dear B.,
Thank you for your letter and Xmas wishes, I thought it was time
I answered it, as one of Williams' men called today and asked if I
knew any details of your demise.
Mrs Mills* had written to them asking for details. I tell them it
must be a mistake, but all the same answer this by return old chap,
will you, as a little natural curiosity (between old pals) exists.
We have had some pretty wild weather, but the only casualty is
your gate which was blown off its hinges.
I have got about half the garden dug and hope to get on with it a
bit more next week. It is very mild here and your violets are in full
bloom, really a very pretty sight.
If you can give me a day's notice next time you come down I will
have a fire going and your sheets aired.
Mrs Correll and Philip both send their love,
And I can only inscribe myself
Your old pal,
Baggy.

All too soon, poor old Baggy was to learn the truth – or, rather, as much of the truth as was up to this time known – about the demise of the friend whom he knew as Byron Smith.

---

*Mrs Maude Mills was the owner of the Polperro cottages leased by Brian Sullivan.

Chapter Thirteen

Hoaxers

Every criminal *cause célèbre* brings the hoaxers and the cranks out of the woodwork, if not actually confessing, speciously remembering. And as weird and wonderful a collection as any comes capering like a troupe of acrobatic clowns out of the Cheltenham Torso Case files.

At nine o'clock on the evening of Tuesday 1 February 1938, a telephone rang at the Cheltenham Headquarters of the Gloucestershire Constabulary, in Lansdown Road. A woman's voice said:

"If you want to find why Mr Sullivan committed suicide, you must find a Miss Whitfield. She was with him last." And the mystery caller, who refused to disclose her identity, rang abruptly off.

Some days after Chief Detective Inspector Worth's arrival in Cheltenham, this message was passed on to him, and, on 15 February he arranged for the insertion of a notice in the local press asking the person who had made the anonymous telephone call to contact the police.

A couple of weeks went by, then, in the time-honoured phraseology of police officialese, 'information was received' which led the detectives to interview, on 1 March, and take a statement from, a 21-year-old girl. Her name was Jean Simpson, and she worked as a wardmaid at Cheltenham General Hospital.

Worth was gravely troubled by this young woman. He regarded her with deep suspicion. No apparent reason for Brian Sullivan's suicide had emerged at the inquest, and the anonymous telephone call had been made two days before the finding of the torso. Moreover, at that time, there had been no evidence of the existence of any connection between the two events.

This was not, said Worth, a case of a person coming forward and giving false information, but one in which, through the medium of the anonymous telephone call, an atmosphere of knowledge and reticence was created. What further worried the Inspector was that he possessed convincing evidence of Miss Simpson's immorality with men. Although not necessarily prejudicial, that did not exactly offer a positive initial impression of character.

However, after overcoming the preliminary automatic officiousness of the matron at the hospital, the girl was seen and, on several occasions, questioned. She claimed that she knew Brian Sullivan, and that she was with him at Tower Lodge on 9 January 1938.

Probably realising the precarious position into which her lies had put her, she attempted suicide on the night of 5 March, by swallowing a large number of Aspirin tablets. Fortunately, she was discovered in time by the duty sister at the

Nurses' Home, who immediately summoned the resident physician. He promptly stomach-pumped her. The girl's brother, William Simpson, of Fence Houses, County Durham, came to Cheltenham and took his sister back home with him on 12 March.

That Jean Simpson was a hoaxer, there can be no doubt, and a week after her departure to Durham a communication was received from Scotland Yard's Records Department stating that she was identical to a woman of the same name who had come forward with a false story in connection with a murder in Shepherd's Bush in 1936.*

Almost certainly, it was Simpson herself who made the telephone call to the police on 1 February. Indeed, she admitted to the use of the name Whitfield, which, she said, was one of her father's Christian names.

The next hoaxer, also a woman, was 24-year-old Agnes Margaret Mary Lucy Browne, of Church Road, Stratton-on-the-Fosse, Bath. Unmarried, she was employed as a lady's companion.

The Chief Constable of Bath communicated to the Cheltenham police that this young woman had stated that she had met a man at Stamford Hill, North London, who told her his name was Byron Smith, and that he came from Cheltenham. The Bath police were requested to take a full statement from Miss Browne.

In it, she said that she had known Brian Sullivan since April 1935, when she met him in London. She had subsequently had meetings with him in Bristol, Southend-on-Sea, and Bath. It was, according to her, on the night of 19 January that she was with him in Bath. He had then told her that Captain Butt was dead, and that he wanted money to leave the country. She had given him £8 10s. She said that he had told her that his mother was an abortionist, and that Captain Butt had attempted to blackmail her.

Worth, after reading through the questions put to Miss Browne by Superintendent Ashworth of the Bath Police, and the answers that she had given, formed the opinion that she was nothing short of a mental case. He arranged to travel to Bath and interview her himself on 20 March.

On 19 March, before Superintendent Ashworth, who had come over to Cheltenham to discuss matters with Worth, left to return to Bath, Inspector Coles telephoned to inform him that shortly after the police observation on Browne had terminated, there had been a telephone call to the Bath police station concerning a woman who was said to have called at Browne's place of employment and attempted to blackmail her.

Coles, accompanied by several other officers, had immediately proceeded to the house, and Browne was proved on the spot to be a liar. She had then attacked the Inspector, scratched his face, and generally behaved like a lunatic.

The following day, Worth, in the presence of Sergeant Shewry, interviewed her

*Edward Lloyd, aged 36, was charged with the murder of his wife, Lizzie, undergoing skin-grafting operations in the LCC Hospital at Shepherd's Bush. (See: _Bernard Spilsbury: His Life and Cases_, Douglas G Browne, EV Tullett (Harrap, 1951), pp 371-2.)

and reached the conclusion that she was a romancer, and knew nothing of the case beyond that which she had read in the papers. He was subsequently informed that she had undoubtedly sent further anonymous telephone messages to the Bath police, who agreed that the woman was an unbalanced hoaxer.

Representing the male of the species hoaxer, there was 40-year-old James Burke, head porter at London's Queen's Park Station (LMS Railway). A native of Cheltenham, Burke said that he knew Mrs Butt before her marriage to the Captain. He had a clear memory of Miss Hogg's marrying Captain Butt at Ashchurch parish church. In 1924 he had been living at Kemerton, near Aston-on-Carrant, and was then a porter at Ashchurch railway station. At that time Nurse Sullivan was living with the Butts in Aston-on-Carrant. He had also known Brian Sullivan during his schooldays.

Between April and June 1936, Burke had met Brian, whom he had not seen for many years, in London, in Lane's Club, in Baker Street. They met many times in public-houses in the West End, but always by chance, never by appointment.

It was in October 1937, he stated, that they met – as usual, by chance – in the Kings Arms public-house in the Edgware Road. Sullivan, who was in the company of another man and two women, told him that he needed £10 quickly, and, without even asking him why, Burke had, he said, returned home to Queen's Park, taken ten £1 notes from a drawer in his room, and given them to Brian, who was still at the Kings Arms with his three companions. Only then, did Burke ask him why he wanted the money. "Call it blackmail, if you like," had been the reply. With an additional: "Don't blame me. Butt's in it."

Sullivan and the others then left, leaving Burke behind in the Kings Arms – £10 the poorer.

It came out later that Burke had been paid three guineas for an interview by a Sunday newspaper, and Worth, who questioned him at Scotland Yard, decided that he was another incurable romancer.

Among the many fantastic happenings which Burke related, was that of his finding, years ago, of a body in a river near Aston-on-Carrant, after a three weeks long search by police had failed. He also claimed to be gifted with extraordinary powers, and had psychically 'seen' the head of Captain Butt facing the head of a woman in a cupboard in a building situated near Haw Bridge.

Once more, Inspector Worth was driven to conclude that he was dealing with a mentally rickety informant. This diagnosis seemed to Worth to be confirmed when, on 13 March 1938, the *Sunday Dispatch* published an exclusive interview with Burke.

In it he told of an attack on him in Kilburn Lane, near Queen's Park station, at 1.15am on Saturday 12 March, by two men in a motor. One of them had jumped out and drawn some sort of sharp instrument across the back of his neck.

"I turned and a struggle took place. Suddenly someone whistled, and my assailant got away."

He showed Worth a scratch on the back of his neck, caused, he claimed, by the men when they knocked him down. A sceptical Worth pronounced:

"The scratch had obviously been made some days before the date of the alleged attack. His story was false."

Equally short shrift was meted out to George Woof, a self-described gentleman of independent means, living in Worcester Street, Gloucester. He stepped forward with his testimony that at 4.15pm on Sunday 9 January 1938, when he was sitting on a seat at Leckhampton Road, Cheltenham, he had seen a large limousine pass at a fast speed. The driver of the car, who had on a previous occasion in Cheltenham been pointed out to him by his nephew, and whose photograph he had seen in the local paper, was, without a shadow of a doubt, Brian Sullivan.

Seated beside him in the front of the car was a man of 50 to 55 years of age, who appeared to be frightened. In the rear was a young woman. He judged her to have been about 24. She had bobbed hair and ringlets at the back. On the seat beside her was a large bundle, covered by a dark green, yellow and red mixture tartan travelling rug.

Enquiry made it plain that Mr Woof's story had been put together from newspaper reports.

William Rea, who was the manager of Messrs Bastin & Son, the electrical engineers in Bath Road, Cheltenham, came up with, considering his responsible position, some extraordinarily, and unexpectedly, unreliable evidence.

He said that on 3 December 1937, Brian Sullivan called into the shop saying that he wanted to have Tower Lodge wired for electric light. The next day, Rea went up to the Lodge. It was then that he saw, or thought that he saw, a .22 rifle standing by the window in a corner of the sitting-room.

Pointing to the rifle, he had asked Sullivan if he was interested in shooting, to which Sullivan had allegedly replied: "I use it for potting blackbirds".

Now to anyone who knew Brian Sullivan, this reported response would immediately have caused every last hackle of suspicion as to its veracity to rise, for he was a notoriously gentle and soft-hearted man where animals were concerned. The very idea of 'potting' a blackbird would have been absolute anathema to him.

Rea did not, he admitted, actually handle the 'rifle', which, incidentally, evidence would tend to show was an umbrella! But he did see a pair of white tennis-shoes by the fire in the same room, and may well have recalled the finding of a tennis-shoe by Dudfield and Ball on Haw Bridge. They had also discovered there a chamois-leather glove. And, with a wink-is-as-good-as-a-nod significance, Rea remembered that upon each occasion that Brian Sullivan came into the shop he was wearing cream-coloured, chamois-leather gloves.

Shrewdly, Worth decided to:

"attach no importance to Mr Rea's statement. The information he gave followed the publicity given in the local press to the finding of a small bore, single barrel rifle in the river Severn on February 6th [1938]. This rifle was shown to Mr Rea, who said it was very similar to the one he saw at Tower Lodge."

But Harold Cox, of Langton Lodge, Charlton Kings, Cheltenham, who had examined the recovered rifle at the police station on 12 February, said that it was the one which he threw into the river at Haw Bridge in September 1937. He had bought it when he was a boy, in 1899, from another boy. For many years it had been kept in his mother's house at Cheltenham. He came across it again in August 1937, when that house was being cleared preparatory to sale. The rifle was very old, and he did not want to declare it, or obtain a firearms certificate, so he disposed of it in the manner stated.

Since William Rea was the only person ever to suggest – and with no satisfactory evidential backing – that Brian Sullivan had a rifle in his possession, Inspector Worth was not inclined to give serious consideration to this proposition. Rea was neither hoaxer nor crank, but something just as bad in its way – a careless misinformant.

On 21 February 1938, a Mrs Flora Orchard, employed as a resident cook at Ovenden Hall, Halifax, Yorkshire, telephoned Ovenden police station. She had, she said, followed the newspaper reports of the Torso Crime most carefully, and felt that she might have some information which could be of assistance to the police.

After the application of a little pressure, together with the promise that her name would not be divulged, she stated that up to about six months ago she had lived with her husband, Thomas Orchard, and her daughter, Peggy, at 'Fairview', Longhope, Gloucestershire. However, in August 1937, she had had to leave with her daughter, as she was afraid that he would murder her.

Her husband had, she said, on many occasions attempted to do so. He had dug a grave in the garden, and laid in a store of cement, which he told her he would use to hide the body. He had always said that he would cut her corpse up, describing in detail the procedure he would take, which was similar to that taken in the Torso Crime.

Her husband had a sister, Mrs Cecil Gardener, who was the proprietor of a dance and billiards hall, at Islington, in London. Mrs Orchard felt that there might be some connection between her husband and Brian Sullivan. In fact, until about five years ago, Mrs Gardener had had a dance and billiards hall – Glevum Hall – in Gloucester.

Thomas Orchard, whom she described as 56 years of age, five foot nine inches tall, with a slim build, dark hair, small moustache, and a certain swagger when walking, was a builder by trade. He was also a very heavy port wine drinker. He owned an Austin 7 motor-car.

The motivation which, on 15 March 1938, brought 38-year-old Mrs Carol Elizabeth Millicent Ghetti into the Gloucester police station, with her distinctly sinister burden of information, was of a very different kind.

She was, she said, the wife of John Carlo Ghetti, a licensed horse slaughterer. She first met him in the summer of 1937. They were married on 22 December that year, at the Gloucester Register Office. He had not supported her since. She had lived at 202 Linden Road, Gloucester, with him, her father and mother, and an adopted boy.

John Carlo was her second husband. She had not seen her previous one, James Perkins, for eleven years, although she had several times been the cause of his arrest under a maintenance order.

The story she had come to tell was an odd one. Her husband had told her that at Cheltenham he had met Sullivan, who had given him £30 to keep his mouth shut. About the time of the bloodstains being found on Haw Bridge, Ghetti had returned home in the early hours of 9 February, with bloodstains on his grey lounge suit. He had said that it was paint. He had continued to wear this suit until he left her – which he did on 1 March – when he took his bloodstained clothing away with him in a sack. But, after 9 February, Ghetto's manner became nervous and he would not go out at night. He was afraid of being arrested for a job in London. There were four of them in it, he said, and between them they had shared £300. He showed her the full amount in notes, and also confided that he was associated with the Sabini brothers, who, according to him, lived at Number 7 Seal Street, Hackney.*

Mrs Ghetti remembered reading in the local paper of the finding of the human torso at Haw Bridge, and her husband's remarking, "They will never find that out, we are too artful for them".

She further said that she knew Brian Sullivan, and had been intimate with him for the past three years. She last saw him on 2 January 1938, when he gave her a present of a box of handkerchiefs.

A statement was taken from John Ghetti on 22 March. He said that he was aged 23, and that for some years past he had been employed as a slaughterman. He emphatically denied his wife's allegations, saying they were a tissue of lies. He had never mentioned anything about the Sabini brothers. He did not know them and that he had never shown her a bundle of £300 in notes. He neither knew Brian Sullivan nor made any remark about the finding of the torso, as alleged by his wife. He did not tell her where he was going when he left her on 1 March, as she would have followed him.

Later on, Worth interviewed Ghetti and his wife at Gloucester Police Station. She had been known in Gloucester for many years as an active prostitute. Ghetti, whose real name it transpired was Alfred George Currell, struck him as a strange type of man. He was said to be a boaster. Worth felt certain that he had been led into marrying his wife, an overbearing woman many years his senior. Since leaving her, he had been working for Miss Payne, an animal slaughterer, of Long

*Five brothers – Charles, the leader, better known as Darby, Harryboy, Joseph, Fred, and George – born of an Italian father and an English mother, in 'Little Italy', the Clerkenwell district of London. Undoubted leaders of the London underworld in the 1920s, they were essentially a racecourse gang, providing protection against menace – from themselves – to bookmakers. They progressed to Metropolitan club protection and branched into highly organised robberies. Darby was said to have Mafia connections. The brothers reached their apogee in the mid-1930s. They were interned during the Second World War, released in 1942, and were soon thereafter a spent force.

Buckby, Northamptonshire. The bloodstained suit of which his wife had spoken was obtained from him and handed over to Dr Roche Lynch. No trace of human blood was found on it. Mrs Ghetti finally admitted that her allegations against her husband were all untrue. She had made them in a fit of rage because he had left her. Her story about her connection with Brian Sullivan was likewise all nonsense.

As Congreve so truly observed:

Heav'n has no rage, like love to hatred turn'd,
Nor Hell a fury, like a woman scorn'd.

As the shoals of his eccentric communicators thinned, and the wells of their misinformings dried up, Inspector Worth began seriously to wonder if his feet would ever touch bottom in this plaguey aqueous case.

Chapter Fourteen

Byron ...

Dredging through the papyraceous detritus of letters and diaries silting-up the departed Brian Sullivan's left-over space at Tower Lodge, the embattled detectives, at a dead-end, prepared to go to any lengths in search of illumination, set in train enquiries to various police forces countrywide in an all-out effort to discover the significance or otherwise of a tangled complex of names and addresses occurring in the trawled-up correspondence.

The result of all this frantic activity was disappointing in the way of affording any suicide-murder revelations, but it certainly did provide a clearer picture of Brian's Byronic *alter ego*. There was, too, the odd unexpected glimpse of the Cheltenham lad before he had evolved into the flash-footed West End gigolo.

For instance ... Barrow-in-Furness police were asked to visit Mr William Joseph Cookson, at 109 Oxford Street, whose name and address had been discovered among Brian Sullivan's papers. A retired foreman sheet-metal worker, he was baffled. He had never heard of Brian Sullivan. But it transpired that he had a son, also William Joseph Cook, who, back in the 1920s, had left home to work in Cheltenham, where he had lodged with a Mrs Sullivan, at Number 1 Andover Terrace. He had left there only because she had felt that she could not give proper attention to lodgers, as she had her invalid daughter, Eileen, and son, Brian, to attend to in addition to her nursing duties. It would have been about 1925, Cook reckoned, when he bumped into Brian, then 14 or 15 years old, who told him that he was employed in a brush factory in Cheltenham. This must have been before he got the job at Paynter's motor-cycle shop.

Similarly, Oswald Claridge, traced by the Devon Constabulary to Number 2 Barbican Terrace, Barnstaple, remembered Brian from the 1927-28 period, when they were both employed as dance instructors at the Winter Gardens, Cheltenham. He had not, however, spoken to him since, although he thought that he might have seen him on Boxing Day 1937, when he (Claridge) had attended two dances – one in the afternoon, one in the evening – at Cheltenham Town Hall.

Another phantom from the past, Lemuel Morgan, was tracked down, via the Monmouthshire Constabulary, in Markham Village, near Tredegar. He had first come to know Brian sometime in 1928, through answering an advertisement in a paper which was asking for paying-guests. As a result, he subsequently stayed with Sullivan in a cottage at Deerhurst, near Cheltenham, from 11 – 16 August 1928. He had also stayed with Brian's mother at Maida Vale for one week from 16 May 1931. During that time Sullivan visited Morgan at his (Brian's) mother's home on four occasions. The last time that Morgan had seen Brian was in the

August of either 1932 or 1933. There had been no communication between them since.

Reminiscences of Byron Smith, the light-fantastic-tripping Terpsichorean of Piccadilly, surfaced a'plenty.

The Wilde-Rices, of Fanfrolico, Southport Road, Formby, in Lancashire, for example. Actually, it was Mrs Wilde-Rice who knew Byron best. Her husband, Allen, met him only once, and that was no more than a brief introduction. But Mrs Wilde-Rice had first come across Byron in 1929-30, when she was on a visit to London with her invalid mother, and the pair were in fact staying at the Piccadilly Hotel, where Mrs Wilde-Rice would be partnered on the dance floor by the winsome Byron most nights.

During the next five years, she was to visit London with her mother at least four times a year. They always stayed at the Piccadilly. She always danced with Byron. Indeed, she would regularly write to inform him of the date of her intended visit.

Interviewed by the Lancashire Constabulary, she stated that for the past four years – that is since 1934-5, she had not seen Byron Smith, although she had received Christmas cards from him. Occasionally, in the past, he would take her out to a nightclub, but he never spent money freely and always gave her the impression of being short of cash. His conversation was chiefly concerning his mother, of whom he seemed to be very fond. He also used to say that he bought old motor-cars, painted them up, and sold them again at a profit. When she first knew him, he was a teetotaller and a non-smoker, and gave the impression of being a sober, inoffensive, but slightly effeminate, man, who was very dissatisfied with the manner in which he earned his living.

Mrs Wilde-Rice was not, I suspect, telling the whole story. There is in existence a letter which was found among Brian Sullivan's papers. It was signed simply 'Me', with a single kiss-cross, but bore the address Pyecot, 50 Waterloo Road, Birkdale, Southport, which was Mrs Wilde-Rice's former residence.

Here, *res ipsa loquitur* is that letter.

Pyecot,
50 Waterloo Road,
Birkdale, Southport.
13.8.31

Could I ever forget -
Darling, it was terribly sweet of you to write, I never dreamed until then that you cared even a little. As I read your letter, a thought as little and frightened as a young bird fluttered thro' my mind, that perhaps for a little while, you did almost.

I am going to be painfully candid now, my dear, my racy dear. You never once told me you loved me! You were sweet always, and sometimes tender – but that isn't love, unless a girl is unworldly and conceited, and I have had too many declarations of love to mistake one for the other. I often waited for you to utter those three words, then I concluded I must only have been very amusing, or that you were just flattered because I was young, and not totally without attractions (I hope) and I came down to the field to see you so often – (there was no <u>*real*</u> *necessity for one to come down, you know!)*

I was growing so fond of you too – when I used to read your letters – it gave one a queer little pain near my heart. Then I weighed the pros and cons upon the scales of my experience – I had never before been 'just amusing'; I had never before been kissed as you kissed one without, whatever [you] call being loved – I felt – and baffled, thus I did not answer your letters.

I don't know why I am telling you all this – kisses are stupid things – I shall never forget your gentle teasing – your tenderness. The fun we had at coffee stalls and in 'Gladys'. Do you remember the night we took Phoebe Roe home – how you wanted to get rid of her?

Life, when one is young, is such a glorious adventure, exploring is so terribly wonderful. Do you remember the boats on B_____ Bridge, and the dim barge escaping quietly upon the dark water?

I am going to be married in September. I don't love him. God alone knows why I am marrying him – isn't it ridiculous? It will be no social asset, he has no more money than I. The only thing I can put it down to is that he never left me alone. He is terribly persistent and very good to me – that is all that can be said. Ok, by the way, darling, why was it you would never come down to the station to see me off?

I hope to be down in London soon – will you take me out again? Write to me, darling – if you want a photograph of me I will send you rather a good one.

As ever –
Me
X

Equally enthusiastic in report about the young Byron was Mrs Doris (Joy) Butler, of Bournemouth, remembering from 1931:

I was living in London and visited the Piccadilly Hotel with my husband and family, where we met Byron Smith. I saw him on numerous occasions when visiting the hotel, and about two years ago this coming May – ie in May 1936, he came to visit friends in Bournemouth. He rang me up and said he would like to come and see us, so we invited him for tea. That is the only time he came to our house.

I knew nothing about his family, only that he was very attached to his mother. I had always the highest respect for him in every way, and as he would not accept any payment whenever he danced with me or my daughters at the Piccadilly, we always sent him a Christmas present. The presents were always addressed to the Piccadilly Hotel as I never knew any other address, and I have not seen or heard of him since the weekend when he was in Bournemouth.

When he visited us, he had with him an Austin saloon motor-car, and in the course of conversation he told me he had got married. I did notice when he came to tea with us that he was very nervy, and I asked him what was the matter. All he said was that he had left the Piccadilly and got married.

Less flattering to Byron Smith's self-esteem would have been the view as to his character confided by Mrs DM Peck. Her evidence was given to the Caernarvonshire Police when they paid her a visit at Green Tub Cottage, Bettws-y-Coed, where she was living apart from her husband. She had, she said, previously lived for about 18 months in London, and attended dances at the Piccadilly Hotel, where – at a fee of two guineas or more – she had on several occasions employed Smith as a partner.

These professional dance hosts, she observed, appeared to carry with them small diaries, and to obtain the names and addresses of those who hired them. It was in this way that Byron Smith had got hold of her name and address, and wrote a friendly sort of letter to her from the Piccadilly Hotel on 15 October 1935. She had heard nothing from him after that date, and he had not visited her in Wales.

Before she left London, 'Buck', as she called him, had tried to induce her to rent Tower Lodge from him at a rental of £2 per week. She had refused the offer. His mode of life had been, she believed, not unlike that of a large number, if not the majority, of professional dance hosts. In addition to claiming fees for their services, they often importuned wealthy women – usually having outlived or otherwise lost their attractiveness – with whom their occupation brought them in contact, for money to live on, or to spend frivolously. Mrs Peck thought that in 1935 – she left London at Whitsun that year – Byron Smith was financially embarrassed.

It was, however, Mrs Helen Susannah Berthet, the former Miss Durrant, run to ground in Beachley Road, Chepstow, who was able to speak with first-hand authority of one of Byron Smith's affairs of the heart.

In the summer of 1935, when she was one-and-twenty, she was sharing a West End flat at 34 Clarges Street with Miss Lilian French-Browne, and was very friendly with Byron Smith.

I knew that he had a flat at Radlett Place, St John's Wood, and was running a motor business in the same locality. Miss French-Browne and myself often went to the Piccadilly Hotel and danced with him, and many times we went with him for motor-car rides and picnics. Lilian, who was a sweetheart of Byron's, eventually transferred her affections to a Major McMasters, whom she later married, and he took her with him to Kenya. The last time I saw and spoke to Byron Smith was about the time that Miss French-Browne went away to Kenya. That must be nearly three years ago.

By 1937, the whilom Byron's amatory relationships had slipped quite a few notches down the calibrations of the social scale.

Kathleen Cole, an 18-year-old domestic servant, of Belmont Road, Cheltenham, and 16-year-old Ethel Spear, a housemaid, of Evesham Road, Cheltenham, both spoke of going out with Byron in his car. Furthermore, Miss Spear referred to a date with him in December 1937, when he took her to Tower Lodge and attempted to interfere with her indecently.

Annie Thick, aged 19, who served in the bar at the Crown and Cushion, a public-house in Bath Road, Cheltenham, which Byron used to frequent, had also been out with him in his car. She spoke of the evening of 7 January 1938, when he came into the Crown and Cushion and told her that he was going to London on the following day, but would not be long in returning. And, later, her parents had heard him say that he would subsequently be going away for a long time. This, presumably, was in reference to his plan to up sticks and settle in Cornwall. He had seemed quite normal and did not, she added, appear to be in any way troubled about anything.

Another of Byron's romantic episodes was, tacitly, testified to by Mrs Constance Preece, a young widow of Ross-on-Wye. She had, she told Police Sergeant JE Keyte, of the Herefordshire Constabulary, met the dashing Byron at the 'Bristol Blue' Dance, held at Cheltenham in December 1937. After the ball was over, he had gallantly accompanied her back to her lodgings at 136 Bath Road, Cheltenham. She had never met him before, or since, that one night stand.

An interesting sidelight on Byron's off-the-dance-floor interests was brought into focus by William James Parvin, a jockey, from South Bank, Lambourn, whose name had cropped up among Sullivan's papers.

Interviewed by Sergeant John Church, of the Berkshire Constabulary, Parvin said that he had first met Byron Smith in 1935 or 1936 at the Piccadilly Hotel, a place frequented by the racing fraternity. Smith was, he said, known to all the leading jockeys, both on the flat and over the sticks, and to quite a few trainers. He was not actually a close friend of his, but he remembered telling Smith to call and see him at Lambourn if he ever came that way. And one day in 1936 he did so, saying that he was on holiday and *en route* to see his mother, at Pewsey, in Wiltshire. He stayed only about 15 minutes, and that was the only time that Parvin had seen him outside the Piccadilly Hotel. He had never heard of him since – until he read of his death in the newspapers.

Mrs Colin Rowe – formerly Miss Irene A Jesse – of Ghanistan Kennels,

Chessington Road, Hook, confirmed Byron's interest in racing. She had met him at the Piccadilly, and, until September 1934, attended various race-meetings with him. She had not seen him in the last four years.

What could just possibly be a homosexual link, suggestive of Brian Sullivan's bisexuality, was supplied by an investigation carried out by the Cheshire Police regarding the name of Norman James Dewison – address: Blue Cap Hotel, Sandiway – found lodged among the Tower Lodge papers. The Cheshire Force, in the persons of Sergeant Worth and Police Constable Welch, reported:

> There was no entry in the hotel register of the names of Brian Sullivan, Byron Smith, or Captain William Bernard Butt. I [PC Welch] also questioned the licensee, and he informed me that he had no knowledge of any persons of these names ever visiting the hotel.
> We [then] went to 5 John Brunner Crescent, Castle, Northwich, where we interviewed Dewison, aged 22, car park attendant, employed at the Blue Cap Hotel.

Questioned respecting the entry of both his home and work place addresses in the diary of the late Brian Sullivan, Dewison could not account for it, saying that he had never given his address to anyone, and denying any knowledge of Sullivan, Smith, or Butt. PC Welch stated:

> Dewison is of rather an effeminate nature and was concerned in cases of buggery and gross indecency at Sandiway in June 1936. At the time there was not sufficient evidence against Dewison to charge him with the offences, but he was called as a witness for the prosecution when other men were convicted for this offence. Dewison is well known to me, and I would describe him as an inveterate liar.

Brian was forever impressing upon his not entirely to be convinced mother what a fine, capable and 'hard' man of business he was. The sad truth was that his rating was lowly, as exposed when Mr Gordon Waddilove, a prominent Bradford businessman, one of the principals of the Provident Clothing & Supply Company Ltd, was interrogated as regards the business acumen and ability of Byron Smith.

Smith had, he said, been introduced to him in 1935 at the Piccadilly Hotel. Upon learning of Mr Waddilove's line of business – the nationwide issuing of credit cheques negotiable with certain tradesmen, the amount of the cheque being subsequently collected in weekly payments – Smith said that he had a scheme to offer which would be of benefit to Mr Waddilove. The latter gave Smith his card and told him to let him have the details of his proposition in writing. In due course they were sent to him, but the scheme was useless, and Waddilove did not bother to reply.

It may have been another master-stroke of business that Byron had in mind when he wrote to St Benet's Abbey, Laniver, near Bodmin. Respecting this correspondence, Sergeant GH Fradd, of the Bodmin Station of the Cornwall Constabulary, questioned Mr FT Nettleinghame, the promoter of several concerns, one of which related to the sale of a lucky charm called 'Joan the Wad'. He said that in all probability the order received from Smith was in regard to an offer relating to a birth stone or a lucky charm. The company had an antique shop at Polperro, where visitors were invited to write their names, addresses, and birth dates in a book. Then, prior to their birthday, a circular letter would be sent, offering for sale a lucky charm or some article featuring their particular birth stone. Byron was either superstitious or ambitious.

Byron's Cornish image seems, generally speaking, to have been good. Mr F Plumridge, the proprietor of the Old Royal Tourists' Hotel, Polperro, said:

"I knew Byron Smith well. He often came to dances in the hall attached to this hotel, and I often drove with him to other dances. He was popular with everyone, and a great favourite with women. He never spoke to me of his wife. He showed such interest in the women he met at dances here that it never occurred to me that he might be married."

But there was at least one young woman in Cornwall for whom Byron Smith, or Barry Symons as he called himself to her, was far from being a 'great favourite'. Her name was Barbara Joyce Cradick. She was a domestic servant in the employ of Mrs Eastoe, of Waratah, Lamellion Cross, Liskeard.

It was in September 1937 that a man identical to Byron Smith followed Miss Cradick in a motor. He got into conversation with her and told her he lived near Looe, and that with his pal he would be going to London at the end of the month or the beginning of October. He asked the girl to go for a ride with him in his car. When she refused, he snatched her diary from her hand, saying she could have it back next day if she agreed to come for a ride. She met him again by chance the following day, but still refused to go with him, and he drove spitefully off, taking her diary with him. That stolen diary was found among the dead dancer's possessions.

So bleak an outcome was unusual in the Byronic calends of casual love, but however solid his emotional deposits in the Bank of Romance, those in the bank of fiscal reality were exceeding slender.

Copies were secured from the St John's Wood Branch of the Midland Bank, at 1 Finchley Road, NW8, of the recorded transactions of Brian Sullivan's account from its opening on 8 August 1934, with a deposit of £27, to its closure in January 1938. The dealings were all of a strictly petty cash calibre. His culminatory credit balance on 8 January 1938, after a final payment of £2 10s in favour of WB Butt, was £4 6s 6d.

An account was opened in 1931 with the Abbey Road Building Society with an initial deposit of £75 7s 1d. After various vicissitudes, it peaked in 1935 with £217 5s credit. It slumped by 1937 to a mere £25 19s 10d, and was closed on 5 August 1937, by the withdrawal of the then remaining £6 7s 8d.

Brian's total monies at the time of his death were in the arctic region of £30.

In October 1937, his solicitor, Theodore Thompson, was certainly uneasy, writing, on 11 October to Nurse Sullivan:

> *I am sorry to have to trouble you, but I have not heard from Brian since the 1st September, although I have written to him twice since then, but can get no reply. I am a little troubled over the matter, as I have had certain commitments to make on his behalf, and should be glad if you could kindly let me know if he is still in Polperro, as I am most anxious to hear from him.*

Throughout the long stretch of years of his periodic financial embarrassment, Brian incessantly sought replenishment from the frankly low-water coffers of his mother, as revealed in the following three extracts from such correspondences:

> *Dear old girl ...*
>
> *Now do you think you can let me have £100 if I repay you say £150. You need not worry as the money is quite safe. Let me know by return as I shall have to have some capital and I don't want to have a partner if I can help it, otherwise I shall have to share and the profits, and you might as well have the share with me. Now I know you will do this for me, you know I won't let you down, and I am recognised as a hard businessman.*

> *Dear Mrs Sullivan*
>
> *You told me you were getting the money on the 1st Sept. How are you paying the Building Society instalment?... It is plain you cannot let me have that money as I have a splendid chance just now of making money, but of course it needs capital, and with cars £100 is very little... Can't you possibly manage it? I am sure you could if you tried, and you know it is for your sake as much as mine...I should be glad if you will let me know by <u>return</u> about this as I am in real earnest... Now please write by return, there's a good old girl.*

> *Dear Mrs S*
>
> *What's up? You are a <u>rotter</u>. What about that cash? You know how I needed it, just now. Why haven't you sent it? I have been waiting for it by every post. Please send it by return. I promised to repay you and you know I will. So DO send it at once, there's a good old girl.*

Barry Byron-Smith was still more or less in credit – the last quarter's rent owing in December 1937 apart – with Mr Collier Smithers, of Roland Gardens, South Kensington, the man who, in 1932, had leased to him flat Numbers 2 and 4 Radlett Place, with leases still valid for another five years. However, his situation with Mrs Maud Mills – formerly of Hillcrest, Polperro, since moved away to 68 Aberdare Gardens, London NW6 – was, as she was to testify, considerably less

Brian Sullivan's cottage at Polperro, Cornwall. Captain Butt and his wife spent a fortnight's holiday there.

satisfactory. In fact, he was substantially in debt to her, owing her money for rent, rates, electric light, and so on for the two cottages at Polperro which he had rented from her at £32 *per annum*, paying quarterly. About the beginning of October 1937, he had sent her £5 on account, but no further monies had been received, and his dues were by this time running at £11.

According to sundry reports, Byron Smith was scarcely more satisfactory to deal with in his capacity of leasor of holiday cottages. Typical in this respect is the statement of 47-year-old George Herbert Jones, an engineer's designer, of 72 Attleboro Lane, Water Orton, near Birmingham, made to Detective Sergeant JH Waghorn, of the Warwickshire Constabulary.

> Sometime in May 1937, my wife and I noticed an advertisement in *Dalton's Weekly Advertiser*, about a cottage at Polperro, which was to let for the summer holidays. My wife wrote to the person advertising, Byron Smith, and eventually it was arranged that we should take the cottage for a week in August.
>
> My wife, child and myself duly arrived at the cottage on Saturday, August 13th [in actual fact 14 August], and instead of finding it unoccupied and ready for our complete occupation of it, as we had been led to believe that we should, we found some of the rooms occupied by an elderly couple. The woman was apparently a painting artist, but we never got into close contact with them and I don't even know their names.
>
> We remained at the cottage for a week, and during that time the man, Smith, lived in a corrugated iron hut or building at the rear of the cottage. I did not at any time have much to do with Smith, and my wife and I regarded him as rather a mystery. He did no work, and I never saw anyone with him at his hut. Six or seven minutes' walk up the hill from the cottage, Smith either rented or owned a field, and in it he kept a pony, which he sometimes rode. There was also a caravan in the field, and while we were at Polperro two young ladies were occupying it.
>
> During the brief conversations I had with Smith I gathered that he used to travel in his car to Gloucester every week, usually on a Wednesday.

A receipt for £1 15s, in respect of rent for the cottage was signed 'B Byron-Smith'.

By means of the careful following-up of clues provided by this useful cache of private papers at the Lodge, a beam or two of light was shed on Brian's last activities.

Detective Constable Victor Tuffley, of Stroud, learned from Miss Winifred Hinton, daughter of the licensee of the Woolpack Inn, at Slad, near Stroud, that Brian had come into the inn at about 9.45pm on Christmas Eve 1937. He ordered a drink, a bottle of beer she thought, which he drank, before ordering another drink – what it was she could not remember – which he took outside to someone in a car. Sullivan stayed only a few minutes before leaving. He was never seen at the Woolpack again.

On 6 January 1938, Brian wrote, as from Hedgey Ditches, Polperro, to Mrs Page, at Cheriton, 25 Highfield Grove, Westcliff, Essex:

> *I have not been in Polperro much this winter, but I hope to be going down in a week or so. I shall be jolly glad to get back there. For one thing, it is much warmer. Did you have a nice Christmas? I expect it kept you busy, anyway. I went home, so was well looked after. Bimbo is very well. In fact he is lying in front of the fire while I am writing this. One of the first things I am going to do when I get back to Polperro is to write you a real letter.*

Mrs Page never heard from him again.

On 8 January 1938, just two days before his disappearance, Brian wrote, from Tower Lodge, his last letter. It was addressed to Captain CE Correll, New House, Talland Hill, Polperro:

> *Dear Baggy,*
> *Many thanks for the Calender [sic]. How attractive the Warren looks on paper. I hope you had a nice Christmas. I have had a rotten time, had the worse [sic] cold I think I've had, was in bed most of the time. Still, plenty to eat and drink, you know Bunter Court style.*
> *Tell Philip I did enjoy the two Bunters he sent, especially the Ghost one. It was jolly nice of him to send them. I am going to London Wed. week, and then I hope to return to Polperro, so will see you soon I hope, meanwhile my very best wishes to all.*
> *Yours sincerely,*
> *Billy*
>
> *Pea ess [sic]*
>
> *Eye am eggspecting a P.O. any*
> *monument eye howep eyes*
> *nott the type of felowe too*
> *fourgett mye awled pals.*

This piece of elaborate epistolary play-acting needs explanation. Byron and Baggy were both old Greyfriars men; that is to say devotees since schooldays of Frank Richards' tales of Greyfriars and St Jim's schools, chronicled in weekly instalments in the popular boys' magazines, the *Magnet* and the *Gem*. Either Philip or John Correll took them weekly, and it was Byron-Smith's habit to borrow them and pass them on to Baggy. The written extension to the letter is clearly an exercise in frank nostalgia.

Byron christened Captain Correll 'Baggy', the reference being to one of the scholars of St Jim's – Baggy Trimble, of Trimble Court.

Billy (William George) Bunter, of the totally chimeric Bunter Court, the Fat Owl of the Remove, was perpetually waiting, Micawber-like, for his eternally expected, but also chimeric, postal order, on the strength of which he borrowed from his chums, to turn up. In this Polperro game of verbal make-believe, Barry Byron-Smith, also as it happened a chimæra, assumed the rôle of the rotund Bunter, so christened perhaps, tongue-in-cheek, by very reason of his physical sparsity.

So much, then, for Byron-Billy Bunter.

What, the detectives were wondering, was there to ferret out about Billy Butt?

Chapter Fifteen

... and Billy

The information contributing to a closer focus picture of the unbuttoned Captain Billy Butt has proved much scantier in supply than that which was available for a portrait of 'Byron' Sullivan.

As we have already hazarded, the Captain's marriage to Edith Hogg was surely a cynical and materialistic move, designed to secure to himself her quite considerable monies. He knew that his bride-to-be was psychiatrically unsound. He got in a nurse to keep her off his back. He got rid of the Manor House, and spent as much of her money and as little of his time as he possibly could with his wife. That is a start; albeit not a very pretty one.

Seeking to build a rather wider character profile of Butt, one begins by calling into evidence the testimony of two of his relatively close associates, Hubert Brooke and George Yeates.

Brooke, of Danes Court, Barnwood Road, Gloucester, was the manager of a firm of dairy produce merchants. He and his wife became acquainted with Mrs Gertie Prew in 1930, and in due course met her brother, Captain Butt. In 1935, the Brookes moved to Shurdington, just three miles from Cheltenham, and that was when Mr Brooke started to come into contact with the Captain more regularly, principally through a shared interest in shooting.

It was about 1930 that George Yeates, a farmer, of Chacely Court Farm, Chacely, near Tewkesbury, got to know Butt. He, too, was a shooting man, and, with Brooke, made up the Butt sporting trio, which raked the shooting ground at Chaceley and Aston-on-Carrant.

In February 1936, Brooke introduced Harold Moffatt to Butt. The acquaintance remained casual until September 1937, when Moffatt went along to Number 248 Old Bath Road with the request that Butt rent him some of the shooting at Aston-on-Carrant. Butt refused, but took Moffatt out for several days shooting with him at both Aston and Chacely, as his guest.

Moffatt met Butt by chance at the Glentworth Club on four occasions during December 1937. The Captain used especially to enjoy a game of bridge there, and would always journey to and from the club by himself.

The last time that Moffatt saw Butt was 19 December 1937. The Captain had telephoned him that day at the Glentworth, explained that his own car was out of order, and asked him if he would pick him up in his car. Moffatt had duly set out for Old Bath Road, met him *en route*, and driven him to the club, where he left him. Before they separated, Butt had said that he would see him after Christmas, but did not mention any particular date.

Moffatt did not receive any communication from Butt and, on 19 January 1938, when he returned to the club, he heard from Mrs Ferguson, the club secretary, that Captain Butt was away. Moffatt told her that he would telephone the Captain on the following Wednesday [26 January], if he had not heard from him in the meantime.

About 7pm on 26 January 1938, he had telephoned Butt's home and learned that he was not there. He spoke to a Mrs Sullivan, who had proceeded to tell him about the death of her son. As a result, Moffatt called at Number 248 later in the evening, and Mrs Sullivan told him that Captain Butt had gone away without stating his destination, but, she said, it was possible that he had gone off on a cruise. Moffatt made enquiries at the club, and the next day Mrs Sullivan telephoned him and asked if he had any news of the Captain. He told her that he had none.

George Yeates, interviewed by Inspector Worth, said that at the end of a day's shooting Butt would often complain of pains in his knee. He would massage it, and say that he had been wounded there by shrapnel in the Great War.

Butt's brother, John, stated categorically that the Captain had no shrapnel wound. This was borne out by the many enquiries, including those at War Office Records, made by the police. There is no evidence to support the contention that Butt had ever received such a wound, and Spilsbury had found nothing other than slight indications of arthritis on the knee joints of the torso-affiliated legs.

Miss Mabel Barton, of London Road, Cheltenham, said that Captain Butt was a member of the Tennis Club in Argyle Road, Cheltenham. She had played tennis with him on several occasions, and she distinctly recalled his complaining of pains in his legs. He had mentioned that he had sprained his knee some years ago.

The detectives were told that in March 1936 there had been a cooling off, a falling out, between Butt and Brooke. What led to it was this. Brooke had telephoned to Number 248, and, in Butt's absence, asked Nurse Sullivan, to whom he spoke, to give a message to the Captain upon his return. The message was of a frivolous kind, and, in view of the fact that it was intended for onward transmission and to be delivered by an employee, probably a tactless thing to have done.

At any rate, the dignified Captain did not take kindly to this, regarding it as an act of impertinence by Brooke. Brooke saw the subsequent six-month silence as inexplicable, and decided, in October 1937, to pop round to Old Bath Road and ask Butt what was wrong, why his calls had discontinued. Making no bones about it, Butt told him that he resented the way he had spoken to one of his employees. Brooke then left the house – and never saw Butt again.

Both Brooke and Moffatt described Butt as most secretive. Brooke said that one could never get to the bottom of the man. He spoke of no one other than his few relatives, but did mention at times that he had visited some of them at Oxford, Mr Hobson at Plymouth, and on one occasion that he went to the Isle of Wight when he was friendly with Miss Cranswick. Moffatt said that Butt never confided in him, was very reserved, and never discussed his private affairs.

It would perhaps be reasonable to suppose that the Captain's brother would be able to fill in some of the more conspicuous lacunae.

Billy's brother, John, aged 51, proved a disappointment. In 1938 he was privately employed as a polo pony trainer by the independently wealthy commanding officer of the 4/7th Royal Dragoon Guards, at Redford Barracks, Edinburgh.

He told the police:

> I have lived very little with him, and only during the last two years have I seen anything of him. In that period I have stayed for two days, and at another time for about a week, with him in Cheltenham. During my visits he used to go out with me in the car and we might have a drink. No person visited him during my stay. He was of very temperate habits so far as I know, with perhaps the exception of a binge at Christmas-time. Up until two years ago, I had not really seen him more than three or four times since I was a boy. On the few times I have stayed with him there was nothing suspicious about his movements. He received letters by post, but none of them seemed to disturb him in any way, and I never knew the contents of any letter received by him. I knew nothing about his financial affairs. He did not inherit money as far as I know. I last saw him alive on Boxing Day 1937, at Greenview, Wolvercote, my sister, Mrs Hobson's house. He and I spent Christmas there. There were no visitors other than the family staying in the house. No person specially called to see him. He never passed any remark that would give any clue as to his death.

Doffing one's cap to the old saw that servants make prime observers of the goings-on in the homes where they are employed, let us see what Mrs Sybil Haycox, who, since 1935, had come to do housework at Number 248 from 8am to twelve o'clock noon every Wednesday and Saturday, was able to contribute.

She harboured no illusions regarding her mistress, asserting that Mrs Butt was a "mental case". She described how Captain Butt spent much time in his garden, and went away frequently. She elaborated further, saying:

"He used to keep two small suit-cases under the bed in his bedroom. One was plain. The other had initials on it – or, perhaps, 'B Butt'. When he went away, he always took his clothes in one of those cases."

She described how he also attended to the garden at Tower Lodge, and would bring produce from it back to Old Bath Road

At times Mrs Haycox did some cleaning up at the Lodge. On one particular occasion having noticed that the downstairs windows there facing the road were boarded up, she had enquired of Nurse Sullivan regarding this, and was told that the match boarding had been erected by her son to keep out the draughts. It was pointed out to her though that it was moveable, and could be taken down when necessary.

Mrs Haycox averred that she had never witnessed or known of any quarrels between the Butts and Nurse Sullivan, and the Captain and his wife struck her as being on affectionate terms. In fact, in the Haycoxian Sibylline books, they all seemed to get on well together, and she had seen Captain Butt and Brian Sullivan chatting amiably in the garden at Number 248.

The police made it their business to look into the Captain's financial affairs. There was an account at Lloyd's Bank, Tewkesbury. This was in the name of the Captain's wife, but it was operated by him through his Power of Attorney. On 5 January 1938, it was £145 5s 9d in credit.

From January to December 1937, the withdrawals, generally, appeared to have been made to defray household expenses connected with the running of Number 248 Old Bath Road. However, on 15 April 1937, and 13 October 1937, cheques were drawn for £9 and £5 respectively, made payable to Miss Cranswick.

On 22 April, 30 August, 13 October, 25 October, and 3 December, 1937, cheques were drawn in favour of Mrs Sullivan for £7 10s, £3 14s, £1, £7 10s, and £2.

The receipts were from properties owned by Mrs Butt, the sale of £100 worth of Bradford Corporation stock, and interest on a War Loan.

There was a second account with the National Provincial Bank, Cheltenham. This was in Butt's own name. The bank declined to furnish a full statement to the police, but counterfoils of cheque books from this bank were found at Number 248. On 5 January 1938, he was £112 in credit. Nearly all the withdrawals were made payable to 'Self'.

The remaining ones were for small amounts, with the exception of one on 4 December 1937, for £10 to the Cheltenham Association Football Club, in which he had shares. On 10 December 1937, one for £6 was made payable to Miss Cranswick, and on 4 January 1938, one for £3 to Mrs Sullivan.

Mr Harry Alec Badham, Butt's solicitor, was visited by Inspector CJ Large, of Tewkesbury, at his office in High Street, Tewkesbury. He said that the income from Mrs Butt's properties was approximately £400 *per annum*. He showed the Inspector the Deed of Attorney made on 4 August 1934, in favour of Captain Butt.

Mr Badham knew of no property held by Butt in his own name, and to the best of his knowledge Captain Butt's assets were derived from his wife's income.

Large also saw Edith Butt's cousin, Mr EA Hogg, of The Nook, Abbots Road, Priors Park, Tewkesbury, and ascertained that of the £3,500 of Bradford Corporation stock which had been purchased on Mrs Butt's behalf on 28 June 1927, amounts had been withdrawn by Captain Butt as follows:

19 April 1933	£500 stock sold
1 August 1935	£300 stock sold
27 April 1936	£100 stock sold
1 April 1937	£100 stock sold

This meant that the Captain's wife's capital had been reduced, by the extraction of

£1,000, to £2,500. Mr Hogg stated that Mrs Edith Butt was under the impression that the original £3,500 remained still intact.

Some puzzlement was expressed as to how the Captain had managed to sell off the £500 worth of stock in April 1933, 16 months before the granting to him of the Power of Attorney. In this context one recalls with distinct unease Nurse Sullivan's tale of the Armenian truncheon.*

Enquiries were made at other banks in Cheltenham, but no trace was found of any other account of Captain Butt's.

When the transfer of Power of Attorney was made to Mr Hogg, he was advised by Inspector Worth to have the safe at Number 248 opened. A representative of the Ratner Safe Company, of Bridge Street, London, EC4, came and duly opened it. Inside were found a quantity of silver-plate and some legal papers relative to the decease of Francis Frederick Hobson, to whose will Captain Butt had been co-executor, and vouchers and receipts for the purchase of Bradford Corporation stock.

Mrs Prew had also directed the police's attention to "a safe in the conservatory at 248 Old Bath Road, with gold and silver in". She had referred, too, to the fact that her brother, "always carried a gold watch with a perfectly plain back inscribed with 'WBB' on it". He had also a gold and platinum watch chain, a gold signet-ring with initials, and a plain gold ring on the third finger of his left hand.

Mr Badham told the Inspector that Mrs Butt and her family had been his clients for a number of years. Butt had had constant interviews with Badham's firm in connection with the property owned by his wife. Often before his departure on one of his mysterious trips, the Captain would mention to Badham's clerk that he was going away, but he never left an address or any information as to where he could be found. He had last visited Badham's office on 24 November 1937. There had been no communication of any kind since. Mr Badham had no idea that Captain Butt had at that time had any intention of going away. He added that he knew nothing of his private life or associates.

To just what extent Billy Butt figured in 'Byron' Sullivan's life remains very much an open question. There were, to be sure, press reports that while Brian was working at the Piccadilly Hotel, Captain Butt visited him many times. However, recent thorough research has found not the slightest evidence to support this. Moreover, although Brian's wife said that she knew Keith Newman, and that, despite Newman's later denials, he and Brian were close friends who used to go driving together for long distances in Brian's car, she admitted that she had never met Captain Butt, although she had heard Brian refer to the Captain and his wife, Edith.

Gertrude Mary Prew, Butt's sister, living at 28 Heathville Road, Gloucester, apart from her husband, said that her brother was always kind to his wife, and that Nurse Sullivan, whom he had engaged to look after her, performed her duty well. She said, too, that Nurse Sullivan had often complained about Captain Butt's habit of going away without saying anything of his intention to do so to her, and leaving her with absolutely no idea of where, or how, to get in touch with him in case of emergency. But she knew of no quarrels between the Captain and Nurse Sullivan.

Mrs Prew was aware that her brother's life with his wife could not have been an

*See Chapter One.

altogether easy or happy one, for periodically Mrs Butt undoubtedly had some bad mental turns. In the course of one of these she had accused her [Mrs Prew] of having immoral relations with the Captain.

Gertrude Prew had absolutely no knowledge of the existence of any friendship between her brother and Brian Sullivan.

Purely by chance, she had run into Nurse Sullivan in Tewkesbury on 3 February 1938 – the day of the finding of the torso. No mention was made of it in the course of their conversation. What was interesting, though, was that Nurse Sullivan had described to her how she had found her son dead and enigmatically remarked:

"Brian had told me that he had an idea that Captain Butt had been using him for something".

Mrs Prew had thought that a very strange thing to say, and asked: "Whatever do you mean?"

A bland Nurse Sullivan had dismissively replied: "I don't know."

Speaking of the Butts' return from their Christmas break in Oxford, Nurse Sullivan had observed: "He brought Mrs Butt into the house a raving lunatic. They had had a terrific row on the way down from Oxford, and he went off the next day."

Mrs Prew stated that later, at Number 248, Nurse Sullivan was still harping on the Captain's absence.

"He's never coming back here. If he does, I'll wring his neck. I've got the strength to do it," she told her.

This is undeniably a quite extraordinary piece of dialogue.

Another of the Captain's sisters, Mrs Mary Agnes Hobson, of the Hobson Riding Stables, Greenview, Wolvercote, with whom the Butts had spent Christmas, said that her brother would customarily visit her about once a month, but never discussed his private affairs with her. She had, one occasion apart, never heard him speak of Brian Sullivan. The exception was when his mother, Nurse Sullivan, had gone to London to visit Brian.

The Captain's brother-in-law, Francis Mott, also of Greenview, Wolvercote, a retired land agent, made reference to a tattoo on the inside of the lower part of one of Captain Butt's arms. This was rather odd, for in a previous statement Mr Mott had thought that the Captain had no scars or tattoo marks.

A distinctly less rebarbative Butt emerges from the pages of a letter written to him on 5 January 1938, from 2 Polstead Road, Oxford, by Miss Ida Cranswick.

Wednesday

Billy, Darling,
Its so nice to sit down and write to you again, cos I always look forward to writing and receiving your letters, and somehow tho' I have seen you for odd hours I have missed writing to you.
Well the festive season is all over now, and a damn good thing did you say!! I bet you were glad to crawl into bed early, and will be glad to do so for a few nights to get over all your late nights. Did you go home on Monday, or did they persuade you to stay another night?

I had a letter from Carol yesterday and she is coming down on Jan. 15th and has got the Monday off so won't have to return till Monday evening which is fine.

Will be nice to see her again, she will come at 3-0 pm on the 15th, so if you have the car back come over either Sat. or Sunday night, darling, but I doubt very much if it will be done by then, knowing how swift any motor works are!!

The radio man came yesterday and fixed my ariel [sic] – he's put it out of one of the top windows and down through the conservatory and it seems quite good to me. He wanted me to test it well last night, but I went out to see Enid – Anyway have it going now and its O.K. and I can get Luxemburg quite well.

Washed my hair tonight and its been so jolly to have the radio going all the time, bless you, darling, for giving it to me. Betty and I had a good afternoon's shopping on Monday and I got all I wanted. Then we had those two girls I told you about in for dinner, and after we played Newmarket till 10-0 pm. Was so lovely seeing you again on Sunday evening, thanks ever so for a jolly time, my dear. You left the box of cigarettes and I wondered if you had any more for yourself, also lots in the bottles which I shall keep till Carol comes and we can have some then, the gin and ginger will do for her as she doesn't drink whiskey – By the way what about the ginger ale bottles, did you have to pay on them, and what shall I do when they are empty, as I am keeping them all?

I was amused on Sunday night at Leslie, when we went into my room, you were hanging up your coat I think, he went over to my radio and was admiring it, I said nothing, then he picked up the snap I have of you and said "Uncle Bill, is he a brother of yours or some relation?" – I just smiled and said "No relation only a friend." – Then I thought he might spot the other snap I have so when he wasn't looking turned your face to the wall, darling – was rather amusing and tickled me somewhat. I like Leslie tho', he's a nice kid.

Betty went off on Thursday morning and we have had a letter from her this evening. Now I must away to bed, my dear, as I'm tired. Have had headache ever since yesterday afternoon, <u>no</u> not a hang-over. Hope I'm not sickening for something, but I feel quite O.K. except for a tight band across my forehead, good night's rest will put me right I guess.

All my love, sweetheart

Always Yours,

XXXX Idey XXXXXX

Will write again Sunday as usual, when I get back from London. Am going up Sat. on the 3-15 pm.

And that, with a bit of between-line reading, is as near to humanising the Captain as it ever gets!

Chapter Sixteen

Dreamers, Dowsers, Mediums and Red Herrings

On 7 March 1938, a very strange letter appeared on Chief Inspector Worth's desk. It was addressed to him by a correspondent signing herself Ethel L Webb, of 1 Stanhope Road, North Finchley, London, N12.

I wonder if you will smile at what is to follow? Whatever the result I feel that I shall have relieved my mind, but first may I ask you to bear with me a little, in recording this dream I have had, as in many of my previous dreams so much has come true.

On Jan. 3rd of this year I had a very vivid dream, of a man being murdered and his dismembered body being buried, and funnily enough it was just the head and small hands which he was burying; on the left hand and third finger was a signet ring, and the head was very round, jet black hair and dark eyes.

In the course of my dream, I was taken up a slight slope of ground and as in a flash something seemed to tell me it was an allotments or something like that, but the earth itself was black, as if it had been well sooted; and then a man appeared to be digging with a <u>pointed</u> spade (not like the usual oblong). His back was towards me, and as I approached I asked, "What are you doing?" He answered, "I have murdered an Irishman and am burying his head and hands." I said, "But you must not do that here, you will be found out." He answered, "They will never suspect it's me." And with that he seemed to be talking to me as his wife.

The most curious part was I was shown in my dream the mouth of the River Severn, the Bristol Channel, and south east Ireland. This has always puzzled me as to why it was given to me. I told my dream to my folks and a friend even before the Torso Case came up. When the paper (Daily Herald) first published the bloodstains on Haw Bridge, I immediately exclaimed and said, "This is the murder of my dream," – and they just laughed. But even as time went on and the case dropped, I still feel there was my dream attached to that spot. I am still confident that the torso is not of Capt. Butt, as he was the man I saw digging with the spade. I recognised his face at once in the paper.

Then, on Feb. 22nd, the continuance of my dream. I was taken into a field with a sludgy cart track near a hedge, and rows and rows of green saplings, about 6ft. 6 ins. In my dream I asked what trees they were, and a voice said, "Where runner beans were." And in the centre of the 3rd or 4th row was a hand sickle, and a voice said, "This helped with the work" – and it was rusty with blood. The voice continued, "They will find all the evidence they want in the murderer's own house."

Find out if Butt had a cousin, about 35-37 years, dark brown eyes, pointed chin, dark straight hair taken right over the head and small _____ [?] in nape of neck, as she appeared in a very old-fashioned country inn, a bar parlour, and a fellow about 5ft. 6ins. or 7ins. was with her – dark hair and eyes, brown suit – and he was drunk. And she was trying to get him out of the place because he was talking all about the murder as the police entered the bar and asked, "What relation are you to this man?" And she answered, "Cousin."

Is there dark earth in Butt's own garden on a slight incline? Had he a ginger plus-fours suit with maroon pullover or cardigan? Is there a tributary River Nevil there?

This is all my dream.

Twelve days later, on 19 March, Worth received a second letter from Ethel Webb.

Since writing you of my dream, I have since had another, in which the spade I saw belonged to a garden where there is a white bench seat and either a bird bath or sundial with a large overhanging branch of a tree. Does this tally with the garden of Capt. Butt, as it is still there? I am always drawn [to], and strange to say in tonight's paper I see where investigations are going on at, Bristol. All along I have told my friends that Bristol would come somewhere in the picture.

On Thursday last, after asking all day for a name of the man to be given me, the name of Talbot came to me in the night, and with this name a man answering to this description: 5 ft. 10 ins. Dark hair, but rather flat on top of head. Nicely groomed. Dark eyes, and a complexion so clean that it would strike one immediately upon looking at his face.

In fact, Ethel Webb's letter was far from unique, for, throughout the investigation, the days, weeks, months, were punctuated by the arrival of weird, sometimes uncanny-seeming, would-be helpful missives.

Another dreamer – Marjorie Thomas – wrote from Kings Heath, Birmingham:

I have quite a lot of very vivid dreams which more often than not come true. I dreamt last night that I was walking along some fields which were barred round with some white railings and it seemed to me that it was some sort of racecourse, when suddenly two men came up to me, and I was surprised to recognise Brian Sullivan as one of them. He had glasses on and seemed very frightened. The man who was with him was as tall, but he was very hefty, with broad shoulders. I heard one of them whispering about "under the tree". They saw me and I ran.

I was running across these fields and stumbled by the tree they were talking about, and it seemed that it had just been dug over. I jumped into the river then, which was near some cottages, and it seemed as if I had found something which had been lost a long time. I got out of the river and found myself in some old *sheds, and I found some snaps of Brian Sullivan on the floor. I wouldn't have bothered you with writing to you, only the part in this morning's paper is so like what I dreamt about. ***

It would not be unexpected in this context for the spiritualists to come forward with extra-sensorily perceived pointers. Indeed, a letter from one such – a Mr DHD Wilkinson, of Plantagenet Road, New Barnet – marked 'Private and Confidential', and addressed to 'The Inspector of Police, Cheltenham,' was duly delivered to the Central Police Station on 16 February 1938.

On Sunday last [13 February], *a lady whom I had never met before called on me, by the advice of a mutual friend with whom she happened to be spending the weekend. My friend had told her that I have some psychic gift, and believe myself to be often in touch with departed spirits, some of whom come to me for help. This lady told me that she had been an acquaintance of Major Butt's, and that for some time she had been troubled by a feeling that he was near her and wanted to speak to her, and she asked could I help her in any way.*

I tried to get in touch with my father, who acts as my 'control' in the spirit world, and he told me that a spirit was present wanting my help, and that it was the spirit of the murderer (<u>not</u> of the murdered man). I had then (in a separate room) an interview with the spirit. He began by saying (more correctly 'writing' for my method of receiving messages is automatic writing) – 'I am the most miserable spirit that ever could be. My name is Sullivan. I was a professional dancer, and I murdered my own friend, and took my own life and now I am in the greatest misery ... &c.'

He then told me about his life, a long confession which I cannot repeat in detail. It included a statement as to the motive which had made him murder the man, and the method by which he did it. He made a business appointment with his friend near the Severn, hid till he came, joined him in a motor car and suddenly shot him behind the ear. He at first tried to hide the body in the river and make it look as though he had fallen in accidentally. But on finding this impossible he cut it up with a large knife and hid it bit by bit in the mud, except the head which he could not manage to conceal. So he took it away 'and buried it in some sand or in some earth of some kind in some sort of field or sort of quarry not far from the Severn and then I went back to my house in Cheltenham and turned the gas on, and shut the window and lay on my bed hoping that death would end it all and it has not ... '

The rest of the interview has no bearing on the crime itself, but was of the nature which would be more like that which a murderer in a condemned cell might have with a keen chaplain:

On the 14th Inst. I received an intimation that the spirit of the <u>murdered</u> man

---

*As a suicide, Brian Sullivan was buried at the foot of a tree, beside a spring, on the edge of St Peter's, Leckhampton, churchyard.

was present and wanted to talk. In that interview he told me that he had accused Sullivan of a certain offence and added, 'He was terribly angry and alarmed for I knew a lot of his wrong-doings and he feared that I might expose him. Then I suppose he wanted to get rid of me and so he sent me a message about an important business appointment near to some place on the river Severn. I don't remember the name. I met him and we drove in my car towards the place when he suddenly pulled a pistol out of his pocket and shot me dead as I was sitting by his side and driving.

I don't know what he did then, for I was confused and was not able to see or understand where I was, or how I came to be there. But after a bit I saw him cutting up my body with a large sort of butcher's knife and throwing pieces into the water and trying to make them sink in the mud by pushing them down with a long sort of pole.

Then I saw him try to do the same with my head, and he could not make it stay under the water, so he carried it away for about a mile I should think and then went into a field with a sort of quarry in it, and a lot of sand and gravel and other rubbish, and there he dug a hole in a heap of sand, or earth of some light sort, and put my head in and covered it up with a lot more loose earth or sand trying to make it look as though it had fallen naturally on the ground from some overhanging bank. And then I saw him retrace his steps to my car and drive in it to the river-bank, and leave it on the bank near to the place in which he had hidden my dismembered body.

Then I came away very miserable and very desirous of revenge on him. So I haunted him all the way back to his house in or near Cheltenham, and I preyed on his fears and his mind in such a fierce and forceful way that he was scared and terrified, and at last tried to get rid of himself by gas poisoning.'

The rest of the interview had no bearing on the crime but only on his own condition and need. I forgot to ask his name and he did not give it.

I am aware that this is not evidence, but it may possibly provide some clues to the mystery. For your information I may add that I am a clergyman of the Church of England and have been a student of psychic matters for many years, and have published two books on the subject.

The Reverend Mr Wilkinson pens a PS:

Since writing the above I have, I believe, received a further message from my father telling me that Sullivan tells him that the name of the man he murdered was Major Butt.

Another spiritualist medium, James T Southgate, of Tredworth Road, Gloucester, dropped a postcard to the police. He wrote:

I feel a woman, well built, travelled in a car with Brian driving. Seated at the back would be Capt. Butt and a heavy wine bottle was used to hit him on the head. The car seemed to be tied with rough string on front bumper. The woman would wear a long string of pearls.

Miss Dorothy Mann, a self-styled clairvoyant, living in Malvern Road, Worcester, had, she said, received certain definite impressions which kept haunting her mind. Writing diffidently to Inspector Hancock, she was, however, insistent that the torso was Captain Butt – some doubts had been expressed that the evidence was sufficiently conclusive that the corpse really was that of the Captain. She was further convinced that, 'the body in question met death by impact with a lorry'. And she came up with the name 'Scarlett', which, she said, had persisted in her mind as being of value in the case.

She was able, moreover, to supply, 'a perfectly clear picture of a stable, which I feel I could probably recognise if I saw it. It was in open country, had three stalls, separated by wooden partitions, one window with wooden lathes, a large drain, to which my attention seemed to be directed, and the whole place was whitewashed, and seemed quite clean, well kept, and up to date. There were other buildings, but this seemed endways to the longer ones.'

Ernest Slade, of Oakland, near Bristol, offered his assistance and the services of his friend, Stanley Hunt, a water diviner: 'We are both at present unemployed and if you could use us would it be possible to arrange some sort of conveyance to take us to Cheltenham, also to arrange for our welfare while we are on the job?' One suspects that the police authorities found this offer eminently resistible.

Rather more persuasive was the, albeit slightly facetiously couched, proposition put forward by Mr WH Trinder, writing from the Swan Hotel, at Bibury, Gloucestershire, where he was staying preparatory to moving house to Hawling Manor, Andoversford:

I have no wish to 'butt in', but if I can be of any service to you in helping to find the missing head in the 'Torso case' my services are at your disposal … I have been a 'dowser' for a number of years and am on the Council of the British Society of Dowsers. I make no extravagant claims but will merely do my best. … I may also say that I can keep my mouth shut.

Another offer was forthcoming from a practitioner of psychometry.

Having been reading about the missing head, etc., of Captain Butt, I feel sure that if the parts are there about I could locate them for you providing that I could have a garment that no one has touched since the Captain wore it.

Thus confidently wrote Frederick Stone, of Barrack Street, Devonport, adding that the magnetism left in the garment would remain there for twelve months. He continued:

I would like to be of assistance to you by my gifts of locating. I don't care if it is buried in the earth, I could still detect it. If you care to try me, my expenses only is what I ask. After reading this and you doubt it, I am prepared to go through a test by the Plymouth City Police before engaging me. Thanking you in anticipation.

There surely breathes an honest, if somewhat self-deluded, man!

A dignified correspondent, Mr Alfred Thornton, writing from no less august an address than The Athenæum, suggested 'elucidation by sensitive'. There being none, in his opinion, 'sufficiently conversant with the technique' in England, the name of Dr Paul Osty, of the Institute Metapsychique, Avenue Niel, Paris, 'not infrequently employed by the French police', was heartily recommended.

Writing in the light of her 'especial study of Astrology and Crime', a Miss B Adams, of 188 Whiteladies Road, Bristol, despatched the following extra-sensory perceptive dispatch to Chief Detective Inspector Worth regarding Brian Sullivan.

This man has been engaged in drug traffic. I find he had commercial interest with seafaring men going to and from China, and any enemy he had would come through that source, certainly not from women, the position of the moon and other aspects would make him popular with the opposite sex. Yet strangely enough I do not think any person caused his death by blackmail; or any other means. I find from my studies that he died really from fear after the dreadful tragedy that he had witnessed and depressing stellar influences upon Sunday evening drove him to this step. Therefore, I think that he died about 2 a.m. of the 17th January last. His mother knew all about this anguish of mind and fearful of the exposure which was imminent, advised this course, but he certainly would have gone abroad if funds had been available.

I should like to know who gave the milkman orders to discontinue supply of milk.

This man, Brian Sullivan, is not a murderer but an unwilling accessory. He was timid in the face of danger. Some stronger personality made him assist in the dismembering, which would make this type mentally and physically sick.

I am expecting Capt. Butt's ephemeris to be sent to me tomorrow. You will have details by Tuesday.

Those details actually arrived in another letter on Wednesday 16 March 1938.

This man [Captain Butt] *had a very strong temper and as far back as 1936 he had been anxious about certain investments he had made. Undoubtedly he was the victim of a series of frauds, there was much deception and treachery, especially in those he employed. The whole chart reeks with duplicity and fraud. His untimely and violent end was caused through a woman.*

In my opinion he was ambushed, virtually made a prisoner at Tower Lodge, and many and various were the ruses to make him sign one particular document.

Of course you realise I have not been given the time or place of birth which is all-important, but I should say his throat was severed, at any rate there are great afflictions to this man's anatomy, and unfortunately he suffered from sex complaints, and the blame I believe was laid upon the head of Mrs Sullivan and her son.

They are all conspirators. Just a case of Nemesis.

Whereas Brian Sullivan passed out under drug and noxious fumes, this man fought like a tiger. He may have struck the first blow in rage, but the chart is a very scandalous one, showing infidelity over a number of years and much trouble in consequence. There is no doubt he was ambushed. He drove very hard bargains. He was very close in money matters.

The all-important dates are these; Thursday evening, Jan. 6th. Friday evening kept a prisoner. He died on the 8th, a victim of fraud and deceit, and by people he had trusted. I am surprised his wife lived so long. There must be a reason. His legal papers should reveal much. There is no doubt about this man's death. His worst enemies came from Ireland or are of Irish descent.

This man stood to lose everything he possessed, the complicity and fraud are obvious to even the most elementary student of stellar influences. I wish I could help you to find the head. There is no doubt he was somewhat of a tyrant and discounted the power of one particular woman. She had suffered for years. There were many quarrels and much strife.

Miss Adams sent a further letter to Inspector Worth on 28 March. She assures him that he need not have the slightest doubt about Captain Butt's decease, claiming to know that he died on 8 January. She states that the cause was a crystalline substance, poison, causing injury to the throat.

I know I wrote you his throat was severed, but there was so much mutilation and as time is the greatest factor in my especial study of Astrology and Crime, I have to ask you to pardon me, not Astrology, if I err on a fraction of time: you see I merely had the date, but I could help you so much more if it were made compulsory to give times of birth as in other countries when registering births. Brian Sullivan also committed suicide from fear, and his mother, I am afraid, will lose her sanity. I wish you could have trusted me. I feel I know where the head is, and you may be positive it is not burnt.

Dutifully, the Chief Inspector read every word of his eccentric post. Here and there amid the outpourings of the dreamers, the clairvoyants, the spiritualists, a nugget of possibility gleamed, but this was the literature of fantasy. He was in the business of truth.

153

Chapter Seventeen

Whose Body?

As early as 19 February 1938, it had come to Chief Inspector Worth's notice that persistent rumours were being circulated in Cheltenham that it was not the body of Brian Sullivan that was found at Tower Lodge and subsequently buried in Leckhampton churchyard.

Apropos this, he duly reported:

"I was satisfied that these [rumours] arose as a result of a press campaign. Statements had already been taken from persons involved in the finding of the body at Tower Lodge, its removal to the mortuary, subsequent placing in the coffin, and final disposal at the cemetery. The press had circulated the news that an exhumation was to take place as the description of the man found at Tower Lodge did not coincide with Brian Sullivan's."

Worth was not, he said, unduly perturbed, but considered it advisable to make a personal enquiry into the matter.

"The main contention was that a coffin was made for a person about five foot eleven inches, and Sullivan's height was approximately five foot seven inches. I interviewed Mr Selim Smith, undertaker, of Cheltenham, and Joseph Stone, carpenter, in his employ. The latter stated that the body measured five foot eleven and a half inches, and when I asked him how he arrived at the measurement he stated he did so by the use of a footrule and finger. I spoke to Mr Selim Smith on this point and it was agreed that an accurate measurement could not be made in these circumstances."

Maybe, maybe not, but what was at issue was whether or not the body lying there in that upper room at Tower Lodge was actually Brian's.

It is, perhaps, well to remember that the coroner accepted evidence of identification at the inquest from PC Merry, and not from Nurse Sullivan. Merry's evidence was from his identification at the mortuary. Nurse Sullivan's evidence was of the finding of the body at Tower Lodge on 24 January 1938, the only occasion upon which she saw her son – if indeed it *was* her son – dead.

Worth wrote:

> I communicated the result of my enquiry to Mr Lane, the coroner, and he accompanied me to 248 Old Bath Road, where I again interviewed Mrs Sullivan, following which the coroner stated he would not entertain any suggestion of exhumation as he was satisfied that the body interred was that of Brian Sullivan.
>
> It is to be noted that PC Merry knew Brian Sullivan well and the

inference from the rumours was that Mrs Sullivan had wilfully withheld the identity of the body and had committed perjury.

Apart from my enquiries, it is inconceivable to make such a suggestion, in the light of January 24th, when she communicated with Mr Thompson, the solicitor, who had known Sullivan from boyhood, and [she] accompanied him to Tower Lodge. If she had deliberately misled the coroner, the last person she would have caused to go to Tower Lodge was Mr Thompson, as she was unaware until afterwards that he had not seen Brian's face. The letter found on the chair in Sullivan's bedroom on January 24th was undoubtedly written by him. The writing is similar to that on other correspondence found in the Lodge.

An anonymous note, plainly scribed by one of those belonging to the 'Brian Sullivan is alive and well' school of thought, arrived at Police Headquarters.

Detective Department

To whom it may concern. Watch the Langton Garage.
You may find Bryan [sic] Sullivan with his glasses off.
Keep an eye on the Montpellier Café operating in the
night in your supper-time.
Sorry to trouble you.
A Friend.

Interestingly, Nurse Sullivan's doctor – Dr Archibald Condor – had told Worth that when he saw her on 27 January 1938, she had mentioned to him the idea that the body at Tower Lodge might not have been that of her son. In Worth's opinion, "this statement was obviously made by her in view of the considerable alteration due to *post mortem* changes."

Andrew Soutar, a well-known novelist of the day, was specially commissioned by the *Daily Mail* to go to Cheltenham to describe his on-the-spot investigations and conclusions.

In his first article of 1 March 1938, he wrote:

The torso mystery is one that has set the whole country conjecturing. I have my theories about the network of mystery in regard to this torso case – and I do believe it to be a network in which many persons figured. At the moment, I am inclined to the opinion that the mystery will end in the disclosure of a sordid picture of modern life. Without betraying the whole of my theory I will say this: I do not think that the head belonging to that torso found in the river was either buried in the ground or thrown into water. Think that out!

The person who disposed of it, I should say, is a well-read man, if not well educated. He hadn't much time in which to construct what we will call an alibi, but he could think quickly. I should say that he had studied criminology or has some knowledge of the Near East and its religious observances.

The torso and the limbs that were found in the river were thrown there by somebody who took fright or funked it at the last moment. I am satisfied in my own mind that the man who concealed the head had no part in the plan of throwing the rest of the body over the parapet of a bridge. The man who hid the head of the victim is probably out of the country by this time, and I don't think he would take that head with him either.

What follows indicates that Soutar harboured no suspicion that the body at Tower Lodge was that of anyone other than Brian Sullivan. What suspicion he did harbour was that Sullivan's death was the result, not of suicide, but of murder.

It is essential to the master-brain that the weakest will among his associates must be got rid of. Well? Do you really believe that Brian Sullivan gassed himself? It is a theory, a suggestion on my part, that he did not commit suicide. The coroner's jury appeared to be satisfied that he took his life in that cottage, but it isn't only the brain of a fictionist that urges me to consider the possibility of his having been murdered.

I well recall the case of Norman Thorne*, who buried his victim in a Crowborough poultry run. Almost every inch of Norman Thorne's poultry run and garden was dug up … without yielding anything tangible. Then, one day, the diggers thrust aside the argument that it was ludicrous to dig under a growing bush, or a bush that was seemingly growing. The remains were unearthed.

Observe the cunning of the criminal mind. When in the stress of those horrific hours, when he was mutilating the body of the girl, Thorne could conceive of the investigators ridiculing the idea of a body lying beneath that bush. My theory has always been that the more intelligent a man, the more likely he is to make a mistake when he is trying to elude justice.

Again, when you have a number of persons conspiring to commit a crime, especially murder, the police as a general rule have a better chance of solving the mystery. Invariably there is a weak link in the human chain. One of the malefactors is dissatisfied; he threatens to

---

* Norman Thorne, aged 24, unsuccessful chicken farmer of Crowborough, Sussex. He was hanged in 1925 for the murder of his 23-year-old fiancée, Elsie Cameron.

betray the others. And the act of betraying brings to him a crazy sense of self-importance. He attracts publicity to himself, and there is always a prospect of receiving a lighter sentence than the others. Once a member of a criminal clique shows the slightest tendency to betray, the others are faced with the terrible alternative – "His life or ours?" If, as I suspect at this juncture, there were fairly well-educated men concerned in the torso mystery, they might have engaged one of greater coarseness to commit the actual deed. Having placed themselves in his power, and then doubting the wisdom of turning him adrift with his knowledge, they formed a cabal against him. And so it might go on, one murder following another …

Soutar had been in Cheltenham barely three days when he voiced the view, 'based on minute investigation and interrogation', that Brian Sullivan did not die in Tower Lodge.

He further opined: 'If the Home Office should order the exhumation of the body that was buried in the name of Brian Sullivan, it may be found that it isn't the body of Sullivan after all'.

The *Gloucester Citizen*, of 5 March 1938, informed its readers:

> Suggestions which have recently been current that Sullivan's body might have to be exhumed from the grave in Leckhampton churchyard are without foundation, and it is further stated that there is no intention on the part of the officials to adopt this course.

Soutar goes on to provide an account of his personal investigations bearing upon his theory that Brian Sullivan's death – if, he insists, it *was* Brian Sullivan's body – was not the result of suicide:

> He was found lying in death on a bed. The floorboards had been lifted in one corner and the gas-pipe cut. Cut with what? I am told that a screwdriver was 'present' as an exhibit at the inquest. Although I cannot find anyone who can say definitely that it was 'produced in evidence', it is implied that Sullivan severed the gas-pipe then lay down on the bed to await the end.
>
> Right. I called on the gas company, and here is the result: The gas-meter in that cottage demands a shilling in the slot. The idea flitted through my mind that it might be possible (a miracle, of course) to determine fingerprints on those coins, assuming that several were necessary for the deed that was contemplated. I asked the company: "What amount was in the meter when you cleared it?"
>
> "We haven't cleared it! Unless it has been tampered with, it is still there. We have accepted the intimation that it might be inadvisable to enter the cottage at this juncture."

The cut gas-pipe in Brian Sullivan's bedroom at Tower Lodge.

"How do you suppose that gas-pipe was cut?"

"Not having seen it, we cannot make a definite statement. But we were called to the cottage last November, or early in December, to correct a leakage. Our men found that a length of piping under the floorboards (not necessarily in this particular room) had been gnawed by rats, and there had undoubtedly been an escape of gas. A new length of piping – known as compo, a mixture of lead and tin – was put in. The diameter of that piping would be half an inch or five-eighths."

I pursued: "Could that be cut fairly easily with a chisel or screwdriver?"

"You could cut it with a knife to such an extent that it might break fairly easily," was the reply.

I then wanted to know what could be expected for a shillingsworth of gas. Answer: 216 cubic feet.

Would a shillingsworth be enough to cause death if it was allowed to escape into that bedroom – a small amount? Doubtful if it would do more than 'haze' a person.

I want to know how many shillings there were in that meter. I would like to see the contents, but I do not doubt that the police have followed up that line of action and must have good reason for not disclosing any information about it.

Soutar had, in fact, already found the police to be distinctly unco-operative. He had asked Inspector Worth to let him go into Tower Lodge to test a theory in his own way. The Inspector had emphatically refused to allow anyone in. Like any reporter worth his salt, Soutar had persisted, asking what the secrecy was for. Worth's retort had been curt, although not impolite.

"I am in charge and I will not allow anyone in the place. I know you as a novelist, and I am sure that you would not be an obstructionist, but the cottage is forbidden to anybody until my inquiries are through."

But Soutar was by now evolving his own very firm scenario.

If the supposedly neurotic Sullivan did actually gas himself, he went about the grim, self-appointed task with stoicism not to be found in one man in a million. The windows were closed. There was no tubing to carry the gas to his lips. We are asked to assume [that] Sullivan calmly lay down on the bed and awaited the fatal effect of the gas when it should have completely filled the room, mixing with whatever oxygen there might have been there.

By 4 March, Soutar was not only convinced that Sullivan did not take his own life, but also that,

If only to satisfy the increasing demands of the ratepayers of Cheltenham – and they have to pay the cost of the official investigation – the Home Office should order the exhumation of the body said to be that of Sullivan, which lies in the churchyard here. Those persons who knew Sullivan personally say that he was a short man of about five foot five inches at the outside. He was slender of build, almost to the point of delicacy.

Soutar goes on to report that when the body was removed from Tower Lodge to the mortuary, where it had to await the usual shell for interment, the pathologist of Cheltenham Hospital, Dr Thomas Bones Hamilton-Heslett, conducted the customary *post mortem* examination, and presumably opened the lungs had been opened for inspection, surely betraying without question the actual cause of death.

That the body might swell after death is perfectly acceptable. What is not acceptable, is that its height and weight should be enormously increased.

Soutar wrote:

> I have established the fact that the coffin employed was adequate for
> a man of 6ft! An official (not attached to the police) was able to give
> me the report of the orderly who helped to place the body in the coffin
> at the mortuary.
>
> The orderly said: "I didn't know Sullivan, but the dead man I helped
> to place in the shell must have been much taller than me, and I am five
> foot eight and a half inches. But it wasn't the height of the man that
> struck me so much as his bulk. I had understood that Sullivan was
> small, but this man's body was big and bulky – extraordinarily so."

Soutar adds: 'A man who knew Sullivan intimately assures me that Sullivan
weighed 9st and that the man who was put in the coffin must have weighed 15st
– which corroborates the orderly's statement.'

One thing of which Andrew Soutar felt certain was that Brian Sullivan had not
died at Tower Lodge. He believed that he had been killed elsewhere – London he
considered to be a likely place – and his dead body 'brought to that dread room'
at the Lodge. He also thought that, 'the torso of Captain Butt was brought from
a distance – probably London. Brian Sullivan may have helped to heave it over
the Haw Bridge into the River Severn'.

But, he asks:

> Was it the design of the master-brain that the remains should be
> abandoned or jettisoned in that fashion? Or would he have some
> different depository in mind? Something else happened that night.
> The persons in the fateful car that held the ghastly thing probably took
> fright and in frenzied haste got rid of the remains at the first likely
> place – a river with a swift-flowing tide. From that point, Sullivan
> might have lost his nerve completely or his associates feared that he
> would. He may have threatened to tell the police. And the master-
> brain would make a mental note that there was one person too many.

Returning to his main theme, Soutar repeats: 'The body buried in the name of
Brian Sullivan should be exhumed. I say that if it is he in that coffin, he was put
to death. If it is not he – where is Sullivan? And who is the unknown in the
coffin?'

Soutar makes a further interesting point:

> When the body of the gassed man was found in that cottage, his
> [Brian's] car was on the drive and facing *into* the drive. From one who
> was familiar with his personal habits in the handling of his car, I
> gather that Sullivan, such being the awkward contour of the hillside,

always *reversed* from the roadway, and so backed into the drive. What construction do I place on that seemingly minor incident?

There are clear indications that Chief Inspector Worth and his minions were unhappy with Andrew Soutar's lone hand investigations:

> I advanced the argument that Brian Sullivan was murdered after careful inquiry, a study of the evidence given at the inquest, and a collating of what may be regarded by some as minor facts. Officials now say to me: "We cannot understand your motive in pressing this or that."
> My answer to that is: "If you will give me an assurance that there is absolutely no necessity to exhume that body – giving the assurance on some sound irrefutable knowledge that is in your possession – I am prepared to stop my efforts in that direction."

Soutar closed his inquiry emphasising the question of whether the Severn torso was that of Butt or not.

Other reasons were beginning to emerge suggestive of the need to uplift Sullivan's coffin.

At twelve noon on 14 February 1938, PC Mills, of Gloucester CID, had telephoned to Cheltenham to inform the Torso team of an anonymous letter received that morning. Addressed to the Chief Constable, Gloucester, and bearing a Gloucester postmark – '12.2.1938 – 4.30pm' – it read:

> *Dear Sir,*
> *May I suggest that the missing head of the Torso found in the river Severn at Haw Bridge is possibly in the coffin and that the body contained therein is not Sullivan's but the man who assisted him. Why not look and see.*
> *Yours, Severnite.*

Two days later, 16 February 1938, another letter arrived. It was addressed to 'The Detective in Charge. Haw Bridge Torso Mystery'.

> *c/o Colonel H. W. L*
> *Stanley Hall,*
> *Selsley,*
> *Near Stroud.*

> *Sir,*
> *May I suggest that the remains of Captain Butt's body may have been placed in the coffin of Brian Sullivan and buried. Would it have been possible for anyone to have entered the home of Brian Sullivan while he lay dead in his*

coffin and placed the missing remains of Capt. Butt's body at the dead man's feet. This suggestion may not help you. And yet it may, as why was the coffin 6 ft. in length when the dead man was only 5 ft. 4" which I have read from the papers. I hope this suggestion will lead you to some clue.
I remain Sir,
Yours faithfully,
Allan Stuart.
(Brother)

Late on the night of 16 April 1938, an anonymous man telephoned the *Sunday Dispatch* and asked for the news editor. He said he was speaking from Brighton.

"If you want to find the head of the Cheltenham torso, and possibly the hand," he said, "you will have to exhume Sullivan. They are in Sullivan's coffin." And the mystery caller, who would not give his name, rang off before any further questions could be put to him.

This must surely be the most extraordinary case in the annals of British crime. Not only do we not know whether Brian Sullivan was a murderer, or murdered, or even if he was in fact dead. Neither do we know that the victim, the torso dragged forth from the Severn, was definitely Captain Butt. Moreover, as we shall see, the whole question of motive is a maze of conflicting uncertainties.

Chapter Eighteen

Scandal

Rumour was, as we have seen in the last chapter, rife in Cheltenham. The sister of Rumour is Scandal. And Scandal was very much alive and hard-kicking in the town.

It was, once again, Andrew Soutar who was to give concrete expression to the vague and difficult-to-pin-down whisperings that filled the uneasy air.

Born in 1879, Soutar was, at the age of 58, a man of considerable sophistication and worldly experience. The author of some fifty novels and many film plays, he had travelled extensively throughout both the Near and Far East, Spain, Portugal, and America. He had served in the Air Force in World War One, and had been despatched to North Russia in 1919.

In the course of his reportings from Cheltenham, he had reached some very firm conclusions. The trouble was, as he himself expressed it: 'I have my own opinions, and I stand by them. But the law will not allow me to say more than I have said here.' In other words, he was unable to supply the pros and cons regarding those conclusions which he had reached.

Consider what he had to say on 1 March 1938, the day after his arrival in Cheltenham; his very first report.

> Here in this beautiful town of Cheltenham, a seat of learning, a health resort for invalids, the death of Brian Sullivan, gigolo in a London house of entertainment, is the axis of a small unsavoury circle out of which rises the hideous idea of perversion linked with the more hideous word, blackmail.

The use of the term 'blackmail' is clear enough, but to just what Soutar is referring when he writes in so general and unspecific a way of 'perversion' is, at this stage, anybody's guess. One suspects that he is casting a wider net than that of simple homo-eroticism, but to exactly what class or classes of perverse conduct he is alluding remains opaque.

So far, so vague.

On 3 March 1938, he wrote:

> Brian Sullivan was a member of a vicious circle which included both men, and possibly, women, who were making money out of the relatives of weak-willed creatures in their clutches. There would be a master-brain sufficiently cunning to let the tools do the actual work.

He would exercise supervision and be on the alert for any sign of 'ratting' or 'squeaking'.

Again, everything is couched in the vaguest way. The 'master-brain' is conjured forth out of a clear blue sky; not a hint as to identity. The peccancies of the 'weak-willed creatures' remain undefined.

But, on 4 March, Soutar's copy hardens. Delivered is an actual accusation: 'Brian Sullivan was done to death by members, or a member, of the vicious circle into which he had slithered his curiously complex character'.

Yes ... but ... into *what* vicious circle? Mr Soutar's reader is still up in the desert air.

However, in the *Daily Mail*, of Monday 7 March 1938, Soutar commits to print that which is to open him up to an accusation of libel.

> I am playing a lone hand in the investigation of this mystery. I have motored hundreds of miles in pursuit of elusive clues, and questioned so many persons likely to have some knowledge bearing on the problem that it would be unfair to myself to abandon even the tiniest argument I have advanced ... If my theories as a whole had met with no more than official complacency I might have been disturbed in mind. It is part of official diplomacy to let the other fellow 'talk through his hat' on the principle that such publicity tends to create a false sense of security in the mind of the man they seek to arrest.

He then proceeds:

> I will now reconstruct the whole crime as I see it, basing my statements on evidence given and collected, inspection of many places, and natural deduction.
>
> The evidence at the inquest on Sullivan implies that the cottage [Tower Lodge] was unoccupied from January 10 to January 17. The latter date is given by the pathologist as the approximate date when Sullivan died.
>
> I am going to say that between January 10 and January 17 that supposed silent cottage was a hive of criminal activity. Floorboards in the hall were raised and a hole dug. A hole was cut in the plaster of the bathroom wall and re-plastered. Obviously all this did not take place before the death of Captain Butt.
>
> Now I am advised to keep in mind the possibility of Brian Sullivan's being fairly strong in spite of his lack of stature. He is said to have been something of an athlete, but could he have accomplished all that dread work in the cottage by himself? Would a man, supposedly half demented by the fear of Captain Butt's death being discovered,

undress, put on his pyjamas, cut the gas-pipe with a screwdriver and lie down on the bed to await death? Remember, there had been no questioning of him by the police about the Butt torso. [Sullivan had been dead at least a week before the torso's discovery.]

I offer this explanation. That cottage, Tower Lodge, was used principally for illegal practices in which women were concerned. Captain Butt, I reason, was killed because there had been a quarrel about the dividing of the spoils. What of Brian Sullivan? I suggest he was done to death by gassing outside that cottage. There had been more quarrels. [Among other members of the 'vicious ring'.] The body was placed on the bed and the gas-pipe cut to convey the idea that he had committed suicide.

The following day's paper, of 8 March, contained this tantalising statement by Soutar: 'I have been making inquiries at the London end and have proof that Sullivan and Butt were frequent companions in the West End'.

Just that. No proof was then – or ever – forthcoming.

He does, however, confide in the 11 March issue:

I slipped back to London to make inquiries in the West End of women of a certain type. Butt and Sullivan were known to them. I returned with the conviction that illegal practices were carried out in Tower Lodge, that women were brought from a distance. I had one or two callers of a type that made me wonder how many psychopaths were involved. Today there is dread in the hearts of many young women that their secret may be revealed. They enlisted the services of Butt and Sullivan and others, and now they find themselves in the soul-corroding atmosphere of blackmail.

I end with these vital questions:
• Was Brian Sullivan a suicide or was he murdered by a stronger will that regarded him as a possible tell-tale?
• Was it Brian Sullivan who was found in the sealed cottage?
• What was the *true relationship* between Sullivan and Captain Butt?
• Was the Severn torso that of Butt?
• Who cut the gas-pipe?

Let us restate in plain language, dispensing with all the interlinear insinuendo, the picture presented by Andrew Soutar; the picture which was to be so resented by Nurse Sullivan.

Brian Sullivan, aka Byron Smith, in the natural course of his job came to know a number of young ladies, both of wealth and of good society, some of whom found themselves, as a result of youth's folly, in a very delicate situation. Nowadays, to have a 'love child', or what used in more robust-speaking times to be called 'a bastard', is virtually – if not virtuously – a status symbol; a badge to share, wear and vaunt with free-wheeling actresses and pop stars. But in the England of the 1930s, it was a badge of shame, a social disaster bearing a stigma which brought ostracism, and sometimes even suicide, in its wake.

For the relief of such nightmares, fallen ladies of means were willing and able to pay well. No doubt in the importunity of the situation they neglected to heed the possibility of blackmail, which could well follow, providing Brian Sullivan – and his ilk – with money enough, to fund, not only frequent and lavish parties in Radlett Place, but also the acquiring of fresh properties in, for example Polperro – as well as more than one discreet cottage in respectable Gloucestershire – for letting out at splendidly pocket-lining rents.

A smooth-running abortion racket of this kind would ideally require the services of a medically experienced, although not necessarily medically qualified, practitioner – such as Nurse Sullivan. It would also need somewhere where the operation could be carried out, and where the patient could afterwards convalesce – such as Tower Lodge, technically tenanted by Brian's mother.

All this could be held, *was* held by Nurse Sullivan, to amount to a libel on her by Associated Newspapers Limited, and Andrew Soutar. An action in libel was duly brought by her against both parties in April 1939.

On 21 April 1939, the settlement of the action was announced. Mrs Sarah Elizabeth Emma Sullivan, described as 'an unregistered nurse, who specialised in mental cases', sued for damages in respect of two articles written by the second defendant and published in the issues of the *Daily Mail,* of 7 and 14 March 1938.

The case was brought in the High Court of Justice, King's Bench Division, before Mr Justice Greaves-Lord and a special jury. Mr Gilbert Beyfus, KC, and Mr RE Manningham Buller appeared for the plaintiff. Mr Norman Birkett, KC, Mr Valentine Holmes, and Mr Harmsworth for the defendants.

Announcing the settlement, Mr Beyfus said that Mrs Sullivan was a woman who for some 30 years down to last year had lived in Cheltenham. Although she had not been mentioned by name in the articles complained of, they were to the effect that Tower Lodge, her house, was used principally for illegal practices in which women were concerned, and that Brian Sullivan and his friend Captain Butt were members of a vicious ring concerned with this unsavoury aspect of modern life.

It was further suggested that women who subjected themselves to these practices, which clearly meant abortion, were afterwards the victims of blackmail. It was repeated time after time that there was a gang concerned in the matter. Whatever might have been the intention of Mr Soutar, a great number of people drew the conclusion that these articles meant that the plaintiff – who was the mother of one of the men and the employee of the other and the tenant of the house referred to, and who, above all things, was an unregistered nurse – was a party to the abominable practices alleged. Life in Cheltenham had become impossible for her, and she had to move to London. In those circumstances she was bound to bring the present action, not for the purpose of making money, but in order to vindicate her reputation.

The defendants had met her in the spirit which was to be expected from the *Daily Mail*. They were prepared to say, as the fact was, that the plaintiff was a woman of unblemished character and stainless reputation. In their defence, they never suggested that there was anything to be said against her, but only pleaded that the words complained of were not defamatory, but that if they were they were not defamatory of the plaintiff and did not refer to her. They were now prepared to make it clear that the words used were never intended to apply to the plaintiff. They were willing to agree that there should be judgment for her for the substantial but by no means excessive sum of £1,000, representing £500 for each of the two libels complained of, and to pay 500 guineas in respect of her costs.

Mr Birkett, on behalf of the defendants, said that in view of the full statement made by Mr Beyfus it was unnecessary for him to say much. From the narrative given it was clear that the matter out of which the publication complained of arose was one of absorbing public interest, and he dared say that his Lordship would be able to take judicial notice of the fact that there was a great vogue at the present time for detective writings. When Mr Soutar, a novelist of distinction and a specialist in matters of crime, investigated the circumstances he put forward certain theories. Counsel wanted to make it clear that, so far as Mr Soutar and the newspaper were concerned, it was with the greatest surprise that they learned that it was considered that Mrs Sullivan's name could be brought into the matter at all. Mr Soutar never had the smallest intention of reflecting on her, while the newspaper took the view that it did not agree with the construction which was put on the words by the plaintiff.

It was recognised, however, that that view might be taken, and when Mr Beyfus, on behalf of the plaintiff, said that such a view had been taken, Mr Birkett agreed that if the matters stated could apply to the plaintiff they were of a very grave character. The defendants desired him to say that there never was any ground for imagining that the words applied to the plaintiff. Her character was quite unsullied. He desired to express the deep regrets of the defendants for having put forward the matter complained of.

Mr Justice Greaves-Lord concluded the proceedings saying that it had been made perfectly clear that that construction was never intended and that what remained to be settled was judgement in the terms of the settlement.

Nurse Sullivan must have felt well pleased with her out of court victory, her apology, and her £1000 in hand.

One must, of course, accept for what they are worth those legally essential denials of Mr Soutar's. Unquestionably, at the time of writing his on-the-spot reports from Cheltenham, he suspected Nurse Sullivan's involvement, but to precisely what extent is another matter. Unfortunately, his newspaper writings apart, he has left us no clue, no indication of the sources from which he garnered the justificatory – if, indeed, it was justificatory – material for the fairly fierce theories which he publicly delivered.

We do know that his hunting-ground was the West End of London, which, in the 1930s, although less hectically perilous than in the 1920s' days of characters such as Brilliant Chang and Eddie Manning, and victims, Billie Carleton, Freda Kempton and Brenda Dean Paul, was still a pretty dangerous place. Soho was especially a territory of dubious daytime drinking clubs, and night clubs, infested with drug-peddlers, pimps, perverts, prostitutes and their attendant parasitic blackmailers.

On 9 October 1938, 31-year-old Mrs Lynda Woods, an attractive blonde dance hostess, was found dead at Drake House, Dolphin Court, Westminster, in a gas-filled room of her luxury flat overlooking the Thames.

A few hours before she died, she had received a telephone call. That call had made her cry out, "I can't stand it. I'll kill myself. I'll commit suicide". And now, there she lay on green silk cushions, cold to the touch, and clasping a stuffed toy dog in her arms.

Her friend and confidante, Miss Patricia Palmer, of Rodney House, Dolphin Square, told a *Daily Mirror* reporter: "Lynda was being blackmailed. The blackmailer was threatening to show her new fiancé certain letters which she had previously written to another man".

The *Daily Mirror* reported a close friend of hers as saying: "I noticed a great change come over her. She seemed worried and depressed. Then one day she whispered, "I am being blackmailed for a hundred pounds." A few weeks ago she told me she had paid the price of silence, but I was worried lest the blackmailer should repeat his demands."

The *Mirror* revealed:

> An earlier friend of Mrs Woods' was Brian Sullivan. He and Mrs. Woods occasionally attended parties as dance partners, and at one time they considered opening a select dance club in the West End. They went for long rides in the country in motor-cars which Sullivan was able to borrow from friends.

Brian Sullivan was nine months dead by the time of Lynda Woods' self-destruction, nevertheless that tragic event does provide a rationale for Soutar's suspicions as to the sort of thing that was going on. And who is to say the letters regarding which she was being blackmailed had not perhaps been written by her to Brian, and had fallen into the hands of one of his criminous associates after his death?

Posted in Hereford at 6pm on 15 February 1938, an anonymous letter, marked 'Confidential', signed 'Yours Truly, Public Spirit', and addressed to the Chief Inspector of Police, Cheltenham, opened with the enigmatic observation: 'I wonder if it would be worth your while to make a search of piggeries in Cheltenham or Charlton Kings – particularly at Bafford Farm'.

'Public Spirit' went on to explain that he or she had read in the newspapers of a Miss B Dighton, whose name had cropped up in the Torso Case. The letter informed the police that Miss Dighton had an aunt, a Miss (*sic*) M Dighton, who kept kennels at Charlton Kings and who probably knew Brian Sullivan. Intriguingly, the letter went on to explain that Mrs M Dighton had once remarked to the sender that if she had a body to dispose of she would give it to pigs as they left no trace of anything – admittedly this had been said in a half joking way. It seemed that there was a Dr Dighton and also a brother in the family, and they were well known people in Charlton Kings, much visited by what the sender referred to as 'all manner of odd looking people'.

A report, dated 20 February 1938, arrived from Detective Sergeant William Rennie, of the Bucks Constabulary, Slough Police Station. It informed the Chief Constable, Gloucestershire, that a Mr George Collins, a brush salesman, of 23 Kings Road, Slough, had read in the papers that the whereabouts of a girl dancer, Peggy Dighton, were being sought. He stated that, about two years ago, a dancer of that name was living at The Barge House, Raymead Road, Maidenhead, and at that time used to advertise in a periodical called *The Stage*. Mr Collins thought that information as to her present whereabouts might be obtained at that address.

Enquiries set in train at Maidenhead by the Berkshire Constabulary had, by 24 February, established that the parents of the girl dancer had resided at The Barge Club, Lower Cookham Road, Maidenhead, until about six months or so before, when they moved to, it was believed, Blackpool.

On 7 March 1938, there was handed to Inspector Hancock, of the Cheltenham Force, the following letter, undated but believed to have been written a year or two previously by one Betty Dighton to a Mrs Walton.

Plough Hotel,
Cheltenham Spa,
Glos.

Dear Mrs Walton,
    This is a rather difficult letter to write and I hope you won't mind.
    The position – I put it plainly – is this. I am three months pregnant. It is absolutely imperative for me to get rid of it and quickly. I have tried every sort of medicine to no avail and so the only course left is abortion. I asked Nick Millward, who is a great friend of mine, if he knew of anyone in Birmingham and Cheltenham who might do something for me and he told me to come to you as you were the only person he could trust and who might be able to help me. If you <u>do</u> know of anyone I should be most terribly grateful if you could tell me. I want if possible to have it done this afternoon. I am sending Nigel Mould, my fiancé, up to you with this, but as you can understand, I am desperate as my family <u>must not</u> know.
    Sincerely Yours, Betty Dighton.

By 1938, Mrs Walton was employed as a secretary at Westons Limited, Biscuit Manufacturers, Slough, and was separated from her husband. It was her estranged husband who handed the letter to the police. The mention in it of Nick Millward, known to have been connected with Brian Sullivan and others, was what particularly interested the detectives.

Letters from the public continued to flow in. A widow's mite, addressed to Cheltenham's Chief Constable, reached his headquarters on 5 March 1938. The letter explained that the 'scraps' of overheard conversation which the correspondent was sending, were to add to the other pieces of the 'jigsaw puzzle', in the hope that they might be of some help. He explained that

> A man who was doing some work for me said: "Curiously enough,
> my wife employs the same charwoman as Mrs Sullivan, and she told
> my wife that Sullivan's mother was not married and that Brian had
> said if he ever found out who his father was, he would kill him. Then
> my own helper said, 'I have been told that girls used to go up to the
> home [Tower Lodge] for illegal operations.'" I know no more, and as
> a widow I do not wish to be drawn into the trouble.

He did not think it was Sullivan lying under the wreaths in the churchyard, although he had been criticised for offering suggestions as regards such 'sordid matters'.

Couched in a rather more authoritative vein was the following communication:

12 Ladbroke Road,
Notting Hill Gate,
W11
Confidential

To The Chief of Police.   *8.3.38*

Dear Sir,
Some time ago I wrote and suggested if the body presumed to be Sullivan was
exhumed it would simplify matters etc. but evidently you did not think my idea
feasible.
I am glad Andrew Soutar is away at the Paris [Probably 'Exhibition', original
script is indecipherable]. *He is a brilliant writer. May I suggest Sullivan and*
Captain Butt may have been on very intimate terms – the [indecipherable]
dressed as a woman? There are other theories.
I am the daughter-in-law of the late Sir George Savage, mental specialist, have
lived always in the Far East and often worked with detectives and am avid
reader of crime.
Sincerely Yours, Helen Savage.

The *Empire News*, of Sunday 20 March 1938, contained an, all things considered, extraordinary article from the pen of Bernard O'Donnell:

> The police are checking up on certain people in London in the company of whom Captain Butt and Brian Sullivan are known to have spent much time.
>
> The police are also in possession of definite information regarding the homosexual habits of Captain Butt and have been investigating this angle during the past few days. It is known that he was a member of a coterie of perverts in Cheltenham who are keeping sternly silent in order not to be drawn into the present inquiry. That is why the police have encountered such difficulty in tracing the movements of the missing captain round about January 4 when he disappeared from his home.
>
> I am also in a position to state that the police are in possession of the information that Captain Butt at one time took part in black magic rites and ceremonies held at a house in Cheltenham. I have spoken with a man who accompanied the captain to this house and witnessed certain rites, which he described to me:
>
> "I did not know anything about black magic at the time I went with Captain Butt, and it was not till afterwards that he explained to me the significance of what we had seen. It was a large house run by an elderly but remarkably well-preserved woman. In one room which was heavily draped and in semi-darkness the floor was marked with a circle in which was a cross. There was also an altar-like structure on which were candlesticks and a number of torn and mutilated Bibles.
>
> Captain Butt explained afterwards that everything in that room – Bibles, candlesticks, crucifixes, in fact everything, had been stolen from churches. He told me that desecration of anything holy was one of the main objects of those gathered together in that house. I have never known such ghastly rites as were carried out in that place. Coming from various parts of the room, shrouded in darkness, I could hear the beating of flesh upon flesh, accompanied by the hysterical, almost maniacal shrieks of women. I should mention that for the best part everyone there was naked. I could not imagine what it was all about, for I was in a state of horror at the cries I heard, which were more like those of beasts than anything human. Captain Butt did not appear to mind it in the least, and in fact seemed to enjoy the experience."
>
> As I have stated, all this information is in the hands of the police, and they are endeavouring to find out whether the known perversion of Captain Butt has any relation to the Haw Bridge mystery.

Chapter Nineteen

An Unknown Male Now Lying Dead

The inquest on 'an unknown male person, now lying dead' – otherwise the Cheltenham Torso, officially unidentified, but which, there was little doubt in anybody's mind, was that of William Bernard Butt – was opened on 8 February 1938. After a series of formal adjournments, it reopened on Tuesday 29 March 1938, at Cheltenham Police Station.

The Police Court, wherein the coroner, Mr JD Lane, sat with a jury, was jam-packed, not a seat to be had. The only solicitor present, *qua* a solicitor, was Mr J Eric Green, of Ivens, Thompson & Green, Clarence Parade, Cheltenham, who attended with his partner, Theodore Leslie Thompson, of Albert Road, Cheltenham, who was to be a witness in the case.

Exhibits were piled high on a table: an axe; a number of sealed glass jars, including those containing the recovered right arm and both legs of the torso; glass phials; several brownish-white bricks and half-bricks; pieces of frayed rope and twine; a brown check overcoat; and a pair of brown shoes.

The coroner began by reminding the jury – all male, all Cheltonians – of their oath, and told them that they must disregard all that they might have seen or heard concerning the case over the previous weeks.

He then called evidence of the finding, on 10 January 1938, of the pieces of flesh and bone, the canvas shoe, and the glove on the pavement of Haw Bridge, the parapet of which bore bloodstains. The flesh and bone, sealed in a glass container, were shown to the jury.

Dr Edgar Norman Davey, the pathologist to whom the examination and identification of these fragments had been entrusted, and whose fundamental error on 12 January had misled all the authorities concerned until the trawling up of the torso on 3 February, was summoned to offer an explanation.

Admitting that it was "in something of a rush" that he had decided that the blood was animal rather than human, he went on, like any other bad workman, to blame his tools. It might have been, he implied, that the precipitating serum which he had used in his first test was faulty. At any rate, a second testing with "some fresh precipitating serum gave a strongly positive reaction," showing it to be human blood after all. Fortunately for the errant Dr Davey, the Court made no reference to his initial statement that his original tests had been exhaustive and had extended over many hours.

Next, evidence of the recovery of the miscellany of remains was provided by Alfred Charles Chamberlain, who trawled up the handless right arm on 5 February and George Poole and John Edgar Bevan, who brought the right and left legs respectively out of the Severn on 8 February. The also handless left arm was not recovered by Chamberlain until 19 February.

There was a stir of expectant excitement as the celebrated Home Office pathologist of the day, Sir Bernard Spilsbury, carrying a bundle of typewritten documents and a small biscuit tin, made his entrance – one is almost tempted to say without a do 'stage right'. Moving with practised ease to the witness-box, he commenced a smooth recitation of the detailed condition of, and inferences to be scientifically drawn from, the torso and limbs.

The trunk, he said, was that of a rather heavily built man. He had found extensive subcutaneous bruising – four distinct bruises on the back, and another on the back of the left hip. It was clearly established that the limbs and the trunk were of the same body.

Endeavouring to supply a visual image of the whole and living man thus piecemeal represented by the chance dredgings-up, Sir Bernard estimated his height to have been probably somewhere between five foot seven inches and five foot nine inches. His hair was most likely medium brown in colour, and might have been partly grey. The muscular development of the limbs was that of a vigorous and active individual. While the absence of serious disease and the development of the muscles and bones showed that he had not been a very old man, the greying of the hair, some degree of disease of the heart, and the onset of commencement of arthritis, indicated his being of middle age, perhaps about 50. When asked by the coroner for the approximate weight of the man, Spilsbury suggested that, very approximately, it would have been around 12 or 13 stone. It might even have been rather more.

As to the cause of death, examination had yielded nothing. There were, as he had said, no signs of any serious disease, and there were no indications of poisoning. He thought, however, the bruising to be of considerable importance. The bruises were distributed almost entirely on the back of the trunk and limbs, and they had all been produced shortly before death. The bruise at the base of the spine was the result of great violence. It was an injury of the kind that would be produced if the man had been struck in the back by a rapidly moving motor vehicle. The bruises on the upper part of the back could have been produced in the same way and at the same time. It was equally possible that such injuries could be caused by a fall from a height, but in that case he would have expected to find rather more injuries to the limbs. Sir Bernard further gave it as his opinion that the torso must have been in the water for at least two or three weeks.

The coroner, referring to the suggestion that the injuries might have been caused by a vehicle or a fall, asked whether they could have been resultant from some other form of violence. Spilsbury replied that the injuries were not the type of bruises expected to be found as a consequence of violence with an instrument in the ordinary way. Blows with a stick or anything of that sort were unlikely to produce such injuries.

Dealing with the question of dismemberment, Sir Bernard said that it had been carried out very roughly, by cutting through the tissues and by the use of a hatchet. Asked if such an act would require great strength, he replied that any ordinary adult could have done it. The coroner asked if the lifting of the trunk over the parapet with the bricks attached to it would have demanded great strength. Spilsbury confirmed that the trunk would have been a heavy weight, and that it was more likely to have been put over the bridge by two people.

Sir Bernard then opened the biscuit tin which he had brought with him and picked out a bone. Holding it up for the jury to see, he said:

"A portion of the right thigh-bone with various fragments of broken bone fitted to it as far as they could be. I produce these bones to show the hatchet marks."

He then walked slowly round the semi-circular jury table, showing the bone to each juryman, asking them to observe the row of notches.

The axe from the exhibits' table was handed to Sir Bernard, who produced another bone from the tin, and, holding the axe to it, told the jury that the centre of the blade fitted very well into the cut. A juryman asked whether the axe had been found at Tower Lodge, which Spilsbury confirmed to be his understanding.

Police evidence was then given that a pair of brown shoes belonging to Captain Butt, found upstairs at Tower Lodge, had been put on to the feet of the recovered legs. They were size eight, and had proved to be a good fit.

PC Merry was called. In the course of his evidence he disclosed a statement said to have been made by Nurse Sullivan. He said that when he had found Brian Sullivan dead at Tower Lodge, on 24 January 1938, he had noticed that floor bricks in a passage at the Lodge had been taken up.

"I asked Mrs Sullivan if she could give an explanation. She said that when Brian was home he was always making some improvement to the place and he was going to put some cement down there to keep the rats out."

Merry had also asked why the bricks were put in the bathroom, and Mrs Sullivan had replied that they were put there so that they could be kept dry. The coroner questioned the fact that Merry had not mentioned the bricks at the inquest held on Brian Sullivan. Merry justified that by saying that at the time the bricks had not seemed suspicious considering Mrs Sullivan's answer.

Detective Sergeant James Shewry, who had given evidence previously, was recalled. The coroner asked him if, when he first went to Tower Lodge in the torso inquiry, he had seen bricks in the bathroom.

Shewry replied no. In the bathroom there had been a quantity of rubble only. He had observed that the brickwork of the bathroom at one point did indicate that something had recently been removed, replaced and cemented. This portion of the wall was taken down by the police.

Adjourning the inquest until 5 April, the coroner asked that the unheard witnesses be bound over. Nurse Sullivan, dressed in black, was brought forward into the court and bound over with the other witnesses.

When the inquest court reconvened on 5 April, the first witness called was Mrs Mary Agnes Hobson, of Wolverton, Captain Butt's widowed sister. She confirmed

Nurse Sullivan in court dress.

most of Sir Bernard Spilsbury's hazarded description of the dead man whose torso and limbs he had examined, although patently differing in some details. She affirmed that her brother had been of medium height, strong, muscular, squarely built, though rather thin, and, she thought, took size nine shoes. He had dark brown hair, slightly greying. His weight would have been, she guessed, about twelve stone, and he was aged 55.

A small piece of cloth and a brown check overcoat, the latter found buried beneath the scullery passageway at Tower Lodge, were handed to Mrs Hobson for her inspection. She said that she was sure that Captain Butt had been wearing that coat when, after staying over Christmas at her house, he and his wife had left for home on 3 January 1938. The piece of cloth was similar to that of a buff-coloured suit he was wearing.

Mrs Sullivan, who wore a black costume, black hat, and a white woollen jumper, to which was pinned a bunch of primroses and violets, was called next.

Telling again, along with other significant matters, the story of her leasing of Tower Lodge, of her life with the Butts, of the Captain's disappearance, and of her discovery of her son's dead body, she was in the box for a gruelling three hours and 20 minutes. Twice she broke into sobs. A policewoman gave her water and brought smelling-salts to her.

Questioned by the coroner about her son's financial position, she told him: "I can't remember through the great strain I've been through". She agreed, however, that she had made a statement that in the past four years she had given him about £360, and that she regarded these sums as loans. He had paid back £17.

On the day after she found Brian dead, Mrs Sullivan had been given his wallet. She had passed it to the solicitor, Mr Thompson, who went through it in her presence. The coroner asked whether he had mentioned a receipt for a car. She confirmed that he had. The coroner continued:

"Some time later did he tell you that the receipt was for Captain Butt's car?"

Mrs Sullivan: "Yes."

"Do you know why that receipt should be in your son's wallet?"

"It is a great mystery to me."

The coroner then asked whether Mr Thompson had told her that he had found the log book.

Mrs Sullivan: "Yes. It was a still greater surprise to me."

The coroner observed that the log book was in the case containing Brian Sullivan's private papers and asked her for a possible explanation as to why. She could offer no reason.

The coroner inquired of her whether she had ever at any time reported that Captain Butt was away. She said that she had not.

"The only thing I said was that he would be away at the time of the tragedy of my losing my dear boy. I had not reported him missing. Why should I? He was nothing to me."

True, no doubt. But hardly the most tactful or sympathy eliciting of answers.

The coroner asked Mrs Sullivan to describe Captain Butt.

"A little above medium height, with biggish bones. I should describe him as decidedly a skinny man. He had brown hair, and he was not grey," she told him.

Next, the coroner referred to a previous statement she had made, claiming that she thought Captain Butt had gone on a cruise. He asked her to confirm this, which she did, saying that she had heard him state as much. When asked if she was aware of his making any preparations or not, Mrs Sullivan said, "Oh, no. If he were making any preparations he would not let me know. He was a very secretive man." The coroner asked why she was not suspicious when she found that her son's dog had been left in the car. Mrs Sullivan parried skilfully: "Well, you know what young men are!"

The questioning turned to the issue of Brian's possible money troubles. Referring back to the inquest on her son, at which Mrs Sullivan had been asked about any financial difficulties that Brian might have experienced, the coroner wanted to know why she had not mentioned the £300 advance she had given him. She excused herself, saying that she had not considered the amount a concern. It had not worried either Brian or herself.

At the conclusion of Nurse Sullivan's evidence, the coroner said that the Court would have a 25-minute break, until 5.30pm.

When the proceedings resumed, George Benjamin Griffiths, the attendant at the Regent Garage, in Regent Street, Cheltenham, took his place in the witness-box. He told the Court that at 10.40pm on 4 January 1938, a man, whom he did not know, brought Captain Butt's car into the garage saying that it would be left there for three nights. He had not seen the man since, and no one had been to the garage to collect the Daimler.

The coroner, summing up, said that there was no direct evidence to identify the torso as that of Captain William Bernard Butt.

"You may wonder," he said, addressing the jury, "why Mrs Butt has not been brought before you. I can assure you it is because of her unfortunate illness.

The first question you have to consider is the identity. Secondly, there is the question of the cause of death, and I should point out that such an eminent and experienced authority as Sir Bernard Spilsbury has not been able to suggest it."

The head, he went on to say, had not been found, and one could only suppose that that was where the fatal injuries were. The jury would be drawn to the irresistible conclusion that death was due to violence, because no one would go to the enormous amount of trouble and risk taken in the disposal of the body unless the violence were of an unlawful nature.

"I don't think that the impossibility of finding the cause of death should in itself preclude you from considering a verdict of murder or manslaughter, but I think you will feel it would be dangerous to bring in any such verdict in the circumstances. If you are satisfied that the house, Tower Lodge, played an important part in this matter, you will also consider that Brian Sullivan played some part in it."

But, he observed, apart from Brian Sullivan, no person had been implicated by the evidence as being concerned in the death of the unidentified man. Sir Bernard Spilsbury had said that it would be difficult for one person alone to move the body and put it into the river. The jury might be led to suspect that two persons might have had a hand in that, but there was no evidence to show who those persons might be. The only direct evidence connecting Tower Lodge with the torso seemed to be that the bricks, twine, and cord found on the various parts of the body were similar to bricks, twine, and cord which had been found by the police at Tower Lodge.

The jury went out at 6pm. They returned at 6.20pm with a unanimous decision, delivering an open verdict on the body of an unidentified person.

And that, officially at least, was that.

Chapter Twenty

Nurse Sullivan 'Tells All'

Well … not quite!

It was Bernard O'Donnell, crime reporter ubiquitous of the 1920s, 30s, and 40s, who netted the plump butterfly or downy moth, *née* Fribbins. Spiriting her off beyond the reach of his fellow Fleet Street scriveners' hands to a 'safe house' at Number 6 Hamilton Gardens, St John's Wood, he set to work 'ghosting' Nurse Sullivan's story for the *Empire News*.

Bernard O'Donnell, whom I knew all too briefly before his death at the age of 83 in February 1969, was, even among the giants and eccentrics of the Fleet Street of his day, a truly remarkable character. It was not just that he had been on the scene and reported pretty well every big murder case between 1923 and the first quinquennium of the 1940s. Neither was it because he was in the slightest degree ostentatious or a player to the gallery: *au contraire*, he was a quiet, inconspicuous man, but he was possessed of the most extraordinary ability to get right behind the scenes of a case, reach to the core, and 'shake hands with the heart' of the accused. It was his especial skill to establish warm, personal relationships with those intimately concerned in the affair. In fact, his experience of attending murder trials – a total of 321 of them over the years – went right back to the trial of Arthur Devereux in 1905. He had poisoned his wife and two children, packed their dead bodies in a trunk, and deposited it in a warehouse at Kensal Rise, North London. Other early classic trials which he had attended included those of Robert Wood (1907), Crippen (1910), Stinie Morrison (1911), and George Joseph 'Brides-in-the-Bath' Smith (1915).

O'Donnell never hunted with the pack. He was a lone newshound. He visited condemned killers in the death cell. He nursed their wives or relatives throughout the time of their ordeal. And he drew the dividend on his perfectly genuine sympathy and kindness to those in big trouble. The seaside house to which he and his wife retired contained a miniature Black Museum of relics and mementoes of his criminous career. There were sheaves of, always very personal, extremely grateful, letters from the prime actors in some of the century's most celebrated murder cases. The mementoes included Captain Butt's ivory-nobbed malacca walking stick and Brian Sullivan's watch, presented to him by a grateful Nurse Sullivan.

I Tell All

by

MRS. IRENE SULLIVAN

This great behind-the-scenes story of one of the most sensational cases of the country will appear

EXCLUSIVELY

IN TO-MORROW'S

SECRETS OF TOWER LODGE

CAPTAIN BUTT, AND MY SON BRIAN

MY ORDEAL IN THE "TORSO OF THE SEVERN" MYSTERY

EMPIRE NEWS

The National Sunday Newspaper

Mrs Irene Sullivan chose to put forward her version of events, through the pages of a popular Sunday newspaper.

Bernard O'Donnell, crime reporter ubiqitous. A close follower of the case, he ghost wrote Nurse Sullivan's story for the 'Empire News'.

Expressing herself through the practised and able pen of Bernard O'Donnell, Irene Sullivan elaborately wrote:

> At last I can break the silence of weeks and say all those things that I have been longing to say. For over six weeks I had to suffer the torture of knowing that I and my boy Brian – who but a few days before had been laid to rest in Leckhampton churchyard – were suspected of murder and even worse; deeds so dark that they could be only whispered or hinted at in veiled language.
>
> I know that in those early days of the inquiries into what has become known as 'The Torso Mystery', both Brian and myself were suspected of those things which were crystallised in the questions put to me during my three hours' ordeal in the witness-box at the inquest.
>
> I knew this from the questions which were asked me by the police. I make no complaint of this probing and questioning. I realise that the police had a duty to perform, and, knowing this, I never once during the six weeks I was living under police protection – entirely at my own request, I would explain – shut off from the outside world, did I ever refuse to see them on any occasion they desired an interview.

During that period I realised that every act and utterance of my boy and myself of recent months had been invested with an aura of suspicion. I am not so foolish as to shut my eyes to the fact that the amazing chain of circumstances – the disappearance of Captain Butt, the death of Brian under such peculiar circumstances, the finding of the torso, and the discoveries at Tower Lodge – to some extent warranted suspicion, but I do insist, and I shall later on show, that there were other mysterious circumstances which throw a different light on the matter.

Can you possibly doubt from the nature of the questions put to me at the inquest that the gravest suspicions attached to me in spite of the coroner's assurance that, apart from my boy Brian, no person had been implicated by the evidence as being concerned in the death of the unidentified man, or that the jury might be led to suspect that two persons might have had a hand in putting the body in the river?

Why had I not informed the relatives of Captain Butt of his disappearance? Why had I taken Mrs Butt to the pictures on the evening he vanished? Every little thing became suspicious, and the implication seemed to be that I had deliberately got Mrs Butt out of the way in order to make the way clear for those concerned in getting rid of Captain Butt, although no motive has ever been suggested why either Brian or myself should be interested in his going.

Why did I take Mrs Butt to Tower Lodge on January 24th, the day I found my boy dead? Even the fact that I took Mrs Butt to sleep at the Lodge on three or four occasions was a matter of suspicion, although, as I explained, she was a mental case, and though on occasions she became almost unmanageable in the presence of her husband, when she was alone with me she would quieten down, and so I took her along to the Lodge. Besides which, if there was any evil intent, or if there was anything going on at the Lodge which I was anxious to hide, should I have taken her there or allowed Captain Butt free access to the place?

Why – why – why? Question after question. But there were also questions I should have liked to put. I have been questioned more than once concerning the arrival of a parcel at Tower Lodge on January 14th from a draper's shop. Why was the assistant not called, who – according to what I was told by the police – declared that I had ordered the contents of that package and that they had been taken in at Tower Lodge by a man with a black dog. I had Brian's dog at that time. I was not at the Lodge that day, and I deny that I ever ordered the essentially feminine articles which were sent there that day. If there was a woman there – who was she?

In trying to establish that the torso was that of Captain Butt, a great deal depended on the description and size. Why were the tailors who made Captain Butt's suits not called to give their recorded measurements? These could have been compared with the measurements of the torso.

Why was nobody called as to the property and finances of Mrs Butt since her husband obtained a power of attorney over her affairs? I could go on putting these 'whys', and as my story proceeds I shall have many questions to ask, as well as supplying the answers to some of them.

I knew all along that I was suspected of having been concerned in the dismemberment of the torso, and having taken part in the disposal of the remains. I am even not sure that I was not suspected of having some part in the murder of the victim. For murder was certainly suspected before the report of Sir Bernard Spilsbury came along to say that the man was probably struck in the back by a rapidly moving motor vehicle.

How could I fail to be aware of all the rumours and suggestions which were made? How Tower Lodge – that picturesque old fourth-century building perched on the top of a hill looking right across to the Bristol Channel – had been the scene of orgies of vice beyond description. And finally, that it was the scene of at least one act in the grim drama of the headless torso.

It was because of these suspicions that the police came to me and asked me questions – very properly, as I have stated – and if the suspicions had been directed at me alone, I would not have cared so much. But they were not. From what transpired at the inquest it is clear that my son Brian, who is no longer here to defend himself or tell his own story to the world, is supposed to have been involved in the happenings at Haw Bridge and Tower Lodge.

It has been my anguish to have read the suggestions published far and wide that Brian belonged to a coterie of people who indulged in unspeakable vices. There have been rumours of dope, blackmail and perversion of every kind, and stories of his affairs with women. The wildest stories of his life in the West End of London, where for years he was a dance host; at Polperro, in Cornwall, where he lived for a time; and at Tower Lodge, where he so tragically died, have been circulated. It is because of this that I have determined to tell to the world the true facts so far as I know them. I do not know them all, and am as much in ignorance on many important phases of this terrible tragedy as are the police. But what I do know I intend to tell fully and frankly, without fear, so that the world may judge.

Brian cannot speak. He lies in his grave in Leckhampton churchyard, branded a suicide by a coroner's verdict. It was a verdict which at the time I was bound to accept in all the circumstances. But now, in view of all that has happened, and what I now know, I do not believe that my son took his own life. Brian lies dead and branded by rumour and suggestion at the inquest – though not endorsed by the verdict of the jury – as having had some part in the death of the Haw Bridge victim and the disappearance of Captain Butt.

The jury are not certain that the torso is that of Captain Butt. But of this I am terribly certain. That behind the death of my son; behind the gruesome finds in the Severn; behind the digging of that yawning grave in the passage of Tower Lodge, with its plastered-up holes in the wall and floor, there lies a story the like of which has never been known even in fiction. It is clear to my mind that between the death of Brian, the discoveries at Haw Bridge, and the disappearance of Captain Butt, there is a link, and I am determined to find that link.

There are those who know more of these things than do either the police or myself. I shall find them. They must speak. The last chapter in the tragedy of Tower Lodge has yet to be written.

I am too much a woman of the world to suggest that Brian was any different from other youths. He would come to me and talk quite frankly. He would discuss his business and private affairs with me and ask my advice. There may have been things he did not tell me. All that I know is that to me he appeared to be open and frank, and as he introduced me to his friends and took me about with him whenever possible it does not seem as though he was trying to hide any dark secrets from me.

Some weeks [after Brian's death] I was asked to go to Tower Lodge by Chief Inspector Worth to see if I could help them at all, and I readily agreed. It did not strike me at the time, but since that day it has come to me that, when I went into the kitchen on that occasion the plate-rack had a great deal of crockery in it. If that is the case, then Brian must have been entertaining visitors there after that day when I entered [4 January 1938], or else, there must have been someone in Tower Lodge after he was dead.

One of the reasons why I do not think that, if he had contemplated taking his life, he would have selected [Tower Lodge], which we both loved so much, as the scene for his suicide [is], I feel certain, that rather than shut the door of Tower Lodge for ever against me by taking his life there, and making it impossible for me to live there again, he would have gone off in his car, taken a room in some other part, and there carried out his intention. He knew what it [Tower Lodge] meant to me, and only a few days before he bade me goodbye for the last time we talked about buying the Lodge outright if ever the opportunity occurred.

Between January 4th – the day Captain Butt vanished – and January 10th [when Brian ostensibly went off to London], Brian came down to 248 Old Bath Road to have his meals as usual. He was in and out at other times during the day. Can it be possible that at this time he had one of the most horrible guilty secrets on his mind that ever a man can have. I say it is unthinkable. And I tell you that anybody who knew Brian will tell you the same. This crime was not the work of desperation but rather the cold- blooded work of one with a cool brain and a calculating mind.

All this time, I would have you remember, if the suspicions of the police were correct, Brian was still faced with the dismemberment and the disposal of the body, whosoever it was. He still had this ghastly thing on his mind night and day – for he was sleeping at the Lodge during this period and must have had for company the remains of his victim – and yet could talk of going to see a friend quite calmly and dispassionately. What is more, he never knew when I might slip up and tidy up for him as I used to do at irregular times. Other people saw him during this crucial time, but there has never been anybody to say that he was agitated or fearful or that he was behaving in anything like a suspicious manner.

I always knew when something was worrying Brian; it is one of those things that every mother can tell by intuition. Yet at this very crucial time I had no hint of anxiety, and he was just the bright, heedless Brian whom I knew so well.

Concerning the finding of certain newspapers in Brian's car, it was pointed out in the press that the papers were dated January 12th to 16th. It was also reported in various quarters that these papers dealt with the finding of the bloodstains on Haw Bridge. But I have since discovered that on January 13th it had been announced that the bloodstains were of animal origin. So that by that time, so far as the Haw Bridge finds were concerned, the police had ceased to make further inquiries. If Brian had been concerned in anything to do with the business of Haw Bridge, then he would have known by this time that any fears he might have had were unnecessary.

You must remember that the suggestion made at the inquest upon the torso was quite definite in its inference that it may have been Brian who was responsible for the death of the unknown victim, and that the grave at Tower Lodge, and the newly-cemented wall, were all part of the mystery related to Haw Bridge. So that if he did take his life, he knew at the time he did so that under the passageway was the partly-filled grave, with the coat of Captain Butt buried beneath a few inches of earth. He knew that in the bathroom were signs of recent labour on the broken-down chimney flue. He must have known that these things would ultimately be discovered, and that something of what had happened within those walls was bound to come to light.

I say it is incredible that, knowing these things, he failed to say something as to the reason he took his life in that last note of his, if, in fact, it be his. I do not believe it, and I am more convinced than ever now that my boy met his death in a different fashion to that recorded at the inquest. I do not dispute that he died from gas-poisoning, but I do not believe that he died by his own hand.

And now I come to a most remarkable incident, one which I related to the police, and which will live for ever in my mind. It was on the 25th [January 1938], that Mrs Butt's brother arranged for her to go into a nursing home. It was the following day that I was feeling all to pieces, there being the inevitable reaction. A doctor was called in, and that night I was given a sleeping-draught, and went to bed. I was alone in the house. I do not know how long I had been asleep, but it was early morning when I was awakened by the sound of Brian's voice calling out to me – 'Mother, Mother!' It was just as he used to cry out to me sometimes when he was a little boy.

In my sleep I felt that he was calling to warn me about something. I opened my eyes, and there, leaning over me as I lay in bed, was the figure of Captain Butt, his hands outstretched in a threatening, strangling attitude towards my throat, and on his face a look of malevolence, such as I hope never to see again. The thought came to me that he intended to kill me. I sprang up, and slithered under his arms, and, with a piercing scream, ran downstairs and out into the back garden, with nothing on but my night-clothes. There, neighbours, attracted by my shrieks, found me trying to clamber over the fence, and one of them, a very charming lady who came to my aid, received a terrible bruise on her hand where I gripped her. The vision – if vision it was – is the clearest and most real thing I have ever known. I do not attempt to explain it. I only tell you as it happened.

Brian was buried on January 28th. Afterwards, I visited the grave on several occasions, to put fresh flowers on it. Once, when I did this, I stood looking down on the little mound which covered my boy and said, as many a mother has said before, I suppose: "That is not Brian lying there". What I meant was that it was only the clay, and not the soul of my boy. That simple utterance was reported to the police, and I was questioned as to what exactly I meant, and whether it was, in fact, Brian buried there.

I would mention here that from the day I found Brian on the 24th, the key to Tower Lodge was out of my possession, and I never entered the place until I went there with Chief Inspector Worth, at his request, to see if I could help them in any way.

Yet, when the police entered Tower Lodge on February 7th – after the finding of the torso on the 3rd – Detective Sergeant Shewry stated that on the floor of the sitting-room he found the suitcase containing the flannel trousers, the hogskin gloves, the electric razor, and a pair of purple-striped pyjamas and other articles which undoubtedly belonged to Captain Butt. That case was one which used to be kept under Mrs Butt's bed at 248 Old Bath Road, and I feel certain that had it been in Tower Lodge when I went on the 24th I must have noticed it. Do you think it possible that having been asked to look for a biggish attaché-case, PC Merry could have failed to notice this and tell me about it, if it had been there? And where is the blue case to which I have referred?*

I told the police about it, for it is not at Tower Lodge. Where has it vanished to?

I have been asked over and over again whether I noticed anything unusual about the passage through from the back-door into the living-room. As I explained at the inquest, when I found the door open, I rushed through that passage to get up the stairs, and I feel sure that if there had been anything very unusual about the place, I must have noticed it. I cannot even now understand how it is that there was no giving of the boards as I ran over that 'grave' in the passage – if, in fact, it was there at the time. You see, originally that passage was paved with hard and unyielding bricks, and even though there was a strip of carpet over it, I cannot help but think that I would have noticed that boards had been substituted. There must have been a hollow sound under my weight. I am a heavy woman. But there was nothing to give me pause, and there was apparently nothing to give PC Merry any cause for thought about the place.

At this point I would like to mention that if I had suspected that Tower Lodge had been the scene of any terrible happenings at that time, I should hardly have been likely to leave the key in the possession of PC Merry, or have asked him to go up to the Lodge and look around for various things on my behalf.

I was asked whether I entered the bathroom, and whether I saw anything suspicious or unusual there. I did enter the bathroom. And, as I stated at the inquest, I did not notice anything unusual there, as I am certain I should have done. You will remember that it was at the far end of the bathroom that Sergeant Shewry stated that he found signs that the brickwork had been interfered with owing to the recent cementing of a certain area. It was on the 24th January that I entered that bathroom, and it was on the same day that PC Merry entered it. I say that if the signs of recent cementing were there on February 7th when Mr Shewry entered Tower Lodge, the signs must have been more apparent when I went in on the 24th January, and we must have noticed them.

I do not know how many times between the 24th January and the 2nd February PC Merry went into Tower Lodge, but however many times it was, he evidently saw nothing to arouse any suspicion, and he had free and complete access at any time. It was on February 2nd that he brought the key down to me at 248 [Old Bath Road].

Just one thing more. When I found Brian dead, I noticed that some blood had trickled from the corner of his mouth on to the bedclothes. It was PC Merry who suggested he should burn these soiled bedclothes and mattress, and it was he who took them into the garden and burned them, and I can assure you that I was extremely grateful for his thoughtfulness in saving me from having to perform this disagreeable task.

And now let me come to the apparently determined way in which Brian is supposed to have taken his life, and see how totally unlike him were these preparations.

He always used to turn the gas off at the meter when he went to bed, on account of the rats once having gnawed through one of the pipes and caused a leakage of gas. When I entered the room where he lay the first thing that met my eyes were his feet beneath the bedclothes, standing straight up. He was lying slightly on one side, and I pulled the bedclothes down a little way. I could see that he was wearing pyjamas.

In the hasty glance as I looked around, I just noticed that the floorboards were disarranged in one corner of the room. This was where the linoleum had been lifted, and the floorboards wrenched up. The gas-pipe underneath had then been cut or severed in some way. I did not see this, but only heard about it at the inquest afterwards.

Anybody who knew Brian would tell you that such cool and calm premeditation on his part is inconceivable. He might in a moment of panic have done something terrible to himself, although that to me is beyond belief. But that he carefully and methodically went to all the trouble of levering up the floorboards, first lifting a washing-stand from over the spot where the boards were moved, and then cut through a pipe, is something I cannot credit.

That he wrote the futile and meaningless message (to me), and then, having turned the gas on at the meter, undressed fully, put on his pyjamas, got into bed, removed his glasses, carefully placing them on the chair beside the bed, is unthinkable.

I do not care what his trouble might be, Brian could never have gone to these lengths to take his life. If he had wished to do so, would it not have been a simpler and easier thing for him to have just lain down, and turned on the gas by means of the ordinary jet? Or would it not have been quicker and easier to attach a length of piping to the jet and inhale it from beneath the bedclothes?

I am convinced now that the whole thing was carefully staged to make it look as though Brian had taken his own life. And I feel certain that whoever was responsible for his death was responsible for staging the whole of the remaining mystery, for that it WAS staged is to my mind the only conclusion possible.

In view of later discoveries at Tower Lodge, it was suggested that there may have been some connection between the torso and the finds at the Lodge. Let us review the facts. Somebody is killed somehow. Sir Bernard Spilsbury suggested that the dead man might have been struck from behind by a rapidly moving motor vehicle, and received head injuries from which he died. It would be a remarkable coincidence if, on the very night when Captain Butt's car was parked at the Regent Garage, the Captain was run into from behind by Brian's car. At 10.40 that night somebody – probably the Captain himself from the description given – left his Daimler car in the garage for three days. Had he left it only for the night, there would not be any mystery about it. If the car were out of order and needed some repairs, the same would apply. But it was being left for THREE DAYS. Where was Captain Butt going for those three days?

Supposing it was Brian's car which knocked the victim down and killed him. Do you suppose that the police did not make the closest scrutiny of his car to see whether there were any signs of damage such as might have been caused by such a crash, whether accidental or by design? I can assure you that every inch of the paint-work and enamel on that car was scrutinised under magnifying glasses. I recall Dr Roche Lynch coming to 248, and, with the aid of electric torches, examining the car inside and out for traces of bloodstains.

That car is now in my possession. There are bits snipped out of the leather upholstery. There is a slice taken from the fabric inside top cover. There is not an inch of that car which has not been subjected to the most minute investigation. And now it has been handed back to me with the assurance that I need not hesitate to ride in it, as it played no part in the tragedy either in the knocking down of the unknown man, or the disposal of the remains.

There is another point to which I must refer in order to clear up any doubt regarding the possibility of Brian having had any part in this horrible and gruesome business. The dismemberment of that body was never carried out at Tower Lodge. If it had been there must have been some traces left. They could not have been avoided.

When I was asked to go to the Lodge by Chief Inspector Worth, I agreed to do so, little dreaming of the havoc I should see there wrought upon my little home.

Apart from the digging inside the house, and the breaking down of the wall in the bathroom, revealing a hole large enough to conceal a body, there was a large trench outside from which I learned drain-pipes had been taken right away down to the main, some feet away from the front of the house. The pipe from beneath the sink had been entirely removed. I can only suppose that it was in order to see whether any blood had been drained away down those pipes. I mention these horrible details to show how thorough was the search made by the police in their efforts to prove that Tower Lodge had been the scene of the dismemberment.

It is the same with Brian's car. If it had been used for taking away the remains and dumping the various parts in the river, there must have been some signs of such use. Yet there were none. And if Brian's car was not used, whose car was it, and where is that car today, and what does the owner of the car know about it?

Is there not something which savours of a direct 'plant' about the whole business? Just as Brian's car was not used for any evil purpose, just as Tower Lodge was not the scene of the worst part in this ghastly tragedy, does it not seem that there were forces at work for some reason or other to make it appear as though there were some connection?

Let us revert to the discoveries at Haw Bridge once more. A person is killed. There is dismemberment of the body. The naked torso is taken, together with the limbs, weighted with bricks, to Haw Bridge. Is it conceivable that the person who can contemplate such an act, and carrying it out with such calm nerve, is going to make the mistake of taking with them a glove with a cleaner's mark, a shoe, a scrap of cloth, a button with threads attached, and the rest of the articles found there, and leaving them all beautifully laid out on the bridge for the first person to find?

It is not as though there had been a struggle on the spot, and the pieces of cloth found, or the button, had been torn from the clothes of the victim. Neither is it as though the dismemberment had been carried out on the bridge. On the face of it, it seems clear to me that whoever engaged in the disposal of the remains was deliberately seeking to make it appear that the torso, if ever it was found, was that of Captain Butt. It is even possible that those things were deliberately placed there on the bridge in order that dragging operations should be started immediately and the torso be discovered, so that it might be identified as Captain Butt, and so put an end to any possible search for him.

← PASSAGE →

WET PLASTER DISCOVERED BY POLICE

EXCAVATED FLUE IN BATHROOM

6 FOOT HOLE WHERE COAT WAS FOUND BURIED

LIVING ROOM

HOLE THROUGH TO LIVING ROOM

BATH MAT

The ground-floor passage and bathroom at Tower Lodge.

If Brian had been guilty of some terrible thing, and had, either by accident or intent, killed Captain Butt for any reason whatsoever, would he have loaded himself up with every evidence of his guilt?

Take the three-day garage ticket for Captain Butt's car. Would it not have been the easiest thing in the world to destroy that ticket? Yet it was found in Brian's pocket wallet. The log-book for the car was found in Brian's attaché-case. Why should he keep this utterly useless thing, and thus incriminate himself?

Quite openly upon the dressing-table in the room where he had lain dead was found a bunch of keys ... one of them being the A.A. key issued to Captain Butt in 1934. A most damning find in all the circumstances. Yet what could have been easier for Brian than to have taken that bunch of keys and hurled them into some stream or place where they need never have been found? The ignition key to Captain Butt's car was also found in Brian's waistcoat pocket.

Next we come to that four-foot grave dug out beneath the passage leading from the living-room to the kitchen. In that, you will remember, buried beneath 18 inches of loose soil, was an overcoat – a black, fawn and white check pattern – similar to one owned by Captain Butt. And instead of replacing the earth and the bricks so that no suspicion would be aroused, the hole is carefully boarded-over for anyone to discover the first time the carpet is removed.

Then there is the bag, which I have already mentioned, containing the purple-striped pyjamas of Captain Butt. I was able to identify these definitely as his, and I stated at the inquest that the last time I saw them they were lying on his bed on the morning of January 4th. Why should that case with its contents of identification be left about so openly when the coat had been so carefully buried beneath the passage? Do you not think that the easiest thing in the world would have been to get rid of the clothing, which could have been destroyed beyond recovery?

It was not the perfect crime as it has been described, for clues were left all over the place. Left with a purpose, as I have indicated.

On February 3rd – a month after the disappearance of Captain Butt, and ten days after I discovered Brian dead – the torso was dragged from the river. Up till that moment, the person or persons responsible for placing the torso in the river had no need to fear anything. Whatever anxiety they may have felt had been removed … the analyst called in to examine the bloodstains, the piece of flesh, etc., had stated that they were of animal and not human origin, and the police had discontinued any further inquiries.

From January 10th to February 3rd, there was plenty of time to get rid of the less important incriminating articles, such as the clothing. There was no occasion for any sort of panic. Why then should Brian take his life at the stage when he is supposed to have done so, presuming that he had anything at all to do with the tragedy?

At the inquest I was handed the scrap of cloth which had been found at Haw Bridge. I identified it as like the material of a suit which Captain Butt wore. To me it looked like an oblong pattern which is sent out from the tailor's, and I had seen it in the second drawer of the left-hand side of the bureau, where Captain Butt used to keep some loose coppers and stamps. It was certainly the colour and material of Butt's suit. But if it did belong to him, how on earth did just this scrap of cloth come to be at Haw Bridge, and where is the rest of the suit? If it had been destroyed, that piece would not have been found. It is not likely that anybody is going to take with them a torn-out scrap of their victim's clothing, unless they are trying to call attention to the identity of somebody for some particular reason. When that body was taken away it must have been without a vestige of clothing. That is the only reasonable inference.

At the inquest I saw lying on the table a chopper found in the tool-box at Tower Lodge, which, according to Sir Bernard Spilsbury, may have been used to dismember the body. I was not asked to identify it, but had I been, I could have told the Court that it was similar to one that belonged to Captain Butt, which used to hang up in his garage at 248. I should have told them that so far as the Lodge was concerned all that we had in the way of an axe was one bought at a sixpenny store.

On the table at the inquest, too, were the bricks which were found tied round the torso and the limbs. I saw, too, the bricks which were taken from Tower Lodge, and which were said to be similar to those mentioned above. It is quite possible that the bricks which were tied to the remains came from Tower Lodge, especially in view of the fact that such pains were taken to connect the Lodge with the tragedy. On the other hand, there are thousands of similar bricks in and around Cheltenham, and they might easily have come from elsewhere.

Just a few days ago (in the first week of May 1938) I paid my first visit to Tower Lodge – with the exception of the one I have mentioned in company with Chief Inspector Worth – since Brian died.

In the living-room I saw the signs of Brian's last night there. On the little table beside the fireplace lay his two pipes with a pouch of tobacco. There was the paper bag containing the gramophone records with which he used to beguile the lonely hours he spent there. There were other things I noticed, too. From the arm of the settee on which he lay reading when I entered the Lodge on the afternoon of January 4th, there had been cut a wide strip of material. Little pieces had been snipped out of this strip, doubtless by Dr Roche Lynch for the purpose of testing for bloodstains. Had I been asked, I could have told them [the police] that the stains that there were, were due to the sickness of a patient whom I nursed at Northwood [Miss Daubenny] long before I went to Tower Lodge.

Upstairs in the large bedroom was the wardrobe containing Brian's suits. A tragic sight for me, as perhaps you will realise. Not one of his suits was missing. In the smaller back bedroom where he died, neatly folded upon the bed, was the suit which he was wearing when I last saw him. It was hanging over a chair when I entered the room on the afternoon of January 24th and found him dead.

In the large bedroom just at the top of the stairs, there stood two wooden trunks which I always kept locked. The locks of these had been broken open, probably with the thought that some grim secret was hidden therein, but all that they ever contained was the bedclothes which I kept there.

In the smaller bedroom, I could see where the linoleum had cracked, as it had been bent back in order that the floorboards could be raised for the severing of the gas-pipe. It was over these floorboards that the wash-stand used to be, and Mr Bernard O'Donnell, who was with me on this visit, found the wash-stand so heavy on account of its solid marble top that he had to seek assistance in order to lift it away from where it stood, so that photographs could be taken. Is it likely then that Brian, who was small and rather weak, could have moved this thing by himself?

There is another thing I would point out. At one time there used to be a gas-fire just at the point where a chair stands now. Brian had it removed when the electric light was fitted, and there is a gas-cock clearly visible above the linoleum. Why then should he go to all the trouble of levering up the floorboards and severing the gas-pipe when it would have been the easiest thing in the world for him to have knocked the plug out of this gas-cock and released the gas much nearer to the spot where he lay? Whilst almost above the middle of the bed was a gas-jet from which he could easily have run a length of tubing to his mouth.

Again, I say, I am convinced still more that my boy did not take his life. I know it will sound improbable and fantastic, but there is nothing too improbable or fantastic in this mystery, and that is why I am going to suggest that it is at least within the realms of possibility that the grave [in the passageway] and the hole in the bathroom wall, together with all the other disturbances, were carried out after February 2nd, when the key of Tower Lodge was handed back to me by Police Constable Merry. I realise all that this involves, as I was the one in possession of that key from that day until February 7th, when I handed it over to the police to make their inquiries. But I think that the police will absolve me from any likelihood of carrying out what must have been a heavy task, even for a strong, wiry man. It is only a suggestion on my part, based on the fact that nobody had noticed anything suspicious about that passageway until February 7th, although Police Constable Merry was in the place at least once after Brian's body had been removed.*

Let us come now to the kitchen, which is really only a continuation of the passage with a sink at the end, over which is a plate-rack. I had got Brian into the habit of using only one cup and saucer, and one plate at a time, so that he would not dirty them all before starting to wash up. I pointed out that it would thus be much easier to wash up one set of articles as he went along. This he used to do. On January 4th, the last time I entered the Lodge during his lifetime, I noticed that he had got his cup and saucer, plate, and spoon, with knife and fork, etc., ready on the tray which stood by the window. The other things were all stacked away in the cupboard.

When I visited the Lodge with Mr Worth, sometime in March, I believe my fleeting impression was that the plate-rack contained a number of

---

*This does not square with Merry's inquest evidence in which it will be recalled that he said that he had noticed that floor bricks in the passageway had been taken up. See Chapter Nineteen.

The plate-rack in the scullery at Tower Lodge. Photographed at Nurse Sullivan's request as a record of an important point in her story.

plates and things. When I visited the Lodge last week (with Bernard O'Donnell) I took particular note of this rack, and to my amazement found that there were ten large plates, two cups and saucers, two basins and an egg-cup; whilst in the zinc draining receptacle underneath the rack were over a dozen knives and forks, including fish knives and forks, and spoons. To me it is of the utmost significance as proving beyond all doubt that somebody was in Tower Lodge after Brian was dead.

We know that somebody was there on January 14th, four days after I last saw Brian alive, for there was a man there who took in the package from the draper's shop on that date. There was also a dog in the house, for the assistant who delivered the parcel heard it bark. Who used those plates and knives and forks? Who was the man with the dog in Tower Lodge?

To the left of the plate-rack and immediately facing the back-door is the door leading into the bathroom. Facing this door is the lavatory basin, over which is a shelf. The moment I stood at this door I turned to Mr O'Donnell, who was with me, and ejaculated: "Why, there is Butt's hair cream and his shaving-brush". On the shelf was a little jar of greenish-coloured hair cream, whilst hanging on a nail was the large yellow-handled shaving-brush which I knew to be Butt's. What was it doing in Tower Lodge?

I want now to return to the bottle of milk episode, as since my last visit to Tower Lodge it has assumed a far greater importance in my view. Certain facts have come to my knowledge during the past ten days [the end of April to the first week in May 1938] which are of vital significance. I know now that Bimbo, Brian's spaniel, to whom he was absolutely devoted, was in the car which stood in the drive on the morning of January 11th, when the milkman delivered the milk – that same morning when Brian was supposed to go to his friend's in London. I know now that Bimbo was still there in the car the next morning when the milkman delivered the milk. Up till last week I had considered it possible that Bimbo had perhaps been placed in the car on the twelfth, on which evening I found him.

This is the point I want to make. Brian loved Bimbo as a child. If it was his intention to take his life when he left me that night, Brian could easily have asked me if I would mind keeping Bimbo with me whilst he went up to town. If it was a sudden decision for any reason whatever, then he could have let Bimbo out, and the latter would have come down the hill to me at Old Bath Road. He would most certainly never have put that dog in the car and left him there for two days, as he was left. In the meantime I would point out that the bottle of milk left by the milkman remained untouched outside the front-door on the 11th, 12th, and 13th. But on the 14th it had been taken inside, and stood just inside the door.

You must remember that there was a man at the Lodge on January 14th. If that man had been Brian, Bimbo would have been in the Lodge on those two days that the milkman saw him in the car. That milk would have been taken in as usual. But it was not. And this leads me to the conclusion that Brian died on the night of January 10th, after he left me, or during the early hours of that morning [January 11th]. And there was someone there at that time who can tell all the details of his death. Who was it?

I fully realise that there is the explanation of that death note to overcome. That is one of the greatest mysteries in this case. I suggest that if that note was indeed in Brian's handwriting, then it was written under pressure of some terrible threat. When Brian returned to Tower Lodge after leaving me on the 10th, did he happen upon somebody and something terrible to which he was forced to become a party? Was there somebody there who communicated to him some guilty secret, which Brian threatened to expose? And was his death the outcome of this threat? It is pure speculation, as everything must be in this problem.

There is somebody who knows what happened in that Lodge on the night of January 10th. That somebody took in the milk during the day of the 13th, for the milk bottle had vanished on the 14th. Who could have been there? That it was somebody who knew the Lodge and knew Bimbo is certain, for I can assure you that it would go ill with anybody who opened the door of Brian's car whilst Bimbo was inside unless he was known to the dog. Captain Butt was known to Bimbo and knew the Lodge. He used to go digging in the garden there.

The police knew that on either January 17th or 18th, there was somebody in the Lodge, for on that day somebody noticed particularly that the blinds of the two top bedroom windows were drawn back. They had been drawn to for several days – ever since the 11th, and this was the first day they had been opened.

Let us return to the disappearance of Captain Butt. Is there any conceivable motive why Brian should be concerned in his disappearance? There were only a few hours between [Butt's] return on the 3rd and our going to the pictures on the 4th in which anything could have happened for Brian to have cause to try and get Butt out of the way, or to make the necessary preparations. The idea is ludicrous. Does it not look rather as if his disappearance was a carefully-planned affair?

I believe that Captain Butt is still alive, and that the torso is that of some other victim. After Easter I decided to go down to Polperro, where Brian's cottages are, to open up the place. I learned there a very peculiar thing. It appears that a well-known London bookmaker was staying down at Polperro during the middle of January (1938), and one evening was standing talking in the narrow street to a local tradesman, when he observed a man hovering about on the other side of the road. This man was dressed in a fawny-brown overcoat, made on the full side, a trilby hat, and a sort of pepper-and-salt suit. He nodded across at the bookmaker, and murmured good evening, and the bookmaker thought he was known to the tradesman. He thought no more of it until having returned to London he saw a picture of Captain Butt in an evening newspaper. He at once turned to his wife and said: "Why that's the man we saw in Polperro in January. I wonder what the date was?"

He was so impressed – because he recognised the rather prominent ears and longish thin nose of the man – that he rang up the tradesman at Polperro and asked him whether he could fix the date of that conversation in the street. The tradesman could do so with certainty, because he recalled that he was talking to the bookmaker about his uncle who had died the day previously in Plymouth Hospital. This was on January 11th, so that the date of the conversation is fixed as January

12th, two days after Brian was last seen alive, and eight days after Butt had vanished.

One most important point about the description of this man which even so far tallies with that of Captain Butt. The bookmaker has stated that what impressed him most about the dress of the man was that he was wearing spats. Captain Butt used to wear spats. The fawny-brown, full overcoat described is also similar to that which [was] purchased by Butt last year, and which is missing. The description of the suit is like that which was described at the inquest.

If he is [alive], it is possible that he can explain something of the mystery surrounding the death of Brian and the discovery of the torso, and, I repeat once more, that, even though it involved my own son, I would welcome any solution which can be provided.

My story is finished for the time being. I have lost my boy. I have suffered the agony of knowing him to be suspected of terrible things. After my daughter died I lived for Brian. Now I am living to clear his name.

Chapter Twenty-One

Solutions

The Cheltenham Torso Mystery is like no other classic case in Britain's criminal annals. To begin with, we do not even know for sure the identity of the victim, for the proposition that the torso was that of Captain William Bernard Butt remains officially unconfirmed. Moreover, we do not know for sure how the victim died. Without the head, the precise cause of death is dubious. The verdict that Brian Sullivan committed suicide, although accepted by the coroner, is manifestly still open to question. In the light of further and better particulars, all previous conclusions seem to be no more than presumptions.

As the man in supreme charge of the Torso case, Chief Detective Inspector Percy Worth and the views which he expressed must be accorded considerable weight and importance.

"Once the story of Hancock, the lorry driver, is accepted – and I cannot see how it can possibly be rejected – then, according to our enquiries, something in connection with the killing of the victim*, or with the disposal of the body, took place at Tower Lodge on Sunday, the 9th January, or very early on the 10th of January."

That means that, in Inspector Worth's opinion, "Mrs Sullivan's account of her son's activities on the 10th [of January] must be untrue."

Nurse Sullivan had stated that Brian had been calm and quiet, and that she had noticed nothing unusual in his demeanour. He had left her at 9pm on 10 January, saying that he would telephone her from London on the following day.

Worth felt convinced that she was lying. What, in his opinion, "probably occurred on this day was that she first became acquainted with the happenings at Tower Lodge from her son."

As to precisely what those 'happenings' were, the Chief Inspector does not hazard so much as a guess. Brian's mother had kept to her statement and stolidly denied all knowledge of her son's connection with the Haw Bridge affair.

For his part, Worth found it difficult to think anything other than that Tower Lodge had played a part in Captain Butt's disappearance, whether or not his was the torso fished up out of the Severn. After all, Butt's connection with the Lodge was definitely known. A suit-case containing recognised articles of his clothing and toilet was found there. So were some of his keys and the garage receipt for his Daimler, as well as a buried overcoat of his. Moreover, old bricks, undoubtedly from the passageway at the Lodge where the hole had been dug for the burial of

---

*Worth is punctilious always to refer to the torso as 'the victim', it never having been officially accepted as the trunk of Captain Butt.

Butt's overcoat, and binder twine found at the Lodge, corresponded with bricks and twine attached to the trunk and limbs brought out of the river.

At 7.45pm on 16 February 1938, Detective Constable Slade had received a telephone message at Cheltenham Police Station from Police Sergeant Hills, of Charlton Kings Station. It came from Mrs Fletcher, a fruiterer, of Pitville Street, Cheltenham, saying that a woman who collected old boxes from her had told her that her two boys came home from Leckhampton Hill some time ago in a very muddy and dirty state. When she asked them where they had been, they told their mother that they had been helping Mr Sullivan to dig a big hole in his house, and that they had been carrying bricks out. Intriguing. But of this we hear no more. Not very satisfactory.

The Inspector considered it feasible that the body had been originally taken to Tower Lodge for burial, and that the cavity had been made in the bathroom wall for the purpose of its immurement, but, finding the hole behind the flue inadequate, the river was chosen as a better place of concealment. The 'grave' in the passageway might have been prepared after the disposal of the trunk in the water in order to bury the clothes.

Despite the mounting of a most exhaustive examination, nothing was revealed at Tower Lodge to indicate that it had been the scene of the dismemberment, and both Spilsbury and Roche Lynch agreed with Worth that no such dissection had been carried out there.

Thorough searches of the surrounding countryside, including isolated open spaces and empty houses, flats and basements in and around Cheltenham and Gloucester, brought no clues as to the site of the gruesome work.

What was, however, found in ashes taken from the fireplace at Tower Lodge was a quantity of fire-damaged metal buckles which could have come from sock suspenders and from trousers, as well as partly-burnt shirt, trouser, drawers, or pyjama buttons, the plain relics of clothing that had been burnt there. That there had indeed been a fierce blaze was apparent from the state of the bricks of the fireplace.

As regards the torso itself, Worth could not agree with Sir Bernard Spilsbury that a person standing five foot seven inches to five foot nine inches, and weighing 12 to 13 stone, could be described as being "of heavy build". Other than that, he found himself in accord with Spilsbury's finding.

"I accept without question the suggestion of Sir Bernard Spilsbury that the injuries found on the trunk were probably caused by a fast moving motor vehicle."

Brian Sullivan, the Inspector felt absolutely sure, was either implicated in the killing, or became involved later in the getting rid of the remains and the clothing.

He accepted that Sullivan had committed suicide, but refused to attribute the wretchedness of his financial position as a main cause for his self-destruction. True, he had only £4 6s 6d in cash at the bank, and no other assets, at the time of his demise, and no prospect of any further borrowings from his depleted mother, but his debts, totalling around £150, were scarcely life-threateningly astronomical. On the other hand, Worth acknowledged that it was reasonable to suppose that, *following the death of the victim*, Brian's financial stresses might have been a contributory factor to his final desperate 'solution'.

From the facts disclosed in the course of the police enquiry, it seemed reasonable to suppose that Brian Sullivan was alive on 14 January 1938, and possibly later than that. This was, however, never called into question, never pursued, as police activities stopped through the failure of the pathologist, Dr Davey, to identify the Haw Bridge flesh and blood traces as human.

The discovery of the return half of a railway ticket, dated 15 January 1938, Gloucester to Cheltenham, in the drive at Tower Lodge, showed that somebody had apparently slept at Gloucester on the night of 14 January and enquiries elicited that a man answering to Brian Sullivan's description had left Gloucester for Cheltenham that day by the 8.23am train.

The Inspector had found Nurse Sullivan "a very difficult person to judge". After a series of lengthy interviews with her, he came to feel that she was a party neither to the killing and dismemberment, nor to the actual disposal of the remains. He found that the greatest difficulty in her case probably arose out of the substantial truth of her statements in most matters, with the resounding exception of those relating to the time following 9 January 1938.

As Worth observed: "A person making a long and truthful statement cannot be found wanting on material points, however searching a subsequent interrogation may be, and an untruth regarding one day's events could well be retained and repeated with little risk of detection."

There had been no one seriously to contradict Mrs Sullivan's statements, except her next-door neighbour, Mrs Price. Worth thought Mrs Price's story of her attention to Nurse Sullivan, following the incident on 29 January in the back garden at 248 Old Bath Road, significant. In his view, it showed that Mrs Sullivan had the dissecting of bodies on her mind *before the finding of the human torso on 3 February*.

But ... Nurse Sullivan was emphatic that she had made no mention of her dream to Mrs Price until *after* she had read of the finding of the torso in the newspapers.

Why the terrible dream of Captain Butt with a distorted face and of the dissecting theatre? asks Worth rhetorically. And answers with the suggestion that it was caused by the reaction of her mind on having learned previously of the terrible details from her son.

The Inspector thought that, following the awful disclosures by Brian, his mother might well have advised him on how to dispose of the victim's belongings, and told him that he should then leave Cheltenham for a time.

Worth wrote:

I believe, that Mrs Sullivan knows that Brian was not the actual cause of the victim meeting his death, and through that knowledge she has been able to keep a bold front. It is her secret which she will not divulge.

He thinks that she might have been at Tower Lodge with Bimbo on 14 January, as the delivery boy from Shill's heard a dog barking, and he considered that it would have been a very odd coincidence if there had been another dog there. The sanitary towel incident the Inspector admits to be perplexing. There was nothing to connect it with any action of Mrs Sullivan's.

It has to be recognised that *someone* was at Tower Lodge when the draper's delivery was made, and judging by the description of the man who opened the door and took in the parcel, it was Brian Sullivan.

Inspector Worth weighed two likelihoods. Left high and dry to act alone in a desperate situation, seeing the future as hopeless, young Sullivan took his own life. Or, if he was not implicated, it must be that all the incriminatory articles had been deliberately placed where they were found after his death. No evidence had emerged to suggest that anything of the sort had happened, but what was plain was that Sullivan did not appear to have been alone at Tower Lodge.

So one is left wondering who the other person could have been. Worth considered the candidacy of Keith Newman, having noted, in relation to Spilsbury's opinion that the torso had been in contact with a rapidly moving motor vehicle, the fact of Newman's having had repairs done to the front of his car on 13 January, following an alleged 'slight collision', the more precise details of which he was unable to substantiate.

But every enquiry concerning his movements during the relevant period tended, *as far as the police could proceed*, to show that he was not in Cheltenham. Worth had had a long interview with Newman on 7 February. It yielded nothing. The Inspector reported: "He is an unsatisfactory type of individual ... a ne'er-do-well ... and enquiries concerning him have not ceased."

That there were two people involved in the tumbling of the torso over Haw Bridge into the Severn was evidenced by the lorry driver, Charles Hancock's account of actually seeing two people in the car on the bridge. This was borne out during the reconstruction of the events of the night of 10 January staged by Inspector Worth on the night of 14 February, when he saw for himself that no one would have any difficulty in picking out two men in an Austin car by the powerful headlights of Hancock's Morris commercial lorry.

Further support for the two men theory had been provided by Spilsbury's contention that if only one person had thrown the trunk into the river there would have been a great deal more mess left behind than was the case.

A most disappointing aspect had been the total incapacity of Mrs Butt to help. The Inspector had had several tries at obtaining information from her, but it had proved hopeless.

Neither was Captain Butt the easiest person about whom to glean solid, evidential material. He was not a man of regular habits – he patronised no single public-house or place of entertainment, he had no regular associates or friends. Consequently, there was no place, and no society, from which he would be missed. He was, moreover, very secretive, uncommunicative, and led generally a very deceptive life. He did, however, have relations with other women, about which his wife apparently knew.

Worth sought to find out where exactly he was between 4 January and 9 January 1938. No one had come forward to testify. Assuming that 'the victim' *was* Butt – and he had certainly disappeared completely at the material time and has never to this day reappeared – he was alive *somewhere* during those five days, and *someone* must have been with him or rubbed shoulders with him. It is possible that he stayed at Tower Lodge during this period, and if so the reasons why remain unknown. It seems that round about that time Brian Sullivan had women up at the Lodge, but there is nothing in the way of evidence to connect the Captain with them.

Inspector Worth confessed that he inclined to the view that it was Butt himself who garaged the Daimler at Regent Motors, and that he had every intention at the time of leaving it there for three days, which, incidentally, was about the length of time for which he used to leave it at his usual garage, Steele's.

Worth did not discount the statement of the Regent Garage's attendant, George Griffiths, but felt that it was unsafe to rely too heavily upon it, considering the lapse of time stretching between the events and his remembrance of them. But Griffiths, in saying that, with the exception of a small moustache, the man who left the car answered very closely to the description of Captain Butt, even down to the detail of his most noticeable protruding ears – on which feature he laid great stress – proved pretty convincing.

Coming at last to the paramountly important consideration of motive, Inspector Worth arrived at the conclusion that Spilsbury's findings, coupled with the results of his own enquiries, disclosed evidence of a frenzy's having occurred. The dismemberment, for instance, was so crudely effected that it could only have been swiftly executed against the background of a frantic state of affairs. And that did not fit in with any discernible motive. The facts were insufficient to bear a reasonable theory. He surmised: "A motive for this crime has not been revealed. I suggest there is not one."

Worth rejected out of hand the theory of sodomy as leading up to the crime. Likewise, the theory that a pecuniary benefit might devolve upon the victim's death made no appeal. Indeed, in place of any and all of the postulated theories he substituted the notion that the death had been a sudden, unpremeditated, accidental even, happening, arising out of chaos, and resulting in even greater chaos, triggering amazing actions and behaviour.

He stated his clear belief that this was:

> no perfect crime as suggested in some newspapers. ... The solution
> was a simple one at one stage, but unfortunate events enabled a lapse

of time to ensue that has been the prevailing bugbear throughout the whole investigation.

In a final summation, the Inspector expressed the view that it could not be said that murder was proved or any other particular crime brought to light. The cause of death, and the course of events leading up to it remained unsatisfactorily unsolved.

Nowhere in any of the police documents is there any mention of the question of abortions having been carried out at Tower Lodge, nor the slightest hint of any suggestion of a policy of blackmail in connection with such a practice being pursued.

It seems virtually certain that this admittedly most persuasive and neat-fitting theory of what might have been going on was formulated and solely presented by Andrew Soutar. While bearing in mind the sagacity of the old saw that there is no smoke without fire, one is bound to say that upon what Soutar based his aspersions, whence the smoke issued, there is not the slightest hint of evidence. That requisite proof was at any rate in short supply, or, alternatively, impossible to muster for public demonstration – as if, for instance, people would tell him things in confidence but adamantly refuse to come out into the open upon that particular score – would seem to be borne out by his apparent inability to produce any self-defensive answer to the charge of libel brought against him by Nurse Sullivan.

It is very tempting to fall hook, line and sinker for the scenario peddled by Andrew Soutar ... Brian and his mother as the friends-in-need to the poor little rich girls in obstetric distress, their short-lived good service backed up by an unwanted 'after-care' serving of blackmail. That would account for how Brian came by the wherewithal never to be without his own private motor-car and his mother was able to indulge in those odd modest dabblings of hers in property investment.

Butt is introduced into the previously cosy scene as the villain who imports some blackmailing of his own, threatening to expose Brian, Nurse Sullivan and *ipso facto* any other members of the abortion ring that there may happen to have been; the gallant Captain thereby leaving the threatened ones no safe alternative other than, literally, to liquidate him.

Another implication which, as Chief Detective Inspector Worth openly admits, bites the dust, is that homosexuality was somehow at the root of the trouble.

It was Detective Sergeant Franklin of the Gloucester Police who recalled Butt's name being mentioned when Nelson Gardner, the Gloucester greengrocer, was convicted of sodomy at Gloucester Assizes in 1928. It will be recalled that, interviewed in February 1938, Gardner alleged that homoerotic play had taken place between Butt and himself in 1927, and further alleged that there had been similar carryings-on between Butt, and a Cheltenham tobacconist, Bernard Belcher, and with a number of other men whom he named.

Worth made it his business to interview the persons named by Gardner, as well as many other known Cheltenham and Gloucester homosexuals into the bargain, but from no one other than Gardner could he glean the smallest hint that Butt had been addicted to such practices with males. Neither, incidentally, did similar industrious and wide-netting enquiry reveal any suggestion that Brian Sullivan, physical appearances and mannerisms notwithstanding, was that way inclined.

The *Cheltenham and Gloucester Echo*, of 9 February 1938, informed its readers that:

> the police are also in possession of a bundle of correspondence found at the Lodge which throws a harsh light on the relationship between Brian Sullivan and the missing Captain Butt. It may be that these two men were on 'exceptionally friendly terms'. They often visited Tower Lodge together.

These letters have been lost. They are no longer – if, indeed, they ever were – among the papers lodged at Gloucester Record Office, so it is not possible to subject them and their intimations to personal scrutiny and assessment.

My own feeling is that both Butt and Brian were facultatively bisexual, as mood and opportunity presented.

Nurse Sullivan specifically denied that Brian and the Captain were in any way especially friendly.

Investigations undertaken by members of the press dredged up, or were said in print to have brought to the public surface, both interesting facts and significant pointers.

A fascinating titbit of information provided by a foraging journalist: a woman friend of Brian's, said that he went to see the murder film, *Night Must Fall*, two or three times. She added that for days afterwards he could talk of nothing else but the plot of the film, and was frequently heard whistling the melody, *Mighty Like a Rose*, which was continually on the lips of the murderer, who, in the film, concealed his victim's head in a hatbox.

Similarly, in the *Sunday Dispatch*, of 6 March 1938, it was reported that:

> Scotland Yard has uncovered and broken up a highly organised Soho blackmail gang during investigations into the Cheltenham Torso crime. For years the blackmailers have been operating from an exclusive club of their own, with a small membership of men and women. The members were hotel employees, professional dance partners, and others whose jobs enabled them to watch wealthy West End residents. From headquarters, raids were organised on Mayfair homes, just to obtain compromising letters which afterwards have been sold back to the victims for hundreds of pounds.
>
> Women whose husbands occupy important positions in the Army,

Navy, or Diplomatic Service had also been victimised, as well as men from overseas. Payment was the only way out. For every person who had the courage to face the publicity of court proceedings in recent years there are at least 50 victims who paid the gang its price. In one instance £3,000 was paid by a woman of title for the return of a stolen letter. The club members have always kept in close touch with Mayfair playboys who sell them information on which they could act. Others working in co-operation with them were mere West End 'runners' interested in the vicious and immoral underworld life.

In the *Daily Mail*, of 11 March 1938, Ralph Hewins reports:

> In an endeavour to trace friends of dancer Brian Sullivan who may have been associated with him in the Cheltenham torso murder, Scotland Yard detectives are combing West End night clubs. This move is the result of the discovery of a card among Sullivan's possessions at Tower Lodge. Having visited dozens of clubs and interviewed hundreds of Sullivan's acquaintances among fellow dance 'pros', hostesses, musicians, waiters and frequenters, the police are, I learn, particularly interested in one establishment.
>
> Following information there, detectives are trying to trace a tall, slender, innocent-looking girl with reddish hair and aged about 23, who worked as a hostess until about two years ago. They hope that she can put them in touch with a flashy young man with whom Sullivan was friendly. He is Irish and has been connected with the car trade – also with night club entertainment – and it is thought that he in turn might be able to link Sullivan with a gang of blackmailers and desperadoes.*

And Edwin Tetlow, in the *Daily Mail*, of 15 March 1938, weighed in with:

> London is the centre of inquiries based on a belief that a story of vice, and possibly blackmail, is linked with the [Torso] crime. I learn that the police have established the reason for Captain Butt's frequent absences from Cheltenham, and have found that several times he went to London. Recent inquiries have told them that both Captain Butt and Sullivan knew of the existence of a vice gang operating in London and certain parts of Gloucestershire.

Whence Tetlow derived this information is a mystery. Nowhere among the official Scotland Yard papers is there any reference that would justify the foregoing paragraph.

*This could well have been Brian O'Halloran Devereux Sutherland. See Chapter Three.

Andrew Soutar was still hammering away at his abortion theory. In the *Daily Mail*, 10 March 1938, he wrote:

> From the very first I have argued that several women were concerned in the affairs that have culminated in the greatest mystery for years. I have heard mention of two who are supposed to have fled to France. Hearsay. My theory of illegal practices in that Leckhampton cottage are receiving greater support each hour. ... This is not a one-man or one-woman affair. I said that in the beginning, and from what I know now I am satisfied I was right.

So it was in this way that what had begun as frank speculation hardened up into known 'fact' with the passage of time. This misleading metamorphic process can be clearly seen to have operated over a number of areas in this case, for example the homoeroticism of Sullivan and Butt.

Whatever Soutar knew, or thought, or pretended that he knew, he never, even under the stress of being sued for libel, either imparted the substance or revealed the source of that special knowledge to which he laid claim. I am inclined to regard it all as journalistic smoke-screening, a common Fleet Street ploy, contrived to disguise failure to come up with any hard facts.

There is some degree of justification in stigmatising Gloucester in the 1920s and 1930s as the abortion capital of England. It was there that in 1920 Sir Bernard Spilsbury provided evidence that helped to bring to book the well-known abortionist 'the abominable Nurse Hopton of Gloucester'.

Inevitably, we have to face the question of who actually killed Captain Butt. Doubts that the torso was that of the itchy-footed Captain have surely been persuasively allayed by an absence that has extended now to a period of more than 60 years.

The torso has to hold some indications, some possible clues. For a start, it tells us negative things: how he did not die. Analysis established that he had not been poisoned. The condition of the lungs showed that he been neither strangled nor drowned. His heart and circulatory system were sound for his age. The bruising on his back betokened no fatal haemorrhaging or internal injuries. Spilsbury could find no cause of death. A bullet could well have lodged in the missing head, or it might have disclosed evidence of a lethal battering. The throat could have been cut.

But the torso can also reveal something positive. The fact of its excessive mutilation, making secure identification impossible, is indicative of the mutilator's anxiety to preserve the anonymity of the dismembered trunk. Why? Surely it is because its recognition as the indisputable mortal remains of Captain William Bernard Butt would focus the attention of those seeking the culprit on the circle of the victim's known friends and acquaintances.

But who? Was it Brian Sullivan? Was he even to be counted a member of Butt's circle? I have found no evidence to suggest so. Did he and the Captain share joint-interest in an abortion-cum-blackmail enterprise? There is not a jot of evidence to support such an allegation.

Detective Inspector Albert Victor Hancock, of the Cheltenham Force, had a theory of his own. He reckoned that a sudden quarrel had sprung up between Brian and Butt when they were both at Tower Lodge. Brian, in debt and short of money, had approached the Captain for a loan. Having been brusquely refused, he lost his temper, hit out at Butt and knocked him down the stairs, with accidental and totally unanticipated fatal results. In a panic, Brian had sent for, and, as he always did, confided in, his mother. Then, they either jointly or, more likely, with the help of some friend – such as Keith Newman – dismembered and disposed of the denuded torso in the Severn. After all the trouble they had taken, the local river seems a lazy, stupid, and unimaginative choice of jettisoning place. With a car available, as we know they had, it would have made better self-preservative sense to have transported their awful burden to some much further away watery grave.

Nurse Sullivan's otherwise inexplicable dissecting room nightmare and vision – premonition or recall? – and subsequent attack of hysteria are rationally accounted for by her possession of guilty knowledge, and do not require the postulation of her actual participation in the killing, the dismemberment, or the disposal.

It is interesting to remember that she was described by acquaintances as "A woman of great character – but ruthless". In this context one recalls Mrs Elizabeth Kate Barlow's memory of how Nurse Sullivan seemed to her to dominate and inspire fear in the elderly lady whom she brought with her to Mrs Barlow's house.*

Rather tellingly, or at least interestingly, at the height of the publicity surrounding the case, she put in an appearance at Polperro, and was disliked by the villagers and shopkeepers there.

Whatever Irene Sullivan's involvement may or may not have been, we are still left saddled with the difficult problem of Brian's alleged suicide.

In my view, all the circumstances indicate that the corpse in the small back bedroom at Tower Lodge was that of a murdered man. But was that man Brian Sullivan? His mother never identified the body. PC Merry did so. Was it, though, a case of his seeing what he expected to see? The strong likelihood is that putrefaction had already advanced somewhat and the corpse on the bed – bloated, pink-coloured from the gas, darkly speckled with putrescence – would not be especially recognisable to someone who certainly had not known Brian all that well in life.

Moreover, we have, if not precisely legally watertight proof, strong hearsay testimony from the undertaker's carpenter, Joseph Stone, that the body received and coffined was that of a man of greater physical measurements than those

*See Chapter Two.

ascribed to Brian Sullivan. And, according to Andrew Soutar's unnamed official, reporting to him the statement of the also unnamed orderly at the Cheltenham Hospital mortuary, the body which he placed in the shell there, and was said to be Brian Sullivan, was that of a man of considerably taller and bulkier dimensions – estimated as being well over five foot eight-and-a-half inches in height and some 15 stone weight.

The question of who the body was is unanswered.

Consider this possibility. I would put it no higher, that Brian brought someone, perhaps a gigolo friend, down with him from London. That he and his mother, and perhaps with Newman in on the plot, succeeded in gassing their unsuspecting visitor at the Lodge. They then faked all the clues to make it look as if it was Brian who had killed himself. They had then set to work to seed Tower Lodge with the evidence that Brian had been connected with the death of Captain Butt, thus supplying a plausible reason for his suicide. And the real Brian? Well, he *had* killed Butt – very possibly unintentionally, as both Worth and Hancock suspected – and, with his mother and Newman's blessing, made good his escape to somewhere such as Ireland, to begin a new life and never be heard of again.

If this substitution of bodies theory seems too far-fetched, I would call to your attention the cases of Alfred Arthur Rouse (1930) and Samuel James Furnace (1933), both of whom murdered in the hope that their victim's remains would be taken to be their own. Brian Sullivan would have been by no means the first thus to fake his own demise.

All of this depends, of course, upon the measurements of the body *post mortemed* at Cheltenham Hospital by Dr Hamilton-Heslett being compatible with the known vital statistics of the veritable Brian. However, I am able to reveal that the pathologist measured the corpse as five foot seven-and-a-half inches, which was Brian Sullivan's actual height. And the coffin provided measured four inches more – five foot eleven-and-a-half inches. We may, then, be sure that, for all the conflictions of rumour, the body was undoubtably that of Brian Sullivan.

Was Keith Newman involved? It is tempting to reply with an unhesitating yes. But one must qualify. For sure he was an unscrupulous, lying, morally dodgy, and, to use Inspector Worth's adjective, unsatisfactory character. That he was involved in the disposal of the torso seems incontestable because of the discovery on Haw Bridge of a man's chamois glove bearing his wife's laundry mark. Indeed, this is the one indissoluble link which unites what may be designated the Brian/Tower Lodge faction with the officially innominate torso. But the extent, the how and why, of that linkage so far as the death is concerned remains obscure.

It is, however, at least suspicious that Newman's car – a Jaguar SS, Registration Number DXT375 – bore marks of impact damage, for Spilsbury had stated that the torso had sustained what he suspected to have been car impact damage. The repairs, which were carried out on 13 January 1938, were to the front of Newman's Jaguar. The nearside front horn was straightened and the rim of the spotlight had to be beaten out. This would suggest a collision of some severity. Newman, describing the incident, said that it had happened in London. According to him, he had left the car outside a post office, and when he came out he saw a woman in a standard car driving off. He took her number … but he had lost it!

Chief Detective Inspector Percy Worth was said to be something of a high-flyer, with a fine reputation for solving murders, but one cannot feel that his handling of the Cheltenham Torso murder displayed any such qualities. It was neither particularly intelligent nor imaginative. He was by all accounts a conceited and arrogant officer, who, well-swaddled in his little brief authority, adopted a very high-handed attitude towards the press, whose assistance and confidences might well have benefited him.

Did he, for example, ever check the money in the gas-meter at Tower Lodge for fingerprints – as Andrew Soutar suggested? Was Hancock, the lorry driver who got a look at the two men in the torso-bearing car on Haw Bridge, ever shown pictures of Sullivan, Newman, and Sutherland, and asked if he recognised them? Was Miss Cranswick invited to view the torso to see if she could perhaps recognise the genitalia she knew so well? We don't know. Investigatory details zealously hidden from the press remain obscure.

Two men died in Cheltenham. Two men were murdered in Cheltenham. Two men conspired to conceal the two murdered. A distinct odour of criminality attaches to the affair.

There is no evidence as to abortion. There is no evidence as to blackmail. There is evidence as to homosexuality. That evidence is not strong, but it occurs in two places independently. The intimate letters from Butt to Sullivan quite probably existed. No motive for Nelson Gardner to lie about his improper relationship with Captain Butt is readily discernible.

Both victims – Butt and Sullivan – were connected to each other through Nurse Sullivan. We come to the contemplation of some kind of unholy alliance.

Homosexuality was a very dark secret in provincial towns of the 1930s. It was not discussed and apprehension was greatly feared by its practitioners. As we have seen, the mutilation of the torso must have been done to avoid the making of connections. Some kind of ring or cabal of homoerotic practices and practitioners could have flourished underground in the quiet back streets of Cheltenham. Some respectable persons would inevitably have been associated with more *louche* personnel.

Communal sexual activity can progress or spill over into sadistic byways. One can imagine Butt tortured for pleasure – and then to death. Things can get out of hand. The policeman's suggested 'frenzy' might have come upon the assembled company. We do indeed have a journalist's account of an orgy.*

It would probably be wiser not to push the suggestion further into black magic, although it was rife in the England of the 1930s.

The whole of the murderous aftermath of some terrible occasion was geared to protecting a cell of respectable citizens of Cheltenham. The way to explain the

*See Chapter Eighteen.

intercessions of the outsider, Newman, is to point merely to his association with Brian Sullivan. He was a friend. There was no fanciful connection between the West End dens of vice and the denizens of Tower Lodge.

Brian Sullivan had to be the second victim because he was perceived as the weakest link, liable to break under pressure and bring down the whole closely-guarded circle.

Could children have been involved? Are we looking at a hidden nest of paedophiles, desperate to keep themselves out of the hands of the law.

The police floundered, met with a wall of silence, and their unimaginable suspicions filtered away as, in April 1938, the *Anschluss* set the Hitlerian scene for the world cataclysm that was to engulf us every one, and very soon, amid bomb and shot and shell, the remembrance of the lone torso floating in the river would be submerged in a great sea of war-mutilated dead.

Chapter Twenty-Two

Water Under the Bridge

And suddenly it was all over. Closed down. Cheltenham dead as a dodo. Anticlimatic as an emptied theatre. Only echoes. No answers.

Nurse Sullivan had shaken the dust of the place from her shoes. Fled to London: there to embrace lonely anonymity in the crowded shadows.

The two Yard men had also left. Bowled off in a purring police car, back to London. Sergeant Shewry gently spinning towards promotion. He would be made up to inspector that April – and transferred to H Division, Limehouse. Chief Inspector Worth, to merge back into the bowler-hatted, Crombie-overcoated ranks of his Metropolitan cohort, until, in the fulness of his serving time, he was appointed chief constable, before his tragic death in a car crash in 1975.

But despite their ostensible shutting of the door upon the case, the detectives were careful to leave it a wide enough crack ajar. Reported Worth:

> In order to keep in touch with Mrs Sullivan's movements, a postal warrant has been obtained to examine her correspondence. She is at present receiving some c/o Mr Thompson, her solicitor, of which the postal authorities are aware. … In respect to the possibility of the head being caught up at the weirs from Haw Bridge to Gloucester direction, Chief Superintendent Wayman has arranged with the Catchment Board for special attention to be paid by them during the periodical inspection for the removal of obstacles.
>
> The Chief Constable, through the County Authorities, has issued a reward of £50 for the recovery of the head to the men who are licensed to drag the Severn for salmon over the material stretch of water from Haw Bridge.

What Irene Sullivan did in the seven years of life remaining to her, we do not know. It is said that from time to time she would return to Cheltenham. We know that she is also said to have gone to Polperro, where the local people did not at all take to her. She surely made the odd excursion to Bournemouth. That was where Nesta of the Forest, the clairvoyant she had known, and doubtless consulted, at her abode in Oxford Passsage, Cheltenham, strategically situated opposite the Black & White Coach Station, had migrated.

In 1963, in her seventies, this extraordinary woman, unprofessionally plain Mrs Nesta Lane, was still laying spells, reading people's futures and fortunes, and providing them with psychic guidance and advice at her Bournemouth premises.

Mrs Irene Sullivan (1881-1945) in her younger and less troubled days.

Oddly enough, in 1934, Andrew Soutar had been commissioned by the *Sunday Pictorial* to carry out a secret enquiry into the world of clairvoyants and mediums, and he had investigated Mrs Lane, to whom he gave the name 'The Dryad'. She impressed him:

> This woman startled me. There must be many charlatans in this clairvoyance business ... but I am certain that she is not one of them. I felt all the better for having known The Dryad.

When Mrs Sullivan was admitted to St Columba's Hospital, or 'Home of Peace', at 98 Avenue Road, Swiss Cottage, Hampstead, she was living at Number 1 Down Cottages, Parson Street, Hendon. She died in St Columba's, on 9 August 1945, of carcinoma of the cervix. She was 63. Bernard O'Donnell, presumably financially backed by the *Empire News*, assumed the responsibility for the burial of her body.

As the ladder of the years extended, others were snatched from its steps. Mrs Butt died at Highcroft, Ashchurch Road, on 12 November 1951, and was buried at Ashchurch, near Tewkesbury. Captain Correll died in 1965. He went on believing to the end that the real cause of what he accepted as Brian's suicide had been that he had got into trouble with London gangsters.

Time passed, but the mystery did not fizzle out.

As early as Sunday 8 May 1938, Bernard O'Donnell, in the *Empire News*, had written:

> This week I have discovered vitally important facts in connection with the disappearance of Captain William Bernard Butt ... On the afternoon of January 4th, the day on which he vanished, Captain Butt had an appointment to play tennis with two young ladies at Montpellier, near the Queen's Hotel, Cheltenham. He did not turn up to keep the appointment, and when telephone inquiry was made at his home at 248 Old Bath Road, they were told that he was not at home.
>
> There is significance in this failure to appear, because when he suggested to the two girls that they should meet for tennis that afternoon, he said that he would bring a friend with him to make up the foursome. One of the girls remarked that they hoped his friend would not mind, as they were not very good players, and Captain Butt replied: "Oh, that's all right. You need not worry. He's not much of a player himself. He is a very big man."
>
> The importance of this statement lies in the last five words. Sir Bernard Spilsbury stated at the inquest that the torso was that of a "rather heavily-built individual". The coroner asked whether he was "satisfied that the body was that of a heavily-built man as against that of a medium-built man," and Sir Bernard replied that he was. Captain Butt was not a heavily-built man by any stretch of the imagination. Who, then, was the 'very big man' whom Butt was to meet on this fateful January 4, and take to Montpellier for tennis as arranged? Did he meet him that day, and if he did, why was not the appointment kept?
>
> The Captain returned to his home alone shortly after lunch-time. But whether he went out again during the afternoon or not is uncertain. It was on that same night [4 January] that Butt's Daimler car was parked at the Regent Garage in Cheltenham, never to be called for, and I [Bernard O'Donnell] can definitely prove if necessary that it was Captain Butt and no other who parked that car. Hitherto there has been some doubt about this, but I am in a position to state definitely that the man who went to the Regent Garage that night was Captain Butt.

Another four decades went by. Then, in February 1982, in the magazine *Gloucestershire and Avon Life*, Robin Brooks wrote an article, 'The Haw Bridge Torso Mystery', which crystallised all the local suspicions and speculations which had been voiced over the years; the vapourings of rumour which had solidified into received legend. He rehearsed, and imported current credulity to the old sensational interpretations provided by the newspapers' 'Special Correspondents' of the thirties.

Brooks told how the residents of Leckhampton had read the reports in the local paper of the discoveries on Haw Bridge, on the other side of Cheltenham. "None of them could have imagined that a connection might exist with the 'odd goings on' that were the talking point of the village."

Of this alleged village gossip, I have, in fact, been able to discover no whisper of confirmation. It seems rather to have been newspaper talk of the time. But Brooks confidently and colourfully asserts:

> Everyone in Leckhampton had heard the rumours about Tower Lodge. Standing alone, half way up the hill, the grey stone building with its castellated roof had about it a look that encouraged speculation. During those middle years of the 1930s, Tower Lodge had increasingly become the cause of local intrigue. Eyebrows were raised and voices sank to a conspiratorial hush when mention was made of "the things that went on, up at the Lodge."
>
> The house was lived in, or rather periodically used, by a Mrs Sullivan and her son Brian. They had rented the property some years before, but neither of them lived there on a permanent basis.
>
> Brian Sullivan lived in London, where he worked as a professional dance partner at the Piccadilly Hotel. The nature of this work brought the gigolo into contact with the gay young things of London's affluent society, a section from which, for a person of enterprising spirit and few moral scruples, there was money to be made.
>
> The rumours surrounding Tower Lodge stemmed from Brian Sullivan's willingness to take advantage of these opportunities. He regularly made weekend visits down from London, bringing with him young ladies from the glittering and fashionable circles in which he moved. All the girls shared something in common, they were single and in an unfortunate condition. The whispers around Leckhampton spoke of Tower Lodge as a venue for illegal abortions. Girls were brought to Cheltenham and, for a price, received an operation that would solve their immediate problem. In seeking this solution, however, the girls unwittingly laid themselves open to a different and no less unenviable exploitation: blackmail. For a fee, Brian Sullivan was prepared to say nothing. On the strength of his bought silence he increased his income to good effect. The business of setting up these package deals to Cheltenham proved most profitable. Brian Sullivan had built for himself a most lucrative, albeit clandestine, enterprise; that made the surprise [of his suicide] even greater.

Nor, again according to rumour, was abortion all that went on at the Lodge. In those days homosexuality, even between consenting adults, was not merely illegal; the law referred to it in terms as 'the abominable crime'. And if 'Byron Smith' had a way with ladies, Brian Smith was a committed (and committing) homosexual. That fact interested the Gloucester police.

Brooks continued:

> Going through Sullivan's belongings at Tower Lodge, the police
> revealed some delicate findings … a number of letters were brought to
> light. They exposed the fact that Sullivan and Butt had been lovers.

These letters, if they ever existed, have, as we have already noted, disappeared.
There is no reference to them in either the Scotland Yard file on the case, or in the
records of the Gloucester Police Investigation, preserved in the Gloucester Record
Office. This article of Brooks' aside, the sole mention of them that I have come
upon is in the *Daily Express*, of 10 February 1938, which states that:

> Letters revealing a friendship between Captain Butt and Brian Sullivan
> have been closely examined by Chief Inspector Worth. Passages in the
> letters suggest that Captain Butt had often visited Sullivan at Tower
> Lodge …

Brooks' article was the touchstone, the pioneering role model upon which future
retailments would rely.

The following year, in the *Gloucestershire Chronicle* of 22 October 1983, the
'Crime of the Century – the Haw Bridge Torso Murder Mystery' was once again
in the news. Reference was made to an individual as closely involved in the
investigation as the police, according to the article. That man was Percy Mills,
former assistant editor of the *Gloucestershire Echo*, and the *Gloucestershire
Chronicle*'s long-standing columnist, 'Chatterer'.

Mills, 28 at the time of the Torso case, was then senior reporter on the *Echo*. He
happened to be on late duty on that January day in 1938 when the news of the
finding of the bloodstains on Haw Bridge came through. He wrote three or four
lines for the stop press, and then spent months following the case.

Those months were, he said, "undoubtedly the most exciting, adventurous, and
at times eerie, of my life in peacetime. It was hair-raising. There was a feeling of
never knowing what would turn up."

In those days, of course, murder drew a death sentence, and every case aroused
great public interest from the time of the crime and the capture of the suspect to
the trial and the subsequent hanging. Moreover, unlike murder hunts of today,
Mills, and through him the *Echo*, were in the position of being able to scoop both
Scotland Yard and the local police. Said Mills:

> From the start, the Scotland Yard detective in charge of the case, Percy
> Worth, had decided on a policy of non-cooperation with the press.
> That, as it turned out, was just too bad for him, as the press took his
> attitude as giving them *carte blanche* to pursue their own inquiries. The

result was that in many cases Scotland Yard were left trailing, often following up clues unearthed by the newspapers.

It was, the *Chronicle* claims, Percy Mills who was the first to recognise the connection between Brian Sullivan, the mystery torso, and the missing Captain Butt. Mills explains:

> This was in consequence of Sullivan's name being dropped to me casually by one of the thousands of spectators of the diving operations at Haw Bridge on a fine Sunday afternoon. It caused me to race back to the office and check the files. From the date and other circumstances of Brian Sullivan's suicide, it seemed to me that this could well fit into the jigsaw puzzle. From my point of view it was desirable to have a discreet word with his mother. She welcomed me most courteously, and invited me to tea – an invitation I did not accept.
>
> She asked me if I knew anything about the value of cars, because she wanted to dispose of Brian's 12 or 14 HP Austin tourer, which she said was in the garage of the house. This surprised me, because I knew that it had been left inside the iron gates of Tower Lodge.
>
> She explained: "Captain Butt lets him keep it here if he is away."
>
> The first reference to Captain Butt.
>
> "Who is Captain Butt?" I asked.
>
> "He's my employer," she replied, adding that she acted as nurse to his wife, who was confined to her bedroom upstairs.

Mills had then asked where Captain Butt was, to which Nurse Sullivan had replied: "I don't know … He goes away, without saying anything to anyone, for months at a time. I believe on Mediterranean cruises."

Mills had felt uncomfortable with her response:

> I can assure you that there is truth in the saying "The hairs rose on the back of my neck." At that moment I realised that it was the mysterious Captain Butt whose torso, enveloped in sacks, I had seen being carried in a gruesome cortège along the side of the hedge between the Severn and the bridge over the River Chelt near Wainlode. My story, which undoubtedly would have been the biggest 'scoop' of the whole drama, was not published the next day. It was submitted to barrister's opinion, and considered to be too hot and dangerous to handle.

Mills was convinced that Brian Sullivan was the guilty party. The old reporter was also anxious to right what he regarded as a most unfair wrong: the misconception that Dr EN Davey, the Gloucester pathologist, made a serious mistake over the bloodstains on Haw Bridge.

At no time did he report that the blood was animal and not human. What he reported was that he did not get the reaction to show that the blood was human. From this it was assumed that the blood was that of an animal, probably a straying sheep struck by a car. But later it was established that the serum which had been supplied from official sources to Dr Davey for the test was out of date and had lost its virtues. A fresh supply was obtained for a further test, and as a result of this Dr Davey was able to report that the blood was human.

Not long before his untimely death in July 1989, at the age of 68, my good friend, Glyn Hardwicke, from 1961 to 1973 Prosecuting Solicitor for the Port of London Authority, and thereafter until his retirement Assistant City Solicitor for the Corporation of the City of London, wrote a short, unpublished, account of 'The Haw Bridge Torso Mystery'.

In it, he minced no words. Butt is stigmatised as 'the sleazy ex-military homosexual with the unbalanced wife'.

Regarding the open question of who killed the Captain, Glyn Hardwicke evinces neither doubt nor reticency.

The obvious candidate must of course be sinister Irene Sullivan. She was certainly the mastermind behind the abortion/blackmail racket, her son being merely the weak, vulnerable charmer who was the well-placed bait for the victims through whom, thanks to his bisexuality, she maintained a control over the wretched Butt who could not have afforded exposure.

On the other hand, Butt had his uses. Why kill even a minor goose who was so busy laying eggs of at least a golden hue? Logically the answer must be because at some stage he became a threat greater than his usefulness. The knowledge he had acquired through his liaison with Brian may have given him illusions of some power, making him too big for his size eight boots – but there is no evidence of this and it is perhaps fruitless to speculate.

At all events, Butt, whose role in the profitable racket may have been more cardinal than we imagine, was disposed of … his corpse was reduced to several component parts. That part of the operation, as Sir Bernard Spilsbury remarked at the inquest, would probably have required a strength which, while not abnormal, was greater than that possessed by the sub-normal weakling Brian, although his mother would have proved physically and mentally equal to the task.

So much for Butt. Hardwicke then turns his attention to the death of Brian Sullivan,

[T]he weedy little gigolo who procured abortions and blackmailed the victims through a future that must have seemed endless to them. He neither attracts nor deserves sympathy. It is, of course, always possible that he was 'put down' by a relation of one of his lady victims – that would not be merely justice but the poetic variety, of which there is, alas, all too little in life.

At first sight, though – to use a modern colloquialism – Brian 'lost his bottle' and gassed himself when the bloodstains on Haw Bridge came to light, which was January 11th.

But … he had no motive for suicide. And if he did not commit suicide, Brian Sullivan can only have been a murder victim. Of whom? The question is unanswerable, the mystery insoluble.

Thus Glyn Hardwicke endorses the Brooksian legends. His debt, also, to the more fanciful theorists in the contemporary press-cuttings is patent.

It was one day in 1991 that Keith Smart, a Gloucester-based keen student of the Cheltenham Torso Mystery, received a telephone call. The man on the line claimed to be Nurse Sullivan's stepson. His father, he said, had married Mrs Sullivan in the 1940s in London. They had lived in the St John's Wood area. Mrs Sullivan was killed in the blitz towards the end of the war. It was not until many years later that his father had told him the full story. At the time he knew nothing of the Torso Mystery.

His father was a widower, and when he [Smart's informant] came home on leave, he found his father wed to this woman, who was always known to him as Emma. His father worked for Kelmsley Newspapers and was a good friend of Bernard O'Donnell, and it was O'Donnell, who was the night news editor, who had introduced his father to Mrs Sullivan. O'Donnell had been a witness at their marriage.

The man on the telephone went on to say that O'Donnell had written Mrs Sullivan's life story for the *Empire News*, and she had given him the watch which had belonged to Brian Sullivan and an ivory-knobbed, malacca walking stick which had belonged to Captain Butt. *

According to Smart's anonymous informant, from what he could recall of what his father had told him, Mrs Sullivan had for many years been carrying out abortions for people in high society, and then blackmailing them. This had been achieved with the help of her son, Brian, and a man that he lived with in London. Smart afterwards identified this man as Keith Newman. They threw many 'high society' parties at their property in London. (This would have been the small mews flat in Radlett Place.)

Captain Butt, claimed the mystery informant, either found out about, or was

*This information he could easily have discovered in Bernard O'Donnell's book <u>Crimes That Made News</u>, published in 1954, by Burke, London.

told by Brian of, the sweet little racket that was going on, and wanted a piece of the action himself, threatening blackmail if it were refused him.

Butt was killed by Newman and another person. He did not specify who that other person was. He insisted that Mrs Sullivan had not been actively involved in the killing, but it was she who had disposed of the head.

When she carried out abortions on some of the better-off clients, she would, for an extra fee, promise that the aborted infant would be buried in consecrated ground. Keith Smart writes:

> I have heard from a number of local people that in those days it was a widely held belief that if you were not interred in holy ground your soul would not go to heaven, and there were undertakers who, in return for a small payment, would bury still-born babies in the graves of other people, so that their souls could go to heaven.

Mrs Sullivan was able to make good her promises because of an arrangement she had with Joseph Stone, Selim Smith's carpenter. Suitably rewarded, he would make sure that the aborted foetuses of richer clients were placed in the coffin he had made for someone else, alongside its rightful occupant.

When her son Brian was buried, Mrs Sullivan employed the funerary services of the Cheltenham undertaker, Selim Smith. She told his coffin-maker, her friend Joseph Stone, that she had another still-born baby to be buried, and asked him to put it in with Brian. But instead of a baby, she gave Stone a sealed box with Captain Butt's head inside it.

Keith Smart asked the man on the telephone for his name.

"I think I've told you enough to be going on with," he said, and rang off.

The man sounded quite old and struck Smart as being genuine. A few days later, Smart tried to re-establish contact with him, inserting a notice in the *Gloucester Citizen*, asking the man to get in touch, but he never did.

Almost certainly, he was a hoaxer. He seemed to know a great deal about the case, but there was nothing that he could not have derived from the newspapers and O'Donnell's book *Crimes That Made News*, except the details of Nurse Sullivan's death – and those he got wrong!

The *Gloucester Citizen*, of 2 February 1994, came out with a special 56th Anniversary eve *bonne bouche*, the Captain's head, as it were, on a plate! Former postman, David Gladstone, 50-year-old father of three, shed some startling new light on 'one of Gloucester's most baffling mysteries'.

Gladstone was living in Gloucester, but back in 1970 he had moved into a flat at Number 22 Evesham Road, Cheltenham.

> After I moved in I found furniture from Nurse Sullivan's former home in the cellar. Among the property was a bloodstained table and solicitors' letters about money which was being paid to her by past patients.

Gladstone said that it was while digging in the garden at Evesham Road in 1978, that he made his astonishing discovery. What is all the more astonishing about the discovery is the fact that Nurse Sullivan never lived at this address!

> I have a commercial horticulture diploma and I noticed that there was nothing growing except two varieties of sulphur-resistant weeds in one spot. At a depth of just over four feet my spade sliced through what appeared to be a decomposed head. It was the consistency of soggy cardboard. It was enclosed in an old-fashioned oilcloth table-cloth. I thought it was almost certainly Captain Butt's skull.

Gladstone had immediately called the police. They had attempted to lift the skull out of the hole, but it disintegrated.

> It is obvious to me now that the head must have been soaked in sulphuric acid. Fragments of bone remained and I have saved some of them, but I have never heard anything more from the police.

He had, said Gladstone, decided to reveal his find now, "to clear it from my mind". No one could be blamed for viewing all this with a considerable degree of dubiety.

The oldest surviving relative of Captain Butt surfaced in the following day's *Gloucester Echo*, (3 February 1994). This was Ann Stephens, the Captain's 56-year-old great-niece, of Stoke Orchard, near Cheltenham. She was married and had three children. Mrs Stephens said:

> I was only about six years old when it all happened, so I didn't know much about it. My parents never mentioned it when I was young, so I was much older when I found out. My mother told me he was murdered, but I never knew the full story. Now I'm the only relative of his to come forward.

She was, she said, fascinated by what she had read of the case.

> It sets my mind at rest. ... If they open up the grave we will know if the head is in there once and for all. It would be great to have this strange mystery tied up. I want to know what happened to him, and this looks like being the best if not the only way.

"Police files are still open on the case," said police spokeswoman Elaine Smith. "And any new evidence would be considered carefully. This crime remains unsolved and therefore we would consider any substantial new evidence to help in our inquiries."

'Did the Nurse Really Tell All in Torso Mystery?' An article by Robin Brooks in the *Gloucester Echo*, of 11 January 1997, opened the whole issue up again. This account is brimful of totally unproven asseverations: that Nurse Sullivan and her son had brokered and supplied abortions; that William Butt and Brian Smith were lovers; that when the Brian-Butt affair turned sour the Captain threatened to blow the whistle on the Sullivans' unsavoury service; that instead of paying the Captain off, mother and son arranged to see him off – permanently; that reports of the time alleged that his body was dismembered by Nurse Sullivan.

What Brooks was doing was repeating in terms the libel at which Soutar, in 1938, had only hinted. Stirred by this article of Brooks', Ann Stephens emerged again, in both the *Gloucester Citizen* and the *Western Daily Press*, of 24 January 1997.

The *Citizen* reported that she was calling for a grave to be opened in a hunt for a severed head. She wanted the grave of her uncle's alleged gay lover, Brian Sullivan, to be opened and his coffin exhumed.

The vicar of St Peter's, the Reverend Adrian Berry, was predictably unavailable for comment, but churchwarden Roy Crompton told the *Citizen*: "The churchyard is our responsibility so I would think the parish priest would have to be approached". And so far as he knew, no such approach had been made.

"To exhume the coffin, relatives would have to convince the police that by digging the body up it could help solve the murder," said Cheltenham coroner's officer Robert Plowright. "The police would have to apply for permission to the Home Secretary and, if granted, carry out the exhumation in the presence of a Home Office pathologist who would examine the remains."

Keith Smart backed Mrs Stephens' bid to have the body exhumed. "I'd like to be there to see if there's anything in the coffin with Sullivan's body. It would be very interesting."

Smart said that he believed that Sullivan, his business partner Keith Newman, and his mother, Irene Sullivan, were involved in the murder. A glove found on Haw Bridge could be traced to Newman, even though he had an apparently good alibi. He also believed that Butt died after being run down by a motor. Injuries to his legs suggested a low-fronted vehicle. He would have died on or about 10 January 1938. On 13 January, Keith Newman's low-fronted Jaguar car went into a garage for repairs to its damaged front.

The next day's *Daily Telegraph* (25 January 1997) picked up the Stephens and Smart story and in a piece by Sean O'Neill, reiterated all the quotations, 'facts' and insinuendos vouchsafed by the West Country papers, and incorporated a few errors of its own – namely that 'Sullivan's Jaguar, it was discovered, had undergone bodywork repairs,' and Keith Smart had 'spoken to relatives of the Sullivans.' They had no relatives.

This article, however, brought in an interesting letter to the Editor from a Mr G Rowberry, writing, on 28 January 1997, from Ascot, Berkshire.

I was closely associated with the Cheltenham coroner at the time, and I can now add some details, albeit from a memory which may prove not to be precisely correct.

Captain Butt's next door neighbours were a highly respected and well-known chartered accountant, a member of an established firm in Cheltenham, and his wife. Mrs Sullivan was in the habit of chatting to the lady, whose name I know but need not disclose [It was Mrs Price]. Before the body in the river was found, in the course of talking to her neighbour Mrs Sullivan had said two odd things, namely that she was of the opinion that Captain Butt did not intend to return to his home and subsequently she dreamt that he was dead.

Shortly after the body was found there was a somewhat dramatic meeting in the coroner's office between him, and his partner and the chartered accountant. Mrs Sullivan's observations were conveyed to the coroner, who informed the police, and Scotland Yard were called in, with the consequences that are now well known.

Among those consequences arose what was almost the certainty that the remains were those of Captain Butt. In fact, if he had been alive the national sensation which the events caused would certainly have come to his knowledge and caused him to surface.

The remarks alleged to have been made by Mrs Sullivan were never put to her in the course of the police enquiries or at the inquest.

Mrs Sullivan gave evidence about Captain Butt and his absences in a completely cool and clear-headed manner at the inquest. She was obviously, and no doubt correctly, regarded as being involved in whatever happened to Captain Butt, but there was no sufficient evidence to support a charge, as indeed there might have been if Brian had survived, because he was not a strong character and might well have disclosed whatever the truth was.

There seems no doubt that Mrs Sullivan was a 'back-street' abortionist.

All of us involved at the time had our own theories as to what actually happened. For what it may be worth, mine was that Captain Butt died at Tower Lodge, not necessarily murdered but possibly as a result of pitching down the narrow staircase there and injuring his back and possibly breaking his neck. Or there may have been a furious dispute between him and Brian Sullivan. Whether or not Mrs Sullivan was there at the time, her son would undoubtedly have sent for her.

Any enquiries by the police as to the death, accidental or otherwise, would probably have led to the disclosure of the abortions and of the homosexuality, which, if proved, would have landed Brian Sullivan and his mother in prison.

It seems unlikely that Captain Butt was blackmailing Mrs Sullivan or her patients since that would have involved him in knowledge of what was going on, itself a criminal offence. It would almost certainly have disclosed the relationship between the two men.

Neither Brian Sullivan nor his mother stood to gain from Captain Butt's death.

They may, of course, have plotted to, and did, kill him, but Tower Lodge was a very dangerous place deliberately to do so because the body had to be disposed of. I think the chronology of events indicated that Captain Butt's body had been kept at Tower Lodge for some days, possibly while the Sullivans were deciding what to do, and also performing the very gruesome operations relating to the head and the limbs.

The journey with the body to Haw Bridge, and disposing of it and the limbs over the bridge, was itself fraught with danger. It seemed obvious that if it were deliberate murder it would have been effected elsewhere, particularly out of Cheltenham, and after the perpetrators had planned the disposal of the body.

It is most unlikely there was a gang behind the abortions, which habitually were carried out with complete secrecy for obvious reasons. With all respect to the suggestion, the prospects of finding the missing head in Brian Sullivan's coffin do not exist.

Some of the theories, and possibly including my own, were what PG Wodehouse used to call "a lot of apple sauce"!

Apple sauce or not, the theory that Butt's death was the result of a row and an accident rather than deliberate murder, was also held by no less a person than Detective Superintendent Hancock, who, as a detective inspector at the time, was actually on the case. Responding to the *Daily Telegraph* article, his daughter, Mrs Pat Taylor, wrote from Aldebury, Salisbury, Wiltshire, to Keith Smart:

From time to time over the years my father referred to the case and would talk to me of it. He never mentioned any homosexual connotations, however, homosexuality was very much a taboo subject then and he would not have discussed such a thing with me at my then tender age.

He told me that he thought the most likely explanation was that Brian Sullivan, frequently in debt, went to Captain Butt's home to borrow money (not for the first time), a row ensued, and Sullivan accidentally killed the Captain, disposing of the body, with which he would have had help. Local gossips believed he was aided and abetted by his mother, though that could never be proved.

In those days, if a Constabulary had not solved a murder within a certain time scale, they were obliged to call in Scotland Yard, hence their presence.

During investigations, a very agitated Mrs Sullivan approached my father in the street and asked him to visit her. She told him she had something very important to tell him. I must explain that my father was well known as a mild-mannered man, gentle, compassionate, and very easy to talk to.

He dutifully reported this encounter and his intention to see Mrs Sullivan to the Scotland Yard Inspector, something he always regretted doing, as the London detective insisted on seeing Mrs Sullivan himself.

The detective concerned was, apparently, a high-handed, arrogant man, and when he went to see her, Mrs Sullivan clammed up and wouldn't divulge a thing, whereas my father was sure, as she had approached him personally, she would have told him a great deal.

This evening I rang my aunt, who had not seen the article. She was particularly interested as she was at school with Brian Sullivan and knew him reasonably well. She and her husband had been speaking to Mr Sullivan only a week or so before the story hit the headlines, and of course remembers the incident very well. She said he was a renowned gigolo and frequently visited Tower Lodge with ladies from London.

On the night of Saturday 1 October 1998, an hour-long film attempting to unravel the mystery of the headless torso had its première before an audience of forty at the George Dowty Memorial Hall, at Arle Court, near Cheltenham.

The film had been made by the Dowty Cine Society, a group of ten cine-film enthusiasts, all of who had been employees of the Dowty firm, and who, for the previous 15 years – since 1983 – had been researching and filming an amateur documentary. They used police records, contemporary photographs, accounts from local newspapers, and conducted interviews with people who had lived nearby, or been otherwise involved, at the time of the discovery of the torso.

The Society's Honorary Secretary, Douglas Symes, said: "The documentary attempts to shed some light on the murder because there has been so much rubbish written about it."

We have already considered a fair sampling of that so-called rubbish. The confident allegations of abortion, blackmail and homosexuality – without the remotest backing up by uncontroverted evidence.

We have indicated the delicacy of balance regarding the issue as to whether Brian's death was suicide or murder – not to mention the difficulty of the apportionment of blame if it was indeed homicide.

We have duly noted the official verdict that it was impossible to say whether or not the torso in question was in fact that of Captain William Bernard Butt, taken cognisance of the circumstance that while the torso was described by Spilsbury as being that of a rather heavily-built individual, such a description would hardly seem to apply to Butt's physique, and registered Nurse Sullivan's – possibly not disinterested – insistent: "I believe that Captain Butt is still alive, and that the torso is that of some other victim".

What also remains unanswered is, if Butt was not still alive, if he was murdered, where was the deed done? Was he killed in Cornwall? There is no record of the police's having checked thoroughly into that possibility. Was he killed in London? Again, there is no record of the police's having investigated that possibility. Was he killed in Cheltenham? If so, then was the *coup de grâce* administered, or the accident enacted, at Tower Lodge or, as the late Superintendent Hancock suspected, at Number 248 Old Bath Road?

We must now, after all this time, surely conclude that the answer is written in water … the water that has flowed under the bridge …